THE EARLY AMERICAN WILDERNESS

AS THE
EXPLORERS
SAW IT

BILL LAWRENCE

PARAGON HOUSE · NEW YORK

FIRST EDITION, 1991

PUBLISHED IN THE UNITED STATES BY

PARAGON HOUSE
90 FIFTH AVENUE
NEW YORK, NY 10011

COPYRIGHT 1991 BY PARAGON HOUSE

LIBRARY OF CONGRESS CATALOGING-IN-PUBLICATION DATA

LAWRENCE, BILL.
WILDERNESS : NORTH AMERICA AS THE EARLY EXPLORERS SAW IT : FROM
NORSE SAGAS TO LEWIS AND CLARK / BILL LAWRENCE.—1ST ED.–P.   CM.
INCLUDES BIBLIOGRAPHICAL REFERENCES.
ISBN 1–55778–145–1 : $19.95
1. AMERICA—DISCOVERY AND EXPLORATION.   2. NATURAL HISTORY—NORTH
AMERICA.   3. NORTH AMERICA—DESCRIPTION AND TRAVEL.   I. TITLE.
E121.L38   1991
970.01—DC20   90–44556
CIP

MANUFACTURED IN THE UNITED STATES OF AMERICA
10 9 8 7 6 5 4 3 2 1

For Joyce, who hates history

TABLE OF CONTENTS

PREFACE

Even today there is speculation about a link between the Old World and the New World long before the first travels of Christopher Columbus, even before the Norse voyages. Books on the matter regularly appear, many of them inferring that we should credit one people or another with the real discovery of America.

Which people? To name a few: Egyptians, Assyrians, Phoenicians, Carthaginians, Cretans, Hittites, Israelites, Etruscans, Greeks, Romans, Chinese, Arabs, Celts, Libyans, and Basques.

Such suppositions are intriguing, but all historians can do is look at the record. And what the record shows is that the Norsemen came and went around 1000 A.D. and that Columbus made his first voyage about five hundred years later. The Norsemen departed quickly and without leaving a significant trace, yet everything that is America today—good and bad—is a result of Columbus's voyage.

But Columbus does not figure at all in the scheme of this book. On his first trip he landed in the Bahama Islands and then turned south, and on three later voyages he explored South and Central America. On no voyage did he get so much as a peek at what is now the mainland of North America.

Columbus was one of a number of Italians who were important in the early exploration of America. The other notables were John Cabot (Giovanni Caboto), who sailed for England; Giovanni da Verrazano, working for France; and Amerigo Vespucci, hired first by Spain and then Portugal.

Even though many Italians sailed for other countries there was no Italy, just a conglomeration of small city-states, each jealous of the others. By the beginning of the sixteenth century only a handful of European countries had achieved political unity and a sense of national purpose: Portugal, Spain, France, England, and the Netherlands. Czarist Russia, still a sleeping giant, awaited its moment of overseas expansion, a time that would not come until the eighteenth century.

A lot of changes had taken place in Europe during the fifteenth and sixteenth centuries. The continent had at last regained its composure after the fall of Rome in the fifth century. The Renaissance brought a rebirth of learning and the opening up again of an inquiring spirit and the Crusades had inspired an interest in trade with the Orient for spices, precious stones, medicine, silks, dyes, and perfumes. In return European countries provided wine, glassware, silver, and wool.

Towns had grown swiftly, and with their growth came the rise of a wealthy middle class. Many among the new middle class were merchant princes, those with money to spare in a search for overseas trading routes. And so were born the first corporations, backed by wealth and power.

Portugal and Spain showed the way. Before the 1492 voyage of Columbus, Portugal sent ships down the East Coast of Africa and established trading posts as far away as India. Portuguese captains found the Canary Islands, the Azores, and finally the Cape Verde Islands halfway between Africa and Brazil. This exploring spadework was necessary before the work of finding America could begin, though few realized it at the time.

But Portugal did not have the population to support any far-flung expansion. Soon other nations, beginning with Spain, challenged Portugal's supremacy. Portugal had turned down Columbus's proposal to find the Indies by sailing west instead of east—the venture seemed too risky and too expensive. Indeed Spain, though not wholeheartedly, took up the offer. Ferdinand and Isabella, joint sovereigns of a newly unified Spain, considered the risk of a westward voyage and took the chance anyway. Their gamble paid off a millionfold.

England, France, and the Netherlands were not far behind, all with an eye toward colonization rather than the conquest and exploitation favored by Spain.

The unfortunate Columbus died in obscurity, apparently still unaware that he had discovered not the Indies but a giant continent not known to exist.

The discovery of America was the greatest surprise in the history of the world.

Columbus called the native inhabitants of the Western Hemisphere Indians, but of course they were not. Where did the original inhabitants come from and how did they get there? By most accounts they crossed from Asia to Alaska twenty-five thousand to thirty thousand years ago, during the last Ice Age. They might have crossed on the thick ice sheets or have walked dry-shod on a land bridge during a period of melting glaciers.

Why did they come? Probably they were in pursuit of the large mammals of the Pleistocene epoch that had preceeded them—mastodons, woolly mammoths, deer, moose, and giant beavers. Apparently the horse and camel, believed to have originated on this continent, went the other way at about the same time.

Once these emigrants arrived they found the way south blocked by ice from shore to shore in present-day Canada. They stayed in the North until the ice fields parted and left a long, clear passage down the eastern flank of the Rocky Mountains. The North American population was well settled by about 3000 B.C.

For ages the emigrants lived as primitive man always did, by hunting and fishing. But as temperatures rose and the land dried out, the thick vegetation became scarce and the usual prey began disappearing from the earth. Facing extinction themselves, the new inhabitants switched to small-game hunting, fishing and gathering, and in some cases agriculture. The settled life made necessary by the pursuit of agriculture brought great changes in their lives. They were no longer nomads, roaming the land in search of dinner. Now they were members of stable communities—hunting, gathering, farming—and increasing the population.

Native Americans were living in this essentially neolithic culture when the first Europeans arrived. Their way of life prompted some European thinkers to call them noble savages.

There were about ten million Native Americans living in North America. They were spread thin in many areas, but in others there were more people than in some parts of Europe in Columbus's time. The Northeast, Deep South, and Pacific Northwest, for example, were heavily populated.

In the Northeast, between the Adirondack Mountains and the Great Lakes, lived the Iroquois. The Iroquois were not a tribe, but a federation including Mohawks, Oneidas, Senecas, Cayugas, Onondagas, and later Tuscaroras. The league—one the Iroquois hoped would spread over the entire continent—was begun through the work of Chief Hiawatha and the prophet Deganawidah. The league put down internecine conflicts within its own membership and presented a united front to the encroachments of its neighbors and then the white man.

In the Southeast, from the East Coast to the Mississippi River, lived a number of advanced tribes, notably the Creeks, Seminoles, Cherokees, and Choctaws. The first Europeans were impressed by the looks, order, and agricultural success of these natives. The tribes, thickly settled in places, cultivated extensive lands and maintained far-flung trading operations.

Along the east bank of the Mississippi River lived the Natchez, the most striking culture of the region and indeed in all of America. An older culture, called the Mississippian, had left them in possession of the large mysterious mounds they used for erecting temples and the elaborate homes of their kings, believed to be descendants of the sun god. When the French came that way they were greatly impressed by the Natchez, entering their villages peacefully and treating their chiefs as the equals of French leaders.

Native inhabitants of the Pacific Northwest—Coos, Nootkas, Chinooks, Yakimas, Walla Wallas, Modocs, the Yuroks of northern California—were at times blessed with abundance. Their environment was rich in fish and edible wild plants. Life was good when the fish, especially salmon, made their spring runs up the streams to spawn. Natives caught them in nets or ingenious weirs, and the tribesmen developed ways of preserving them so that the lean times would not prove so disastrous.

Among Pacific Coast natives there was an opulence of dress unrivaled by any other native society except perhaps the Sioux of the central plains whose home stretched from Canada to Texas, from the Mississippi to the Rockies. In these plains also lived the Pawnee, Omaha, Oto, Iowa, Cree, Ojibway, Kansa, Osage, Crow, Cheyenne, and other tribes. There was some farming, but mainly these natives hunted their mainstay—the buffalo. We are not certain that the plains have been continuously inhabited over the ages.

Inhabitants of the desert Southwest—Apaches, Yumans, Pecos, Hopi, Zuñis—often lived a precarious existence. Those who lived along large streams, especially the Rio Grande and Pecos River, farmed extensively and generally prospered. Those elsewhere developed techniques of dry farming—catching ground water runoff in terraces—and made the best of a bad situation. Much of the time denizens of these arid lands lived on small animals, rodents, birds, insects, seeds, berries, and yucca fruits.

Native Americans did not live *in* the wilderness—they were as much as part of it as the animals, plants, and trees. The wilderness provided their entire livelihood: food, weapons, clothes, homes, tools, and hiding places. Native societies were self-contained, importing nothing and not having to worry about trade deficits or national debts.

Europeans adopted such wilderness devices as snowshoes, moccasins, canoes, kayaks, ponchos, dogsleds, toboggans, parkas, and even enema tubes. Native American words insinuated themselves into the King's English, words such as wigwam, teepee, hominy, succotash, moose, caribou, skunk, papoose, tomahawk, mackinaw, hickory, and pecan. Today the

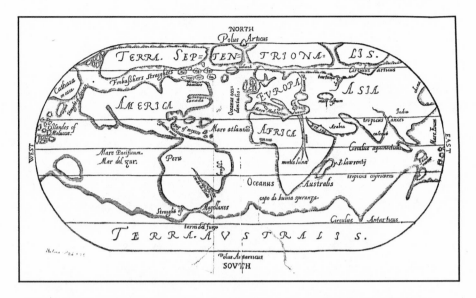

map of North America is peppered with the native names for locales from Millinocket, Maine, to Yuma, Arizona, and from Miami, Florida, to Tacoma, Washington.

Perhaps that is as it should be.

~~~~~~
~~~~~~

INTRODUCTION

When the first Europeans came to these shores they saw the North American wilderness in its pristine glory—its birds, beasts, trees, plants, streams, mountains, deserts, plains, aboriginal inhabitants. It was an incredibly beautiful land, beautiful and dangerous.

Many early comers searched for gold or for the Northwest Passage, a mythical waterway through the continent. But few explorers realized the value of what they had stumbled upon. Most saw the marvels of this New World as obstacles to overcome in pursuit of a greater goal—the marvelous Indies.

What *did* they see, these first venturers into the North American wilderness?

Before they saw, they smelled. The fragrance of the continent's primeval forests wafted far out to sea, breezes carrying the scent of pine, cedar, laurel, magnolia, sassafras, mulberry, and other aromatic trees. Countless flowers blended their scents with those of the trees, creating the distinctive sweet smell of a New World, a world relatively undisturbed by human hands since time began.

The trees were part of a great forest stretching almost unbroken from the Atlantic Ocean to the Mississippi River and along the coastal areas beyond. Some trees were gigantic; the mammoth redwoods and sequoias of the West Coast are legendary, yet the East had its prize oaks, cedars, and pines that seemed to touch the sky.

Where these Paul Bunyans of the plant world lived, the forest floor was remarkably free of undergrowth. Spreading canopies of leaves, assisted by massive grapevines, blotted out most of the sunlight and allowed little to grow beneath them except darkness-seeking wildflowers.

These were the foreboding "dark woods" often spoken of by the first European explorers. In places where the trees were not so large and protective, thickets and impenetrable tangles made the going difficult, especially in the South, where the sun shone hot and long. Growing in the clearings were tall grasses, masses of flowers, thick stands of cane.

Beneath the branches or within them were the forest creatures, large and small, meek and dangerous, beautiful and repulsive. Almost everywhere were bears. The black bear—more of a cinnamon color in the West—called most of the country home. The toughest customer in the bear family, the grizzly, dwelt in the western plains and mountains. On two occasions a grizzly came close to ending the life of Meriwether Lewis of Lewis and Clark fame. In the early days the polar bear, then called the white bear, rode the ice floes as far south as Cape Cod, Massachusetts.

Roaming the country were the cougar and its smaller cousins, the bobcat and lynx. Early comers called these beasts panthers, cats, tigers, or "lyons." There never were any real lions in the New World though, and there have been no tigers since the saber-toothed species became extinct.

There seems to be a little evidence that the great woolly mammoth still existed in the interior of North America almost into the historical period of the continent. One charge President Thomas Jefferson gave to Lewis and Clark on their famous expedition was finding out if the legendary mammoth still lived. The partners found no signs of any recent existence but most of the evidence was Indian hearsay anyway. Perhaps, too, Europeans misunderstood when native Americans, through sign language, tried to describe the buffalo.

The first explorers to see buffalo called them "humpbacked cattle." They must have stood awestricken when beholding five or six hundred of the shaggy beasts, unaware of the vast herds numbering in the hundreds of thousands farther inland. The buffalo meant everything—even life itself—to Indians living where it thrived.

Many creatures fascinated newcomers to the continent. They found the opposum a peculiar little beast because it hung from a tree by its tail and when frightened pretended to have resigned from the world. The skunk, though a beautiful creature, gave off a stench "like the odor of sin." Legend soon had it that the porcupine shot its quills like a shower of arrows. Other oddities were the little black-masked raccoon, kangaroo rat, pocket gopher, and the industrious prairie dog that built cities covering hundreds of acres.

Squirrels—red, gray, and the now extinct black—were the most numerous of small animals. Early boatmen found rivers swarming with them, some invading their boats by scampering up the oars.

And a squirrel that flew? Yes, those too. Europeans were especially intrigued by this strange creature and it was some time before they learned that instead of flying it glided from tree to tree with the help of a fold of skin stretching from limb to limb.

On the coasts were seals, walruses, auks, sea otters, sea lions, and whales, including white whales. All life living near the sea ranged farther inland than it does today. The great auks, and their smaller cousins the puffins, flocked in sizeable numbers off the coasts of Canada's maritime provinces. Early explorers called the auks penguins. Indeed they were members of the penguin family, having the black-and-white tuxedos to prove it.

Great sea lions and sleek sea otters lived on the coasts of the western United States and Canada. The fur of sea otters was in great demand, and by the early nineteenth century they had been hounded almost to extinction. Today they are protected by law.

Birds were everywhere—many kinds and in huge numbers. Out west dwelt the unusual magpie. Seeking the shelter of the deeper woods was the great black raven. The hummingbird, never seen by Europeans before, captivated early birdwatchers with its tinyness and grace. Most numerous of all were passenger pigeons, so many they obscured the sky for hours at a time.

America's big game bird, the turkey, flourished in the wild. But turkeys were swift of foot and not easy to catch. A lot of Europeans thought turkeys were the best eating on these shores.

Alligators, hideous beasts to the early explorers, lived in the waters of the Deep South. Europeans who had never seen an alligator before invariably exaggerated its size, and most called them crocodiles. There were then—and there still are today—a few crocodiles hiding in the swamps of southern Florida, but apparently no early visitor saw any.

Indians of the South relished alligator meat. So, too, did some Europeans—after they got used to the idea of eating it.

The great Mississippi River catfish was another formidable creature in European eyes. And well it should have been: By modern standards the catfish grew to staggering proportions, sometimes weighing several hundred pounds.

The armored body and dagger-like teeth of the alligator gar was an even more fearsome sight. It grows to be nine feet long now, and how big it was centuries ago can only be guessed.

Fish, much bigger than today's, choked American waters. Rivers feeding the Pacific Ocean were so clogged with salmon one explorer imagined he could walk on their backs. An incredible abundance of cod from New England to Newfoundland brought fishermen from all over western Europe, some of them apparently arriving before the first explorers.

Shad, mackerel, herring, halibut, bass, sturgeon—all of these abounded. Striped bass, looking for spawning grounds, fought their way up rivers from Florida to the Gulf of St. Lawrence with six footers weighing as much as a hundred and forty pounds not uncommon. Lake sturgeon might be eight feet long and weigh a hundred pounds or more. Sea sturgeon, abundant in coastal waters, were twelve feet or more and might tip the scales at half a ton.

Fish took the hooks as quickly as they were dropped in the water. Reports tell of as many as five thousand being caught in a single cast of the net. Natives used arrows or lances, or simply clubbed them to death.

This, then, was the North America seen by the early explorers—a breathtaking wilderness unspoiled by its creatures and changed little by its native inhabitants. It did not take long, as such things are measured, for this wilderness to all but disappear and many of its creatures with it. As the California naturalist John Muir wrote, "A numerous class of men are painfully astonished whenever they find anything, living or dead, in all God's universe, which they cannot eat or render in some way useful to themselves."

Happily, this numerous class appears to be less numerous these days.

TOUCHING THE SHORES
The Norsemen, Cabot, the Portuguese, Verrazano, and Cartier

T he Norse discoveries of the eleventh century, recorded in the ancient sagas, are the earliest reports of America that can be verified. Just before 800 A.D. adventurous Norsemen island-hopped across the North Atlantic, discovering the Faroe Islands and Iceland. About 985 an Icelander named Eric the Red colonized a huge icebound land which, for real estate purposes, he named Greenland. From Greenland it was a short hop to the North American continent.

But North America was not what Bjarni Herjulfson, the first European known to have seen our shores, was looking for when he was blown off course in 986. He was headed for the Norse colonies in Greenland, but missed the large island entirely and ended up cruising the coastline of North America instead.

But Bjarni Herjulfson did not come ashore and, in fact, saw land only twice. First he came upon "a land not mountainous and covered with forests and low hills." The second time the country was "high mountainous and glaciered." He was probably near Labrador and Baffin Island.

In the year 1000 Leif Ericson followed Herjulfson's route. Not much is known of Leif Ericson's background, except that he was a son of Eric the Red. Leif asked his father to lead the expedition, but the old man

declined. "It is not my fate to discover any more lands," the sagas have him say.

First Ericson came to what probably was Baffin Island. Noticing flat ledges leading to the icy mountains, he named the spot Helluland—Country of Flat Rocks. South of there it was level and wooded, and the Norsemen went ashore.

Leif named this place Markland—Country of Forests. He called a beach there *furdurstrandir,* or Wonder Strands. It must have been the short stretch of sandy beach on the Labrador coast, appearing so remarkable because it was on an otherwise rocky and barren shore. The Norsemen may never have seen a shore like it. Farther on, the expedition landed on an island to the north of the mainland, probably Belle Isle.

On the mainland, "where a stream flows out of a lake," the Norsemen built houses and settled in for the winter. "There was no lack of salmon, either in the river or in the lake, and it was bigger salmon than they had ever seen," say the sagas. "Nature was so generous it seemed to them no cattle would need winter fodder, but could graze outdoors. There was no snow in the winter and the grass hardly withered. The days and nights were more nearly equal than in Greenland or Iceland."

The site, believed to be L'Anse-aux-Meadows at Epaves Bay on the northern coast of Newfoundland, had broad meadows and salmon clambered upstream to spawn in a lake. In recent years archaeologists excavated dwellings there much like those the Norse built in Greenland around the same time. Carbon-14 dating places the settlement within a hundred years of the Norse voyages.

Mention of grapes in the sagas gave scholars problems for years. Would grapes be growing in northern Newfoundland? The likelihood that they wouldn't caused historians to locate Vinland, as Ericson named his settlement, in spots all the way from New England to Florida. Perhaps these were a hardier breed of grapes than we know today, and maybe it was not as cold in the Newfoundland of a thousand years ago.

Perhaps, too, there was no mention of grapes at all in the sagas. Some philologists think the name Vinland is a semantic fluke. They say *vinber*, the old Norse word usually translated as grapes, really meant wineberry. *Vinber* could have referred to wild red currants, gooseberries, or mountain cranberries—people of the day tried to make fermented drinks out of any fruit that grew. No saga, the philologists point out, specifically states that Vinland means Land of Grapes or Land of Vines.

The self-sown wheat referred to in the sagas has been identified as lyme grass. Growing wild with a head like wheat, it is found along beaches as far south as New England and from a distance looks like waving fields of grain.

A tree the sagas call *mosür* apparently is the white birch, which was often used by northern Indians for making canoes. Knobby protuberances in the middle of the trunk, carved into cups or bowls, also made eating and drinking vessels. Today there are no birches in northern Newfoundland large enough to have burls such as these, but they still grow in the middle of the island and they may have grown farther north in 1001.

Encouraged by the news Ericson brought home, his brother Thorvald brought more settlers to Vinland who wintered in Leif's houses, living mostly on fish. Exploring to the west next summer, they found "a beautiful and well-wooded land, the woods scarcely any distance from the sea, with white sands and a great many islands and shallows." After another winter they explored a fjord near "a headland jutting out that was entirely covered by forest." It was so lovely Thorvald thought of building a home there.

In this place the American aborigine and the European met for the first time, according to the sagas. The results were not encouraging for future relations. What the Norsemen took to be three small mounds turned out to be three skin boats overturned, with three natives hiding under each. For whatever reason the Europeans killed eight of the natives, the other escaping to warn his compatriots.

These *skraelings,* as the Norsemen called aborigines, were small with unkempt hair, large eyes, and broad cheeks. *Skraeling* meant barbarian, weakling, or perhaps pigmy. They are thought to have been an Eskimoan people who had moved down from the arctic regions to hunt seals.

Thorvald, wounded in the skirmishing, soon died and his settlers returned home; a third expedition was launched on a grander scale. This time Thorfinn Karlsefni, a wealthy trader hoping to become richer, arrived with some 250 settlers and much livestock. Sailing along the coast in search of Vinland, his group came upon a land with "a great forest and many animals," including white bears. The ships continued past an island—they named it Straumey—covered with sea birds. This could have been Belle Isle, or perhaps Great Sacred Island off L'Ans-aux-Meadows. After finding Leif Ericson's houses, Karlsefni's people settled in for the winter.

As the winter was hard, by spring the settlers were desperate for food and fodder. Meat from a dead whale that had washed ashore made them sick, but after recovering they found the fishing good as well as plenty of birds' eggs. Nevertheless, the leaders decided to go further south to look for better land. They found it at the mouth of a river flowing into a small landlocked bay. The settlers called the place Hop, and it could have been any number of places between Quirpon Harbor and White Bay. Here they found self-sown wheat and grapevines, or some kind of vines. They caught halibut stranded in pools, their cattle thrived, and the hunting was excellent.

In a couple of weeks *skraelings* appeared, making what the Norsemen interpreted as peace gestures. Certainly they wanted to trade and off the natives went well satisfied with cows' milk—they seemed to think it inordinately good—and bits of red cloth.

Come spring the *skraelings* were back, probably anticipating more milk for which they offered furs and salmon. But Karlsefni's bull interrupted the bargaining by making a surprise appearance. Alarmed by the sudden appearance of this strange animal, the *skraelings* quickly dispersed.

When they returned three weeks later, the *skraelings* were in a rebellious mood and fighting broke out. The Norsemen were getting the worst of it until Leif Ericson's bastard sister Freydis saved the day. She charged at the natives, screaming and brandishing a sword. Startled by this sudden apparition, the *skraelings* broke off the attack and retired to the woods.

Soon after the Norse leaders decided to abandon the country. "There would always be fear and strife dogging them there on account of those who already inhabited it," the sagas explained. Before they left, it was said, an *ein-foetingr,* or uniped, hopped down to the beach and fired arrows at them.

The curtain falls on North American exploration for the following five hundred years.

The next European to report seeing North America was John Cabot, an Italian working for England. In 1497 he sighted land, probably the northern coast of Newfoundland. Samuel Eliot Morison believed the spot to be Cape Bauld or Cape Dégrat, both located on the northernmost tip of Newfoundland. He wouldn't have been far from L'Anse-aux-Meadows.

Apparently Cabot went ashore only once. He probably didn't land again because he had only eighteen crew members and did not want to unnecessarily expose them to danger. On the other hand, it may have been because of the mosquitoes breeding by the hovering millions in the rock crevices of that stern coast. Cabot reported them as huge, vicious bloodsuckers.

When Cabot's men did go ashore they found signs of life—animal traps, fishing nets, a stick painted red—but saw no humans. Once, on their ship, they spotted two figures running along the shore, but couldn't make out whether the forms were men or beasts. If they were human they probably were Beothuk Indians, Newfoundland hunters and fishermen.

Cabot may have gone as far south as New England. For no accountable reason he called what he saw the Land of the Seven Cities, referring to an old tale about seven cities of gold founded somewhere in the western sea by seven Portuguese bishops. For generations many in America persisted in believing the myth, though it seems no one ever got rich. The New World protected its secrets, even those that didn't exist.

King Henry VII was pleased with Cabot's work and gave him a small annuity. After swaggering around Bristol for a time in new clothes and his pockets full of unaccustomed money, Cabot departed on a second trip to the West. This time he had five ships and a full complement of sailors. Only one ship returned—Cabot and the other four were lost forever.

Between 1499 and 1502 several Portuguese navigators visited this same part of the New World. João Fernandes, a *lavrador* or small landed proprietor, apparently made two voyages and brought back arctic falcons and three natives. He may have entered Hudson Bay. He left us the name Labrador, the oldest monicker north of the West Indies still in use.

Another Portuguese, Gaspar Corte Real, found "a land very cool and with big trees," probably some other part of Newfoundland. He turned back when he encountered ice floes. Returning later with more ships, Gaspar found the land delightful and rife with "luscious and varied fruits."

The natives, says a brief report of Real's second voyage, "live altogether by fishing and by hunting animals . . .such as very large deer covered with extremely long hair [moose], the skins of which they use for garments and also make houses and boats thereof. . . . They laugh considerably and manifest the greatest pleasure. . . ."

Instead of bows and arrows these natives, the Beothuks, hunted with "pieces of wood burnt in the fire . . . which when they throw them make wounds as if pointed with fine steel."

Two of Gaspar's ships returned to Portugal with fifty-seven natives. Later French and English settlers pursued them like wild beasts until they were literally exterminated.

Gaspar, staying behind to explore further, eventually disappeared. When Miguel, his brother, went in search of him, he also vanished.

John Cabot's son, Sebastian, is also said to have explored some part of North America. His accounts of a voyage or perhaps two voyages are vague. One report tells of a trip so far north that his men refused to continue because of threatening ice. Possibly he traveled the eastern coast of Baffin Island and may have seen the entrance to Hudson Bay.

One can't be sure about Sebastian's alleged voyages, for he was a great fabricator. One tale he told was about bears off the Grand Banks of

Newfoundland surrounding and capturing codfish that came near shore to feed on the leaves of overhanging trees.

But it's possible this story was a greatly exaggerated account of the incredible fishing around the Grand Banks, the world's greatest fishing hole. Part of the continental shelf stretching from Newfoundland to Cape Cod, the Grand Banks have enough water to flood all of North America. Fish must have fed on its lush undersea pastures in astounding numbers. Cod was king and Sebastian Cabot claimed to have given the place its first name—*Bacalos,* the native word for codfish.

Fishermen from England, France, and Spain already knew about the bounty of the sea at the Grand Banks. They were visiting there by the turn of the sixteenth century and may have been coming before John Cabot. The real discoverer of America may have been some lonely fisherman, blown off course by storms.

In 1521 another Portuguese, João Fagundes, explored the southern coast of Newfoundland and sailed into the Gulf of St. Lawrence. He named Penguin Island (now Bird Rocks) though the big birds there were auks, not penguins. Pulling their boats up to the shore, the men killed the auks at will.

Fagundes also visited the islands of St. Pierre and Miquelon and the numerous islets between them and the southern coast of Newfoundland. He named the islets *Onze Mil Virgenes* after an old medieval tale about St. Ursula and her eleven thousand virgins who were said to have wandered around the waters off the coast of Europe. (Other explorers used the name for small islands, such as the Virgin Islands of the Caribbean named by Columbus.) An island "at the foot of the Banks," Fagundes dubbed Santa Cruz, probably present-day Sable Island. He tried to catch walruses there.

Fagundes eventually returned to Europe and organized a group to start a farming and fishing colony in the New World. Their settlement, on Cape Breton Island or Prince Edward Island, was a place "fertile and good, where there is a large [native] population. . . . There are in that country things of great price."

This was the first colony in the New World since the Norse attempts over five hundred years before. It lasted about a year before the settlers were forced to leave by jealous French fishermen and hostile Indians.

As far as we know, Giovanni da Verrazano was the first explorer to sail the coast between Canada and Florida. He already had an impeccable maritime record, one that led King Francis I of France to hire him.

Verrazano's portraits show him to be a strong-featured man with a heavy beard and mustachio. He was well educated and apparently highborn.

Verrazano was the first explorer to mention the smell of the New World. The land, he said, was "spacious and so high it exceeds the sandy shore, with many beautiful fields and plains, full of the largest forests, some thin and some dense, clothed with various sorts of trees, with as much beauty and delectable appearance as it would be possible to express." The trees "for a long distance exhale the sweetest odors."

Many later explorers also remarked on the pleasing smell of the New World which they detected while far out to sea. Sometimes masses of flowers floated out from the mainland, a spontaneous floral offering from the New World to visitors.

Verrazano landed in 1524 at or near Cape Fear off the coast of what is now North Carolina. Put off course by a storm, he went about 160 miles down the shore to reach his original latitude and then doubled back for fear he was too close to Spanish territory. Indians around Cape Fear, apparently Cusabos, "came hard to the sea side, seeming to rejoice very much at the sight of us, marveling greatly at our apparel, shape, and whiteness. They showed us by sundry signs where we might most commodiously come to land with our boat, offering us also of their victuals to eat."

These natives were impressive specimens. Verrazano gives us our first good description of these Indians:

> The people are of color russet and not much unlike Saracens; their hair black, thick, and not very long, which they tie together in a knot behind and wear it like a tail. They are well featured in their limbs, of mean [average] stature, and commonly somewhat bigger than we. They are broad breasted, with strong arms. Their legs and other parts of the body are well fashioned and they are disfigured in nothing, saving that they have somewhat broad visages, and yet not all of them. For we saw many of them well favored, having great and black eyes, with a cheerful and steady look. They are not strong of body, yet sharp witted, nimble, and great runners. . . .
>
> The people go entirely naked except that they cover their privy parts with certain skins of beasts like unto martens. They fasten these onto a narrow girdle made of grass, very artificially [artfully] wrought, and hanged about with tails of divers other beasts dangling about their bodies down to their knees. Some wear garlands of birds' feathers.

It should be explained early that naked, used over and over by early comers, was a relative word. Europeans of the day wore all the clothes the law would allow, considering nude anyone wearing as little as these natives. The skin covering privy parts was the famous loincloth, or breechclout.

Verrazano found the Carolina country lovely, "with beautiful fields and broad plains, covered with immense forests more or less dense, various in colors, and too delightful and charming to be described." He took it for granted he was near Asia and decided there must be gold in abundance because of the golden beaches.

At one of the landings, somewhere between present-day Cape Fear and Cape Lookout, large waves tossed a young sailor overboard onto the shore. When the Indians approached, he "cried out piteously," fearing for his life. The natives stripped off his clothes and built a fire. Seeing this, the young man's shipmates were sure he was about to be roasted and eaten—they had heard awful tales of cannibals in these parts. Instead the Indians warmed the lad, then sent him back to the ship "with great love, clapping him fast about with many embracings."

Sailing on, the voyagers found a strand of islands with what appeared to be open sea beyond them. Verrazano thought he had discovered the "happy shores" of Cathay, but it was the string of islands known as the Outer Banks, around North Carolina's Cape Hatteras. The waters beyond were Pamlico and Albemarle sounds. "For the beauty of the trees," Verrazano named this country Arcadia. It must have been the right time of year to find a land of pastoral bliss, as the ancient name implies, for these deciduous woodlands must have stood out gloriously in their new spring finery. Incidentally the name Arcadia survived, though mapmakers steadily moved it north until it became Acadia—French-speaking Nova Scotia and some of the surrounding territory.

Once the strangers were ashore, natives of Arcadia—Pamlicos or Tus-

caroras—gave them beans "of a very good and delectable savor." But Frenchmen in the party gaped at the huge grapevines twining high in the trees—they were familiar only with the pedestrian vines of the Old World's closely tended vineyards.

The Indians here were more slightly built and had sharper features than those of their northern cousins. Their skin was "shiny," probably because they were smeared with bear fat or some other greasy preparation. They hunted with hardwood bows, using reed arrows with fishbone heads. Verrazano thought the animals wilder than Europe's because the hunters "continually molested them."

Verrazano must have missed Chesapeake and Delaware bays, for surely he would have checked out such large expanses of water as possible routes to the Orient. He may have been too far out to sea to notice them. Closing in on the land again he spotted a coast "green with forests" and named it Lorraine. It was probably New Jersey.

Soon the expedition found "a very attractive place among steep hills. From the hills runs down into the sea a great stream of water, very deep at the mouth." Verrazano had blundered into New York Bay, and the river with the large mouth apparently was the Narrows now named for him. The ship anchored in this waterway with some of the men taking a longboat out for a look around the upper bay, thinking it was a lake. According to Verrazano:

> We found the country on its banks well inhabited. The people were about the same as those we met before, dressed in birds' feathers of different colors. They came toward us happily, raising loud shots of admiration and showing us where we could land our boat safely. We passed up the river about half a league, seeing that it formed a beautiful lake about three leagues in circuit. On the lake about thirty of their barks were going from one side to the other, carrying an infinite number of people coming to see us.

Obviously the natives considered the sudden arrival of white beings from the sea an event of the first magnitude. Perhaps the Indians were the first of the Mahicans.

On this brief tour the sailors probably saw the Hudson River's mouth and the verdant tip of Manhattan. But when strong contrary winds came up, they scurried back to the ship and quickly put out to sea, spending only half a day in the best natural harbor of North America.

Rounding Long Island, the voyagers continued along the coast until they found "an island triangular in form . . . the hills covered with trees and well populated, judging from the number of fires we saw along the shore." This must have been Block Island, just past the eastern end of Long Island. The weather unfavorable, they did not put in.

A few miles farther Verrazano rounded Point Judith and sailed into Narragansett Bay. He anchored off the big island Indians called Aquidneck—now Rhode Island—at the future site of Newport. In this "most beautiful harbor" the group stayed fifteen days, the longest stopover of the voyage.

The Indians seemed helpful and friendly. Some came aboard ship, two of them kings "more beautiful in form and stature than can possibly be described." The royalty wore large chains of colored stones as emblems of office and deerskins decorated with porcupine quills dyed various colors.

"These are the most handsome people and most gentle in their manners that we have met on this navigation," wrote Verrazano. "They exceed us in size. They are of a very fair complexion, some inclining more to a white and others to a tawny color. Their faces are sharp, their hair long and black and which they take great pains to adorn. Their eyes are black and sharp. Their expression is mild and pleasant, greatly resembling the antique."

As for the women, Verrazano described them as, "very graceful with fine countenances and pleasing appearance." Some wore fine lynx skins on their arms and ornaments "such as the women of Egypt and Syria use" in their hair.

These Indians were the Wampanoags, recent victors over the Narragansetts for possession of Aquidneck. Living mainly by agriculture, the Wampanoags were well known along the coast for their farming expertise. They lived in beehive-shaped houses of bent saplings covered with grass mats or bark. The Frenchmen thought their life idyllic.

In particular the Wampanoags were fascinated by the explorers' gewgaws: "They did not appreciate cloth of silk or gold, or of any other kind, and did not care to have such. The same was true of steel and iron—being shown our arms they did not admire or want any of them. . . . The things they liked were small bells, blue crystal glass, and other objects of fantasy to put in their ears or hang about the neck." Surprisingly, the Wampanoags were not interested in mirrors; they merely glanced at them and passed them back with a smile.

During their fifteen-day stay, the Frenchmen explored Narragansett Bay and found the region "very fertile and attractive, full of tall and spreading trees." Surrounding present-day Pawtucket were champaigns, as the French called prairies, "open and without any impediment of trees, of such fertility that whatever is sown will give great return." They were in the most fertile part of New England.

Out of the oak and walnut forests the excited Frenchmen flushed deer and "luzernes" [lynx]. The Indians captured them in nets or shot them with arrows tipped with flint, jasper, or hard marble. Crab apples, cherries, plums, "filberts" (probably hazel or beechnuts), and "many kinds of fruit different from ours" were in abundance.

A short time after resuming the voyage, the sailors rounded an "eminent promontory." Surely this was Cape Cod, the most eminent promontory on the East Coast. Instead of following the land, they apparently sailed north until they hailed the coast again at or near Saco Bay on the Maine coast.

This was "a high land full of very thick forests, with pine, cypress [probably cedar] and such trees as grow in cold climes." The trees of New England were part of a great pine and hardwood forest stretching from Maine to the Mississippi River. Many early explorers remarked on the size of Maine's "stately timber."

But the Maine natives proved to be not so stately. Although they looked like Wampanoags, they did not act like those friendly folk. They were "of such crudity and evil manners, so barbarous, that despite all the signs we could make we could not converse with them. They are clothed in the peltry of bear, luzernes . . . and other wild beasts. Their food, as far as we could perceive . . . we suppose to be obtained by hunting and fishing, and of certain fruits and a kind of wild root." The root was probably the groundnut, a potato-like tuber that later helped sustain the Pilgrims.

Any time the Europeans came ashore these Indians, probably Abnakis, shot arrows at them then fled into the forest. Nevertheless the Abnakis were eager to trade, yet would do so only by lowering baskets from a cliff to receive the visitor's fishhooks, knives, and other tools "to cut withall." Afterward they used "all signs of discourtesy and disdain as were possible for any brute creature to invent, such as exhibiting their bare behinds and laughing immoderately."

It is no surprise then that the Abnakis often appear in early records as intemperate and profane. Most Indians, though, were friendly to the first Europeans they met as long as the visitors posed no threat to them. And the Indians were always ready to trade. It is likely that the Abnakis had already met traders and fishermen—and perhaps slave hunters—along the coast and had been ill-treated by them. Verrazano named their country *Terra Onde di Mala Gente,* Land of Bad People.

Continuing along the Maine coast Verrazano counted some thirty-two islands "lying all near the land, being small and pleasant to the view, high, and having many turnings and windings between them, making many fair harbors and channels." Three islands he named after young princesses at the French court. Today they are Monhegan, Isle au Haut, and Mount Desert. After continuing on the coast up to Newfoundland—apparently missing the Bay of Fundy and Nova Scotia—Verrazano sailed for home.

Between 1534 and 1543 at the behest of Francis I, Jacques Cartier made three voyages to America, all in search of that mysterious strait known as the Northwest Passage. Other than the fact that the navigator was born the year before Columbus left on his first voyage, not much is known about him. Certainly he was one of the period's finest navigators. Not on any of his three voyages did he lose a man or a ship at sea. His only casualties came from an epidemic ashore.

After landing at present-day Cape Bonavista in Newfoundland, Cartier shaped a northern course. Soon he reached an island, no more than a huge rock, filled with thousands of birds. "All the ships of France might load

a cargo of them without anyone perceiving that any had been removed," he said. In the air were "a hundred times as many more." Cartier named this the Isle of Birds.

Today this island is known as Funk Island and every inch of it is still covered with birds: gannets, murres, and kittiwakes. The first thing a modern visitor notices about Funk Island is the screeching and the never-ceasing flapping of wings. When the wind is right, the smell is overwhelming. It is the odor of more than a hundred tons of bird excrement, of rotting fish vomited up by the parent birds and not eaten by the nestlings, of the indescribable stench of a million creatures packed together in a small place.

The stench must have given the island its modern name. In various languages funk means to steam, to smoke, or a great stink.

With one notable exception, this must have been the scene that greeted Cartier. In his time Funk and the craggy islets close by were also crowded with black-and-white birds as big as geese and "so fat it is marvelous." These birds had striped beaks and wings no bigger than a man's hand. They, of course, were the auks that flocked in incredible numbers around the rocky islands off Newfoundland and in those days perhaps as far south as Cape Cod.

The great auks, magnificent birds, were the pride of the New World. They looked splendid sitting on rocky promontories with their heads thrown back while their great, black eyes scanned the water for cod, rock bass, and perch. Spotting their next meal, they swooped down into the waves and used their tiny wings like fast propellers to dart after their prey.

Auks became a favorite food of meat-starved seamen, hunters finding them little trouble to take. In water they outswam the fastest boat, but on land they could barely walk and their miniature wings would not lift their plump bodies into the air. They were good to eat fresh or salted, their eggs a delicacy. Later comers stuffed mattresses and pillows with their feathers, used their bones for fishhooks and needles, fed fires with their fat.

Now they are seen only in the paintings of John James Audubon, for the great auks are no more.

In half an hour's time Cartier's men, after landing, clubbed to death enough auks to fill two boats. Some of these they soon ate, salting down the rest for future meals. Though taking auks was easy work, the men found other birds a different matter. Gannets, the big-billed seabirds larger than gulls, were particularly troublesome; they "bit even as dogs."

The men took birds' eggs as well, and once had to beat a bear to them. The beast, "as big as a cow and white as a swan," escaped the sailors' first attempt to capture him, but the next day the men caught up with him and afterward feasted on red meat as well as poultry. "The flesh was as good to eat as that of a two-year-old steer," wrote the captain.

White bears came farther south in the sixteenth century, riding the ice floes like circus acrobats. They were spotted off Cape Cod and may have drifted as far south as Delaware Bay. Despite the mature male's twelve hundred pounds or more, they were agile. Equally at home on land or sea, the great creatures infested the lands in and around the Gulf of St. Lawrence and were sighted perhaps more than any other animal. The Norsemen mentioned them and Karlsefni named Bear Island—off Labrador—after them. Gaspar Corte Real is said to have brought home "men of the woods and white bears."

No less than twenty places on Newfoundland alone are named Bear something or other. But perhaps man and his ways, especially his destruction of the seals and cod it fed on, drove the white bear into more northern climes and in the nineteenth century the animal became known as the polar bear.

Later explorers found the animal good eating as well, though not in every case. Several Frenchmen fell violently ill after dining on one of the animals and if it hadn't been for the Indians' herbal medicine and sweat baths they probably would have died. The natives claimed the white bear had poison in its liver.

Cartier followed the coast of Newfoundland until he entered the Strait of Belle Isle and then crept along the mountainous southern coast of Labrador. Just beyond Blanc Sablon, at a little island called Greenly, the Frenchman saw large flocks of puffins. Junior-size cousins of auks, the little puffins were red-beaked, red-footed, and built nests by burrowing under flat rocks. Perhaps because of their burrowing habits, it was easier for them to survive than the auks. Today the Canadian government protects the puffin to spare it the similar fate of its cousins.

Cartier was less than impressed with the sterile coast of Labrador. According to him, there were only "stones and frightful rocks and uneven places. On this entire coast I saw not one cartload of earth, though I landed in many places. Except for Blanc Sablon there is nothing but moss and stunted shrubs. To conclude, I am inclined to regard this land as the one God gave to Cain."

The natives of Caindom were "well formed but untamed and savage. They wear their hair bound on top of their heads like twisted straw, sticking into it a pin or something and adding birds' feathers. They are clothed in peltry, men and women alike, but the women shape theirs more to their figures and gird their waists. They paint themselves with tan colors. They have boats in which they go to sea made of birch bark, and from which they catch a great quantity of seal."

These boats are the first recorded mention of the northeastern Indians' favorite means of transportation, the birchbark canoe. According to Cartier, these Indians were not native to the region: "Since seeing them I have learned that this is not their home. They come from warmer lands to take seals and other things for their sustenance." The Indians may have been Newfoundland Beothuks, renowned seal hunters, or they could have been Iroquois from the St. Lawrence Valley—they were apt to go hunting far from home.

Instead of continuing down the Labrador coast, Cartier turned back to Newfoundland and explored its western shore. He found parts of it spectacular, with reddish cliffs and waterfalls.

In the middle of the Gulf of St. Lawrence the Frenchman came upon three islets, "two of them as steep as a wall, so that you cannot climb up." These were the aptly named Bird Rocks, "as thick with birds as a meadow with grass"—gannets, auks, puffins, kittiwakes, and murres. His party landed on the biggest island and killed over a thousand auks and murres.

Nearby, Brion Island had "the best land we have seen, worth more than the whole of Newfoundland. We found it full of beautiful trees, meadows, fields of wheat [lyme grass], and pease in flower as fair and abundant as I ever saw in Brittany." Wild roses, strawberries, gooseberries and a variety of "sweet-smelling herbs" abounded.

Bears and foxes roamed Brion Island and on the shore were "great beasts like oxen, with two teeth in the mouth like an elephant's tusk and swimming about in the water." Of course these were walruses. The crew was impressed by these great water mammals, the big bulls weighing as much as three thousand pounds with tusks as long as a man's forearm. In the days of European exploitation soon to come, a walrus's tusks would be more valuable than an elephant's and walrus skin would be used for making ropes stronger than the day's fiber ones. The animal's oil would caulk the seams of ships.

When the crew tried to catch one of these sea oxen it proved too quick for them. It was just as well, for the walrus, like the white bear, can be a fearsome opponent. A party of Englishmen later passing this way annoyed some of the sea oxen and immediately regretted it: "When we approached nere unto them with our boate they cast themselves into the sea and pursued us with such furie as that we were glad to flee from them."

Four times the Frenchmen landed "to see the trees, marvelously beautiful and sweet-smelling. We found them to be cedar, yew, pine, white elm, ash, willow, and several others unknown to us." The open country was "fair and full of pease, white and red gooseberries, strawberries, raspberries," and the usual lyme grass mistaken for wheat. The great trees seemed "as excellent for making masts for ships . . . as it is possible to find." Apparently the crew thought Prince Edward Island was a part of the mainland.

So far the voyagers had only glimpsed Indians. At marvelous Chaleur Bay on the New Brunswick coast, the best harbor Cartier found on his three navigations, matters changed. Fleets totaling forty or fifty canoes came out to meet the ships, the Indians brandishing furs on sticks to show that they wanted to trade. Afraid to let so many Indians get close, Cartier frightened them off with a few shots from his swivel guns.

Continuing to make signs of friendship, the Indians persisted. The captain sent two men ashore to deal with them, taking knives and a red cap to give their chief. "They showed marvelous great pleasure in possessing these wares," wrote Cartier, "dancing and going through many ceremonies and throwing salt water over their heads with their hands." The shower bath was their way of showing gratitude and happiness.

Their words for hatchet and knife identify these Indians as Micmacs. They must have sprinkled themselves well, for Cartier said they "bartered everything they had to the extent that they went back naked . . . and made signs that they would be back on the morrow with more furs."

At Gaspé Bay, a few miles farther up the coast, the natives were different. "They could well be called savages," wrote Cartier, "for they are the poorest people that can be in the world. All their possessions, except for their canoes and fishing nets, are not worth five sous."

They wore only loin cloths and a fur or two thrown over their shoulders. Their heads were "shaved all around in a circle, except for a tuft on top of the head, which they leave long like a horse's tail. This they do up and tie with leather thongs." These Indians were apparently Hurons; their haircut sounds like the scalplock. They had no sleeping accommodations other than turned-over canoes and Cartier said they were "wonderful thieves."

Accompanying the Hurons was their chief, Donnaconna, up from his capital on the St. Lawrence River—at the present site of Quebec—on a fishing trip. When Cartier ordered a large cross set up and took formal possession of the land for France, Donnaconna followed the proceedings with interest and no little trepidation. Although he didn't understand exactly what was going on, he knew enough to realize his sovereignty was being threatened. In sign language he indicated that no one was going to take over part of his country without his blessing.

Cartier placated the chief with gifts and rhetoric. He must have done a good job since Donnaconna allowed the captain to take two of his sons back to France. Cartier promptly dressed the boys in European duds, complete with red caps and brass necklaces, and promised to bring them back next summer.

Before departing for home, Cartier explored part of Anticosti Island at the mouth of the St. Lawrence River. He described it as, "a flat island composed of white and alabaster rocks." On it were, "many wild animals such as bear, porcupine, stags, does, hinds, birds of all kinds . . . and many wild fowl that keep to the woods and resemble pheasants." Probably the pheasants were grouse.

Cartier returned next summer as promised, bringing back Donnaconna's two sons. By now the boys knew enough French to interpret, and communication went more smoothly. Again the captain stopped at Funk Island to load up on wild poultry before heading into the Gulf of St. Lawrence. This time he approached Anticosti Island from the north instead of the south bringing him directly into the mouth of the St. Lawrence River. With great expectations Cartier's expedition headed up the river feeling assured this grand watercourse was the fabled Northwest Passage.

The abundance and variety of marine life astonished Cartier: "This river abounds with more kinds of fish than man has ever known, for you will find in their season most kinds, both of salt and fresh water. . . . You will find many whales, porpoises, and fish as large as porpoises without any fins and in body and head are formed like a greyhound, as white as snow."

These last were the little white whales known as belugas that lived—and still do—in the salt waters of the St. Lawrence. Reaching seventeen feet, they weigh up to a ton. Sociable creatures, they congregate in bands of several hundred. Twentieth century scientists discovered that belugas have a sort of sonar—they "see" things by echo detection.

But Indians deduced as much long ago and took advantage of this knowledge. In the St. Lawrence's waters they placed reed wands that vibrated with the tide. "Seeing" these as impenetrable barriers, the little whales veered off toward the mud flats where fishermen, waist deep in water, harpooned them.

The river also boasted "great quantities of mackerel, mullet, sea bass, sartre, large eels, and other fish, and in their time there are smelt as good as in the Seine." Elsewhere the captain added pike, bream, and sturgeon.

Once out of the glacier-scarred Laurentian Highlands the scenery improved dramatically. This St. Lawrence Valley then was "as good a land as can be found, highly productive with many fine trees." They included oak, elm, cedar, ash, hawthorn, maple, birch, and beech.

Heading for Donnaconna's capital of Stadacona, the explorers reached a large island where many Indians, the chief's Huron subjects, were camping. The natives "made good cheer and danced. . . . Some of the chief men came to see our boats, bringing us a heap of eels and other fish, two or three loads of maize—the bread they live on here—and several big melons."

Receiving a delegation on board, Cartier gave them small gifts "with

which they were well content." The Hurons welcomed the Europeans with their traditional gesture of friendship—rubbing the visitors' arms and legs. Donnaconna had himself rowed out and greeted Cartier by kissing the captain's arms and then wrapping them around the Frenchman's neck. This must have been the customary greeting among executives in these parts.

Apparently this island was occupied only at fishing time. The Frenchmen were elated by the wealth of grapes, some "as big as Damson plums," and named the place *Ile de Bacchus*. It is now called Ile d'Orleans and is about the northernmost place where one can find grapes.

Just up the coast, on a scarped promontory beside the St. Charles River, Stadacona lay nestled at the foot of the great Rock of Quebec. Cartier found the country rich, "with many fine trees . . . beneath which there grows as good hemp as that of France, and it grows without sowing or labor." The hemp was probably wood nettle, a fiber important to the locals.

The Frenchmen got a pleasant reception here. An elder delivered a preachment, a typical long-winded talk, while the women sang and danced. Donnaconna, it turned out, did not want Cartier to go farther upriver. He was afraid his bitter rival, the chief of Hochelaga a few miles upstream, would manage to ally himself with the powerful strangers and take over his dominions.

First Donnaconna got his son, one of the interpreters, to try to dissuade Cartier. This failing, he offered the white chief a gift of two more boys and a girl, his niece. When Cartier declined all profferments the chief resorted to a sort of morality play. Three "devils," medicine men with blackened faces and long horns, paddled out and circled the flagship, one of them constantly haranguing in the local fashion. Presently some braves came out and dumped the devils into the river. Sinking to the bottom before being carried off to the woods, they were "dead."

According to the interpreter the god Cudouagny was warning the Europeans that going upriver would mean death in the ice and snow. But Cartier said he wasn't afraid. Laughing, he said he had consulted Jesus and his prediction was for good weather. Donnaconna soon dropped his attempts at deception and the ships proceeded.

On up the St. Lawrence, Cartier found the countryside charming: "Along the banks we saw the most beautiful and fertile lands, as level as a body of water, full of the finest trees in the world. Along the river were many vines loaded with grapes as if they were planted by the hand of man. . . . Also we found many houses along the banks, the people at the time busily engaged in fishing. They came over to our boats in as friendly and familiar a manner as though we had been their countrymen." One Indian picked up Cartier and carried him ashore as if he were a small child. Here the Frenchmen tasted their first muskrats, "large as rabbits and wonderfully good."

Wildfowl along the route delighted Cartier—"cranes, swans, bustards, ducks, larks, pheasants, partridges, blackbirds, thrushes, turtledoves, goldfinches, canaries, linnets, nightingales, sparrows, and other birds the same as in France, in great numbers." The captain, though apparently an enthusiastic birdwatcher, must have been confused by the variety. Not all the winged life he mentioned existed in North America. His "nightingales" were probably some sort of thrush, his "canaries" goldfinches, his "turtledoves" passenger pigeons. Bustards? Many French explorers mention them, apparently referring to wild geese.

When they neared Hochelaga a thousand or so natives greeted the Frenchmen, "with as good a welcome as ever a father gave a son." Cartier put on his dress uniform and went off to meet the chief of Hochelaga, three miles away. He was much impressed with the countryside they passed through; it was: "the finest and most beautiful one could find anywhere, with oaks as lovely as any in France." There was also, "fine land with large fields covered with the corn of the country, resembling Brazil millet and about as large or larger than a pea. They live on this as we do on wheat."

Hochelaga was a wooden citadel of the sort eastern Indians built for defense, circular and enclosed in wooden palisades. It had a single gate, closed with bars, and ramparts for hurling stones at invaders. Hochelagans, also Hurons, were in a more vulnerable position than the Stadaconans because their town lay on one of the favorite routes of the ferocious Iroquois.

"There are some fifty houses in the town," wrote Cartier, "each fifty or more paces long and twelve to fifteen wide. They are made of timbers and covered, roof and sides, by large pieces of bark and the rind of trees, some as wide as a table and artfully tied together. . . . Inside are a number of rooms and chambers. In the middle of the house is a large room or space upon the ground where they make their fire and live together. Afterwards the men retire with wives and children to their private rooms." And this is our first report of the multifamily longhouse favored by Indians of the Northeast.

Once ensconced in the central plaza, the Frenchmen sat on bark mats and awaited a visit from the chief. Soon several braves carried him in on

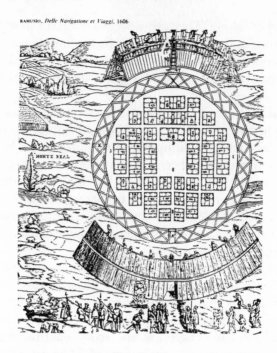

RAMUSIO, *Delle Navigatione et Viaggi,* 1606

a deerskin litter; he was paralyzed. After Cartier had shown his respect by rubbing the chief's arms and legs, the Hochelagan leader presented him with a red headband decorated with porcupine quills, symbol of rank among chiefs. Several blind or crippled Hochelagans were brought out to be touched by the visitors, thought possibly from heaven. "One would think that God had come down to cure them," Cartier said. Later he read from the Gospel and made the sign of the cross over the invalids.

These Hurons slept on bark, covering themselves with animal skins. Their clothes came from the pelts of otter, marten, beaver, fox, deer, and lynx, "but for the most part they go naked." The Frenchmen marveled at how the people of such a cold clime went about with so few clothes.

Cartier's men didn't care much for the Hochelagan's food, not because it wasn't good, but because it wasn't salted. Their principal dish, cornbread, was ground in a wooden mortar and mixed with water before being baked on a hot stone covered with heated pebbles. Pottages of corn, beans, peas, and cucumbers were also common. In the winter the Hochelagans lived on fish and eels, smoked during the summer.

Before leaving, Cartier climbed a nearby mountain. The St. Lawrence still ran for as far as he could see, with today's Laurentian Hills on one side, the Adirondacks and Green Mountains on the other. Between these ranges lay "the finest land it is possible to see—arable, level, and flat." To his dismay, just beyond where he had left the longboats, was "a *sault* of water, the most impetuous one could possibly see." These were the Lachine Rapids. Knowing that nothing larger than a canoe would ever get past them, Cartier realized his journey had ended. The mountain he was on he named *Mont Real,* and around it would grow the city of Montreal.

Although he had gone as far as he could, Cartier was convinced there was a large body of water somewhere inland that led to the Indies. He believed the Indians had told him as much. Communicating in sign language, they probably were trying to tell him of the Great Lakes.

Cartier also got the idea from the natives that there was gold nearby. They had touched the Frenchmen's gold ornaments, jabbered excitedly, and pointed to the west. Probably they thought the European's ornaments were the same as their own copper ones from the Lake Superior region, the ancient smelting pot of the continent. All over inhabited Canada and the United States, there was sharp trading in Lake Superior copper. Had the Indians known of gold they might still have preferred copper—reportedly they loved its smell.

With fall in its early stages, Cartier returned to the fort he had built at Stadacona to prepare for the first winter Europeans would spend in mainland Canada. His men strengthened their fort, brought in great stacks of firewood, salted down fish and game. Soon enough, though, the Frenchmen found out how rough a Canadian winter could be.

"From mid-November to the fifteenth of April," Cartier wrote, "we were continually frozen in by ice, thicker than two arms' length, with snow on the land to the depth of four or more feet. . . . All our beverages were frozen in their casks and the ice was four fingers thick within the ships, below as well as above deck."

Inside most of the time, Cartier had plenty of time to ponder the manners and customs of his native hosts. One that particularly wounded his Christian soul was the *maison de plaisir,* a common brothel for nubile girls. Here men of any age could come and take their pleasure; the girls had to remain until they captured a husband, which might not be easy since Huron men were allowed more than one wife. The Frenchmen visited one of these establishments and found it "as full of girls as schoolrooms in France are full of boys."

Cartier's description of Indians smoking was the first such report outside the tropics.

According to Cartier, tobacco was "carried about the neck in a small pouch, in lieu of a sack, and with it a tube of stone or wood. They crumble the leaf at all hours and put it into one end of the tube, then place a live coal on it and suck on the other end. They fill their bodies with smoke until it comes out the mouth and nose as though from a chimney."

Columbus first reported the use of tobacco after he saw natives of the Caribbean smoking cigars—rolled-up leaves—in their noses. Verrazano tells of an Indian approaching his sailors with a stick burning at one end, surely a tobacco pipe, as a peace offering. In fact the pipe Verrazano's Indian carried seems to have been the same kind Cartier's men saw, not one of the large pipes with an upright bowl seen by so many other Europeans. The former was more like an elongated cigarette holder whose bowl was merely an enlargement of the stem and opened through the front.

"They say these things keep them warm and in good health and they never go without them," said Cartier. "We made a trial of this smoke. When it is in one's mouth one would think one had taken powdered pepper, it is so hot." Of course the tobacco was raw and strong, not the cured product of a later time.

In midwinter "the pestilence" broke out in Stadacona. Gums rotted, teeth fell out, legs swelled and were "blotched with purple-colored blood." Rising to arms, shoulders, and necks, these were the classic symptoms of scurvy. With no fresh fruits or vegetables to provide the necessary vitamin C, many Indians died.

Scurvy was not contagious, but the French captain took no chances; he forbade any Indians to come into the fort. Yet many of his men did contract the disease, for the same reason the natives got it. In two months "out of the 110 men that we were, not ten were well enough to help the others, a thing pitiful to see."

Afraid of letting the Indians know how debilitated his men were, Cartier explained that they were all working inside the fort and had them—all those able to—make loud noises with hammers and stones. At least twenty-five had died and some forty were believed to be near death when, "God, in His holy grace, took pity on us and sent us knowledge of a remedy." The remedy, provided by the grace of the Indians, was a tree called the *annedda*.

One day an Indian who had been seriously ill for ten or twelve days came to the fort. He brought several branches of the tree and showed the white men how to grind the bark and boil it in water. They drank this ill-tasting potion every other day and applied the residue to their swollen legs. Right away they felt better and in a few days were cured. Some claimed it also cured them of the syphilis they had had for several years, perhaps a faith healing in these cases.

We know now that the *annedda* was the northern white cedar, with a foliage and bark high in vitamin C. "All the doctors of Europe could not have done as much in a year as this tree did in one week," exulted Cartier. The men tore a tree apart and took as much of it as they could back home. It is believed the white cedar was the first New World tree transplanted in the Old World, where it got the name *arborvitae*—tree of life.

In the meantime, Chief Donnaconna, a practiced spinner of tall tales, fired up the imagination of the Frenchmen with improbable stories of fabulous wealth and fantastic creatures somewhere up the Saguenay River. In the precious land of Saguenay, said the chief, there was a huge amount of gold as well as jewels, all there for the taking. The people of Saguenay were white and wore woolen clothes, and as an added inducement the chief mentioned unipeds, humans flying with wings like a bat's, and peculiar folk living entirely on liquids because they had no anus.

Cartier had no chance to investigate wondrous Saguenay. Growing alarmed at the arrival in Stadacona of many strange Indians, he quickly set sail for home. Before leaving he abducted Donnaconna and nine other natives, none of whom ever returned to America.

Cartier returned to the New World in 1541, but found little new or exciting. He believed he had discovered gold and diamonds, but the "gold" turned out to be those glittering little frauds, iron pyrites, and the "diamonds" were quartz crystals.

Once it was determined that North America was not part of Cathay, it was impossible for Europeans to imagine the size and nature of such a huge land mass. Three centuries would pass before anyone traversed the continent from one coast to the other, and during that time the American wilderness continued to surprise and bedazzle those venturing into its fastnesses.

Even before European mariners had completely mapped and described the coastline, the Spanish and French were trying to pry loose the secrets of a wilderness known as Florida.

2

FUMBLING IN FLORIDA
Ponce de León, Ayllón, Narváez, Ribault, and Laudonnière

While France and England were preoccupied with domestic squabbles and religious wars, Spain forged a national unity that allowed it to become the premier power in the conquest of the Americas. Although the Spaniards were concerned mostly with the rich lands of South and Central America, they eagerly searched the northern horizon for more splendid civilizations to exploit. They found none, but at the time they had no reason to doubt that they would.

Spanish exploration of North America began in 1513 when Juan Ponce de León landed in what is now the state of Florida. At that time Florida referred to a vast vagueness that seems to have included most of the continent north of Mexico. According to legend, Ponce de León was looking for a fountain of youth that Indians in Puerto Rico had told him about. In their poetic way of speaking, these natives may have been referring to any of a number of hot mineral springs in the present-day southern United States. Or the Spanish may have enlarged the myth later. But Ponce de León was not an old man searching for a means of rejuvenation, as he is often portrayed. He was in the prime of midlife, looking for worlds to conquer and probably for slaves to take.

Coming up from Puerto Rico, Ponce de León landed on the east coast of Florida somewhere between present-day Cape Canaveral and Jacksonville. Tradition claims he first set foot at what is still called Ponce de León Inlet, just south of Daytona Beach. The weather must have been gorgeous, the Indians unfriendly. There was a sharp engagement, the earliest report in North American history of natives greeting their first European visitors with armed hostility. History doesn't record what started the trouble.

The Spanish party reembarked smartly and sailed around Florida to the first good landing spot on the west coast, perhaps San Carlos Bay or more likely Charlotte Harbor. Here Indians, Calusas, swarmed out into the water to meet the Spaniards' longboats, acting in all friendliness. But something happened and quickly the Indians turned on the Europeans, fighting ferociously.

Again the Spaniards left rather quickly, this time sailing back to Puerto Rico. When passing the Florida Keys they captured 170 turtles and some seabirds and eggs.

Eight years later, in 1521, Ponce de León returned. This time he had with him a large party of men and horses as well as cattle, pigs, and goats. Obviously he intended to try his hand at colonizing, and probably landed again at Charlotte Harbor. The Calusas, who hadn't forgiven the Spaniards' previous incursion, once more drove off the interlopers. When Ponce de León was fatally wounded by an arrow, the Spaniards boarded ship and gave up Florida as a lost cause. They left no record that they saw anything other than scowling aborigines.

Five years after Ponce de León's last journey, Lucas Vazquez de Ayllón tried to establish a colony in another part of Florida, today known as South Carolina. Somewhere Ayllón had met a young Christian Indian known as Francisco who told the eager Spaniards about his homeland, the land of Chicora somewhere on the East Coast. Chicora, claimed the youth, was just right for Spanish settlement, "for in it there are many trees and plants of the kinds in Spain and the people are of good understanding. In greater part they are ruled over by a man of giant stature. There are pearls and other things which they trade."

After piquing Ayllón's curiosity, Francisco expounded on his stories more and more. There were, he said, people with tails a few inches long and as thick as an arm, obliging them to dig a hole before they could sit. Their fingers were as wide as they were long, they had scaly skin, and lived on raw meat. Another tribe was ruled by giant kings and queens who grew to whatever size they wished by using a special diet and by stretching their limbs to the desired length. Apparently Ayllón enjoyed what this imaginative and garrulous youth said for he raised about five hundred prospective settlers and hauled them to the South Carolina coast, the land of Chicora. After arriving there they disembarked at a river their leader named the Jordan—either today's Santee or the Waccamaw. Their flagship ran aground while entering the river, losing much of the company's food and equipment.

Now that he was home again, Francisco promptly vanished, never to be seen again. Instead of the spectacular country he had led them to expect, the would-be colonists found a sandy, swampy wilderness. They were left without guides, interpreters, or good prospects.

Ayllón picked up the pieces and moved his colony down the coast to the Gualdape River. The spot he chose was just south of the present site of Savannah, Georgia. Natives here were called Guale, later known as Creeks. Mostly they lived in communal houses: "These are very large and are constructed of very tall and excellent pine trees on which the upper branches and foliage remain. A double file of pine trees forms a wall, the space between them being fifty to thirty feet wide. . . . They cover the entire structure with well-laid mats. In each of the great houses there may dwell two hundred persons." The venerated bones of the dead rested in stone temples decorated with oyster shells.

The Savannah area was mostly a land of pines and oaks, but also thriving were chestnut, laurel, walnut, mulberry, and palmetto trees. Leathery-leaved sumac ran wild, and grapevines festooned the woods. Countless birds—cranes, thrushes, geese, and ducks—resided here as did deer, rabbits, squirrels, and skunks. The Savannah River also held "a great abundance and excellence of fish." Reportedly more than six hundred could be taken in a single cast of the net. One fish was so big twelve colonists once dined on it and still had some left over.

From the writings of these colonists comes the first mention of that beautiful yet repulsive creature known as the "squnck." Early comers quickly learned that this animal could exude a powerful odor. "No sewer ever smelled so bad," wrote one European. "I could not have believed it if I had not smelled it myself," said another. "Your heart almost fails you when you approach the animal." Later comers learned to give this "woods pussy" a wide berth. Despite the big stink, some Indians are said to have relished the skunk as food.

Eventually a plague struck Ayllón's colonizers. According to one report, "many persons died of hunger for lack of bread and because in their infirmity they were unable to fish." Ayllón himself perished before the year was out and the ill-fated colonists returned to their homes in Hispaniola.

In 1528 another Spanish conquistador appeared, the red-bearded and one-eyed Panfilo de Narváez. A rough customer, he wasn't interested in colonization, only in finding gold and other riches like those the Spaniards had come upon in Mexico and Peru.

Knowing of Ponce de León's troubles farther south, Narváez traveled up Florida's west coast to Tampa Bay. Here the Indians, almost certainly Timucuas, seemed friendly enough. They brought the strangers deer meat and other food, then overnight slipped away into the darkness. The Spaniards woke up to a deserted village of small thatched homes and one large family house that would hold perhaps three hundred. Rummaging around, the men found a gold "tinklet" that excited everyone.

Later on some Timucuas reappeared and made signs showing they wanted the Europeans to move on, and to be quick about it. The Spaniards, somehow, got the idea from them that a district a little further north called Apalachee (the country around modern-day Tallahassee) contained gold. Probably the Timucuas encouraged this belief. It didn't take Indians long to find out what Europeans were most interested in—and therefore how to get rid of them.

After a quick tour around Tampa Bay, Narváez split up his forces. Half of the men went north in the ships with orders to follow the coastline and look for good landing spots. The ships sailed out of the bay . . . and were never seen or heard from again.

Narváez took the other half of his men and started for Apalachee, expecting to find gold. So they would not get lost, the troops stayed close to the coast. Narváez's men would not have encountered many problems if it had not been for the rivers, creeks, and fallen timbers in their path.

After marching for fifteen days they came to what was probably the Withlacoochee River, spending much time getting across it. They had not met any Indians or seen any villages during their trip, but at this river they met natives who took them home and gave them maize. They remained friendly, the chief even volunteering to guide them to Apalachee.

Soon the Spaniards reached the Suwannee River and spent a day crossing it. A horse and rider were accidentally killed here. The men buried the rider and had the horse for supper.

Apparently there had been little to eat. The Spaniard's food supply, puny to begin with, quickly ran out and the men were making do with maize and the largesse of the palmetto tree. The large leaf buds of palmettos, the hearts, made a tasty cabbagelike salad. Spaniards called the trees cabbage palms.

Besides palmettos the woods were dominated by longleaf pines. There were also walnuts, hickories, magnolias, bald cypresses, cedars, liquidambars (the scientific name of the sweet gum tree known by that name until more recent times), and live oaks. These trees, dripping Spanish moss, must have been astonishing. Though not towering like some trees, they could measure up to twenty feet in girth and were armed with brawny branches that might reach out fifty feet from the trunk, almost horizontally or in a gracefully curving arc. Indians ate their acorns—after leaching them to remove the tannin—and cooked with their oil.

The forests here, mostly open, were full of deer, rabbits, bears, and "lions" who were actually cougars or bobcats. And there was a peculiar little beast the Spaniards had never seen before: "It carries its young in a pouch in its belly and as long as they are small they are thus carried until they know how to search for food. If they are out searching and people come, the mother does not flee until she has gathered her young into her pouch." This had to be the first mention of that marsupial, the American opossum. It was the first pouched creature the Europeans had ever seen. Pouched animals were common in the age of dinosaurs, but the possum is the only one left in North America.

Early Frenchmen called the opossum *rat de bois,* and one of them described this eccentric character as "an animal that has a head like a

sucking pig and of about the same size; hair like a badger, gray and white; the tail of a rat; and paws like a monkey. It has a purse beneath its belly where it produces its young and nourishes them."

Most observers, like this Frenchman, thought the young were born in the pouch. This belief led to an odd story about babies not being produced in the uterus like ordinary embryos, but developing like buds on the female's nipples then breaking off. The theory seemed plausible because the babies, weighing one-sixteenth of a pound at birth, were immediately placed in the pouch and clung to the nipples as if they really did grow on them.

After Narváez's expedition crossed the Suwannee the men started traveling west instead of north and the pace quickened—the Spaniards were eager to reach Apalachee and load themselves with riches. Certainly many birds covered Apalachee's lakes and much maize waited to be harvested, a lot more already in the cribs.

Once at Apalachee the Spaniards quickly dispossessed the Indians and occupied their homes—round thatched houses like those of the natives farther south. Prowling around the outskirts of town, the Indians harried the intruders as much as they could. They were especially afraid of the foaming beasts the Spaniards rode. Like those elsewhere on the continent, these Indians had never seen horses before. Rumor claimed they ate people.

After all their looting, the Spaniards found no gold in Apalachee. Narváez's scouts reported no change in Indian civilization anywhere near Apalachee and farther west, some Indians told them, was only "great lakes, dense forests, immense deserts, and solitudes." Soon Narváez decided to turn southwest to the coast and wait for sight of his ships.

The march was more like a retreat. Indians, most likely Timucuas, shot arrows at the soldiers all the way to the coast, killing several of them. These were "people of marvelous physique, very lean, and of great strength and speed." A Timucuan skeleton unearthed in modern times was said to be that of a man seven feet tall.

The bows of the Timucuas were "thick as an arm, eleven or twelve palms long [close to seven feet], and used with such accuracy as not to miss at two hundred paces." Tipping their arrows were flint, bone, snake teeth, or fish scales, against which the Spaniards' light armor provided little protection. Soldiers were found with "their corpses traversed from side to side with arrows." More damaging were the reed arrows without heads; they were sharpened points that splintered when striking the soldiers' chain mail, inflicting multiple injuries.

Depleted, the expedition eventually arrived at the town of Aute, either at the mouth of the present-day Apalachicola River or a little farther up the coast at St. Andrews Bay. Wherever they were, no ships were there to greet the weary soldiers. Feeling abandoned, Narváez decided to build boats and follow the coastline to the Spanish settlements in Mexico.

Apparently these foot soldiers and cavalrymen didn't know much about building boats. They also had no tools, no forge, no pitch for holding timbers together. But there was a wealth of good native timber around and the men, anxious to get out of there, started building. There was one experienced carpenter around and a Greek who knew how to make pitch out of the resin of the longleaf pine abounding everywhere in Florida.

Splitting yellow pine trees, the Spaniards made rough planks and fashioned oars from bald cypresses. A blacksmith set up a crude forge, created a bellows from deerskin, and started turning spurs, stirrups, and crossbows into nails, saws, and axes. The soldiers no longer needed their riding gear because they had eaten their horses, carefully saving the skins to make water bottles.

After the men made sails of shirts stitched together, a makeshift fleet of five small vessels set out along the coastline of the Gulf of Mexico. Seven days later they came to an island, or perhaps a sandbar, at what was probably present-day Pensacola. Here they took some mullet and "dry eggs," probably turtle eggs. But soon they were out of water—their horsehide bottles had rotted—and the little fleet put in at a large inlet, perhaps Mobile Bay.

A chief wearing a robe of civet-marten greeted them in a friendly manner and showed them to a village where the Spaniards got water and a good deal of cooked fish. However this friendliness quickly soured and the Indians attacked during the night. Beating off their advances, the Spaniards reembarked smartly.

Soon tongues of land and small marshy islands spread out before them into the sea. On a point of land the Spaniards "took sweet water from the sea because the river entered the sea in a flood. Landing to roast some maize that we had, we could find no wood and therefore went on to the river." Almost certainly this was the great delta of the Mississippi River; these Spaniards would see the river a dozen or so years before Hernando de Soto.

The river's strong current and a north wind pushed Narváez's explorers back out into the Gulf of Mexico. The five boats drifted apart in the night and only three were rejoined the next day. The other two were lost forever.

Narváez had the best boat of the remaining three, and the stoutest

crew. All were trying to reach the Louisiana coast again, at a place where they had seen "many smokes," when the leader of one of the other boats asked Narvaez for a line. The captain remarked that it was too late for mutual help, that everyone should do what was best to save his own life—and then pulled off into the gulf. His craft drifted seaward and Narváez and his boatmates were never seen again.

Those in the other two boats eventually landed on the Texas coast. Their further adventures are part of Chapter 4.

The Spanish government decreed that, for the time being at least, it would waste no more money on Florida. This left the door open for the French, and in 1562 they sent an expedition under Jean Ribault to find a site for a French colony. Ribault's men eventually landed at Anastasia Island near where the Spanish would soon build St. Augustine, the oldest city in the United States.

The French expedition came to the great mouth of what Ribault named the River of May, now the St. Johns River. The country seemed "the fairest, fruitfulest and pleasantest of all the world. It abounded in honey, venison, wildfowl, forests, woods of all sorts, palm trees, cypresses, cedars, bays, and the highest, greatest, and fairest vines in all the world with grapes accordingly, which naturally and without man's help and trimming grow to the top of the oaks and other trees that be of a wonderful greatness and height."

The "fair meadows" were full of herons, curlews, bitterns, mallards, egrets, woodcocks "and all other kinds of birds." In the woods dwelt deer, rabbits large and small, wild turkeys "in marvelous numbers," and "sundry other wild beasts."

The natives, of the Saturiba tribe, welcomed them "without any token of fear or doubt." Chief Saturiba appeared with several hundred men, behind them "twenty pipers making the wildest kind of noise, without any harmony or rhythm, each blowing with all his might as if to see who could blow the loudest."

The Saturibas were dressed in "feathers of different kinds, necklaces of a special sort of shell, bracelets made of fish teeth, belts of silver-colored balls—round and oblong—and pearl anklets. Many of them wore round, flat plates of gold, silver or brass." The gold and silver, the Europeans found out later, were scavenged from wrecked ships and the brass probably was Lake Superior copper. These plates, hung from the neck on chains, signified rank—only the most important men wore them.

The St. Johns area seemed a fine site for a settlement, yet Ribault moved up the coast to see if he could locate something even better. After passing several likely looking rivers, he anchored in a large sound with a wide-mouthed stream emptying into it. The Frenchmen explored this place for two weeks, marveling at "the havens, rivers, and islands of such fruitfulness as cannot with tongue be expressed."

The abundance of fish was clear, the woods full of turkeys and deer. Ribault saw two deer so large he forbade his men to shoot them. On an island at the mouth of the sound there were so many egrets "the bushes be all white and covered with them."

What the Frenchmen saw was typical of the Sea Islands. Ribault named the sound Port Royal, a name it still bears, and the great stream that fed it was the Broad River of South Carolina. After establishing the outpost of Charlesfort, either on Parris Island or near the present town of Port Royal, Ribault returned to France for supplies.

The handful of men he left behind fought among themselves, had trouble with the local Cusabo Indians, and finally tried sailing to Europe in a ramshackle boat of their own devising. They were picked up—except for one man the others ate—by a passing English ship. Later a Spanish raiding party destroyed the abandoned fort.

Back home Ribault became involved in the religious wars then going on and was thrown into prison. He did not make it back to the New World

for three years. In the meantime the French sent over René de Laudonnière, Ribault's lieutenant, to seek out another spot where France could
find "new means of traffic and profit in strange lands." Laudonnière
returned to the St. Johns River.

Once there Laudonnière picked out a bluff covered with cedars, palms,
and laurels, and built Fort Caroline in 1564. The site was on the south
side of the river, near today's city of Jacksonville. The view out to sea was
so lovely, Laudonnière thought, "that melancholics would be constrained
to change their nature." The view inland was of a great green valley "in
which were the most beautiful prairies in all the world and herbage most
suited for pasturing livestock."

Chief Saturiba welcomed the French back and for a time life was
idyllic. The soil was rich beyond imagining, "an incomparable land never
as yet broken with iron plows, bringing forth all things." Florida Indians
raised the same crops as most other natives of the New World, the main
ones being maize, beans, and squash. They tilled the soil with wooden
mattocks or hoes with heads fashioned from fish bones. Women did the
seeding with a planting stick.

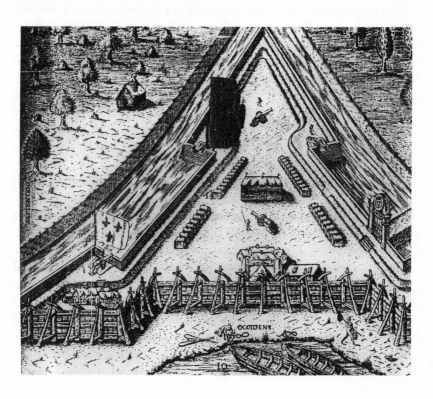

There wasn't much tending to the crops after they were put in—nature took over from there. Rich soil and mild climate allowed for two crops a year on the same land. Putting away the harvest in a common storehouse, the Saturibas distributed it according to rank. There was only a six-months' supply: "in the winter months they retire to the woods for three or four months, where they make huts of palm leaves . . . and live by hunting and fishing."

The Saturibas generally lived in round houses with conical roofs "fitly made" of wood and reeds. Twenty or thirty houses made up a village, everything contained in a high palisade of logs. The village had one narrow entrance with a guardhouse on each side. It was said that the sentinels at the guardhouses had a remarkable sense of smell—so acute they could detect an enemy a mile away. When someone was seen, or smelled, lurking about, the sentinels aroused their fellows inside. Those who didn't respond or didnt' fight fiercely enough were executed in a public ceremony, kneeling while their heads were split open by a sharp-edged club.

In the middle of town was the chief's house, surrounded by those of his nobles. A large ceremonial house with a circle of benches inside adjoined. It was for council meetings.

In these council chambers important men decided affairs of state and downed a ceremonial drink made from the leaves of *Ilex cassine,* a type of holly. Apparently the drink, something like coffee, produced a great fever. After imbibing, when his temperature subsided, a man was supposed to be able to go for twenty-four hours without feeling hunger or thirst. Only those who had proved themselves in battle could partake of this semisacred nectar.

A similar concoction was the black drink, made from another kind of holly. This was a powerful purgative and emetic (*Ilex vomitoria,* botanists call it) meant to clean out the body. It was used both by the sick and by the healthy as a spring tonic. Most Indians of the Southeast partook of this liquid.

Laudonnière's Frenchmen, like the Spaniards of Narváez, were impressed with Saturiban men—most were half a head taller than the Europeans. They were

> mighty, fair, and as well proportioned of body as any people in all the world. . . . They are neither flat-nosed nor big-lipped, but their faces are round and full, their eyes clear and timid. Their hair is very long and they bind it very neatly about their heads. This trussing of their hair serves as a quiver to carry their arrows when they go to war. It is marvellous to see how swiftly they can take the arrows into their hands and shoot them unbelievably straight and far.

To the Saturibans war was a serious and grisly business. They declared war by sticking arrows along a public path with locks of hair attached. The grisly part came after the battle was over.

First the victors scalped the fallen, using a reed knife "sharper than any steel blade," and dried the scalps over a fire started with a live coal carried in a skin bag. "After the battle they invariably cut off the arms and legs of the fallen warriors with their knives, broke the bones with a club, and then laid the bloody bones over the fire to dry. They hung the bones and scalps at the ends of their spears and carried them home in triumph. After they had mutilated the dead, they always shot an arrow into the corpse. They would never leave the battlefield without doing this."

Saturiban men and women pierced their ears and wore small oblong fish bladders in them, "which shine like pearls when inflated and when dried red look like light-colored rubies. It is remarkable that these savages should be able to produce such tasteful ornaments." Both sexes let their fingernails grow long and sharpened them to a point. With the women this was a matter of vanity, but the men used their nails to claw the enemy. Chiefs and their wives tattooed themselves by pricking the skin and rubbing in finely ground charcoal.

Reports said some of these Indians were hermaphrodites, who let their hair grow long and wore skirts like women. Though "considered odious," these natives had their place. In war they carried the army's provisions and at other times they took the sick away and cared for them until they were well.

Treating the ill involved cutting open the skin of the forehead and sucking out some of the blood, in turn this was drunk by pregnant or nursing women: "They believe that drinking it makes their milk better and their children stronger, healthier and more active." Another method of curing the infirm was to have them lie on a platform above a fire and breath in the smoke, "expelling the poison from the body and thus curing the disease." The natives also thought it cleansed them to smoke "tapaco" and blow it out through the mouth and nose.

When a chief died he was buried with appropriate solemnity; his grave was surrounded by arrows and topped by his favorite drinking vessel. All the man's worldly possessions were placed in his house and then it was burned. The chief's subjects mourned for three days, both men and women cutting off their tresses as a token of respect. For six months certain chosen women continued to mourn for the man three times a day with a great howling, a usual native way of expressing strong emotion, good or bad.

Except in winter, the Saturibas did not want for food; wildfowl crowded the lakes and brimmed the streams. Indians went out in their big log canoes, made by burning out the insides of tree trunks, and pulled in fish by the hundreds. Or they built great underwater weirs "so cunningly set together, after the fashion of a labyrinth or maze, as it is impossible to do with more cunning or industry."

The woods here hid many deer, turkeys, and bears. Many early comers to the American wilderness learned to love, as the Indians did, the tender young flesh of bear cubs. Natives hunted deer by concealing themselves in the skins of large ones, peeping through the eyeholes.

When large game was not plentiful, they ate reptiles large and small—lizards, snakes, and alligators. One Frenchman killed and ate an alligator, finding the soft white belly meat tender and much like veal. This one was

> killed by a gunshot, struck between two scales. Otherwise the crocodile is strong enough for any hits. His mouth is extremely large and his teeth straight, like the teeth of a comb. His body is twelve or thirteen-feet long. His legs are short in proportion to his body, the claws strange and cruel. His tail is long and strong. His life depends upon his tail, for it is his principal means of defense. . . . The lower jaw protrudes over the upper jaw, a monstrous thing. The mere sight of it strikes a man with fear.

These and other Europeans thought this animal was a crocodile, like the ones of the Nile River. They did not know that the alligator was a separate species recognizable by its rounded blunt snout rather than the tapered one of the crocodile. The crocodile also has a long lower tooth that shows even when its jaws are closed. The alligator's long tooth fits snugly in the reptile's upper jaw.

There were crocodiles in Florida, but they weren't found until much later. They lived in the deeper swamps around the southern edge of the Everglades, and there weren't many of them. Alligator comes from Spanish *el lagarto,* the lizard.

Laudonnière's Frenchmen arrived at the mouth of the St. Johns River in May, alligator mating season. Big bull alligators made the swamps ring "with a noise like dreadful thunders." Bulls were staking claims to the females—and arguing loudly about it. This courting ritual among the saurian set had been going on for millions of years, all the way back to the age of great reptiles, and it often resulted in pitched battles between two bulls over the affections of a belle. Our earliest description of such a conflict comes from pioneer naturalist William Bartram, traveling these same swamps in 1773:

> They suddenly dart upon each other. The boiling surface of the lake marks their rapid course. . . . They now sink to the bottom folded in horrid wreaths. The water becomes thick and discolored. Again they rise, their jaws clap together, re-echoing through the deep surrounding forests. Again

they sink, when the contest ends at the muddy bottom of the lake, and the vanquished makes a hazardous escape, hiding himself in the muddy turbulent waters and sedge on a distant shore. The proud victor exulting returns to the place of action. The shores and forests resound his dreadful roar.

Certainly Bartram saw a "prodigious assemblage" of 'gators on the prowl for food. He watched transfixed as one big alligator seized "several great fish at a time and squeezed them betwixt his jaws while the tails of the great trout flapped about his eyes and lips, ere he had closed them. The horrid noise of their closing jaws, their plunging against the broken banks of fish and rising with their prey some feet upright above the water, the floods of water and blood rushing out of their mouths, and the clouds of vapor rising from their wide nostrils was truly frightful."

The roaring of these creatures, Bartram thought, resembled heavy distant thunder. When several hundred roared at the same time it encouraged a listener to think "the whole globe was violently and dangerously agitated."

Whether the Frenchmen at Fort Caroline saw and heard anything like this we don't know. We do know that most early comers gave reports that led Europeans to believe the New World alligator was some sort of fire-breathing creature akin to the dragons of medieval times. Their size was almost always exaggerated, some reports claiming they were thirty or even forty feet long. The average 'gator today is ten to fourteen feet, and it is unlikely that any early traveler saw one longer than twenty feet.

To hunt alligator the natives started by setting up an observation post near the water, a small hut with cracks. When an alligator approached, the observer inside called to his fellow hunters waiting in the woods. The

others ran out and jammed a long pole down the reptile's throat, the rough bark preventing it from slipping out. Then they flipped the alligator over on its back where it was helpless.

Hunters then filled the soft underbelly with arrows or beat it to death with clubs. They may have put it to sleep first by rubbing its stomach. Herpetologists think rubbing an alligator's stomach creates some sort of pressure on its brain.

Once in a while a brave—a really brave brave—tried to catch an alligator in the water. He swam in front of the monster armed only with a thick branch of a carefully judged length. When the prey opened its great flapping jaws to their full extent the Indian propped them open by quickly inserting the branch, grasping it in the middle and holding it vertically. Its jaws now useless, the alligator was lugged ashore.

Sometimes, though very infrequently, a warrior inserted his arm instead of a stick. As the alligator started to crunch down on it, the Indian quickly jerked his arm out. The jaws slammed together with such force some of the lower teeth went clean through the upper jaw and sealed the mouth shut.

Hearing of French incursions into their domain, despite earlier proclamations, the Spanish established St. Augustine just down the coast from Fort Caroline in 1565. The same year an expedition from St. Augustine fell upon the French fort, massacring all the colonists. In 1586 the English buccaneers Francis Drake and Martin Frobisher razed St. Augustine, which was rebuilt three years later.

So the French abandoned Florida. The Spanish remained not so much to colonize as to set up bases as havens for their ships that had been ravaged by storms or by French or English pirates. This made the southern coast and the Florida Keys particularly important, so the Spanish tried hard to make friends with the Calusa Indians living there.

In 1566 Pedro Menéndez de Avilés, Spanish captain-general of Florida, paid a goodwill visit to Chief Calusa and succeeded in recovering several shipwrecked sailors and some gold and silver salvaged by the Indians. Later de Avilés built a fort near the main Calusa town, a settlement of about four thousand.

Though only about twenty-five years old, Chief Calusa controlled a large territory: most of the mainland of southern Florida, the Keys, parts of the Bahamas. His lands included one of the largest inland bodies of water in America, the Lake of the Mayaimi, or Lake Okeechobee as it is known today.

Okeechobee was not the usual sort of lake. Its main artery was not a

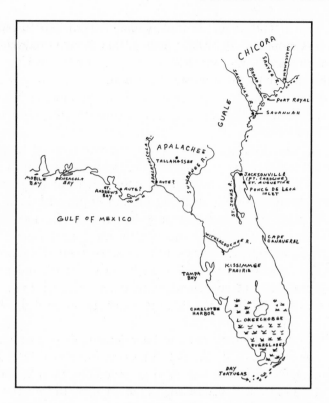

river, but the muddy waters draining into it from Kissimmee prairie just to the north. It had no river outlet either—the surplus water simply drained into southern Florida, creating the soggy Everglades. Spaniards found the lake a fisherman's paradise, packed with huge fish and with eels thick as a man's arm.

The Calusas of the keys lived on fish, shellfish, turtles, whales, as well as the many deer and bears that often swam from one key to another. On the Dry Tortugas (Spanish *tortuga,* turtle), a group of little islands that had once been Keys and were now treeless and paralyzed by the sun, the great sea turtles came ashore at night to lay their eggs. They were "the size of a large shield and have as much meat as a cow, the meat being of several kinds."

Spain kept Florida until 1819 when the fledgling United States bought the territory. During the three previous centuries Florida was a lonely northern outpost of Spain's great colonial empire in South and Central America.

In the early sixteenth century the continent of North America had revealed only a smidgen of its true nature, just enough to pique the curiosity of Europeans over what remained to be discovered. Hernando de Soto in the Southeast and, at the same time, Francisco Coronado in the Southwest, set about to satisfy that interest.

3

TOURING DIXIE
De Soto Looks for Gold and Glory

The fate of the Narváez expedition did not daunt Hernando de Soto. He had already become rich conquistadoring in Peru and Central America, and saw no reason why he couldn't do the same in Florida. Narváez had stuck close to the shoreline, but De Soto's experience had shown that coasts yielded little; the riches of Central and South America had been in the interior.

De Soto landed in 1539 at about the same place Narváez had, Tampa Bay. He had the largest force yet assembled on the North American continent: about six hundred men, some two hundred horses, a pack of vicious bloodhounds, and thirteen pigs.

The bloodhounds were for fereting out the natives, for De Soto delighted in "the sport of hunting Indians." Sometimes he set dogs on them just to watch the mongrels tear the poor victim to shreds. Refusing to do De Soto's bidding could cost an Indian a hand, an ear, or a nose.

As for the pigs, they were insurance against the possibility that this unknown land would afford little to eat that a Spanish stomach could accommodate. De Soto would protect these porkers as though they were sacred cows, rarely allowing his men to slaughter even a few. They were emergency rations, but there never seemed to be an emergency great enough. Before long there were hundreds of them.

These odd curly-tailed creatures fascinated the natives. Given half a chance, they would snatch a pig and have it in their cooking pot in no time; the animals grew fat on all the good things to eat the forest floor provided. It was said that the Indians watching De Soto's progress carried three ropes—one for a Spaniard, one for a pig, and one for a horse.

When De Soto landed in Tampa his men were captivated by the dazzling beauty of the landscape—the blue of sea and sky, white sands of a beach gently curving, the nearby woods of cypress, ash, and magnificent live oaks. Inland, though, the Spaniards found that the lovely appearing woodlands hid dirty ponds, muddy sloughs, and sometimes impenetrable tangles of undergrowth. Much of the terrain was virtually impossible for cavalry to move in; horses sank up to their haunches in quagmires, cut their legs on unseen snags, or became hopelessly wrapped in dense thickets.

Only in Florida a few days, De Soto had an unexpected stroke of good luck, about the only one he would have in his four years of thrashing about in the forest primeval. It happened when an advance party of cavalry came upon a small band of Indians and attacked. The surviving natives fled into the woods, except for one. As lancers bore down on him he cried out in Spanish, "Do not kill me, cavaliers. I am a Christian!"

The man turned out to be Juan Ortiz, a survivor of the ill-fated Narváez expedition. He had lived with the Indians for eleven years. According to de Soto's chroniclers, the tribe that had captured Ortiz was preparing to kill him when an Indian girl arranged for his escape to a friendly neighbor-

ing tribe. Until almost the end of De Soto's travels, Ortiz stayed with him as an interpreter.

When he started north De Soto moved inland, following a line from Tampa Bay to present-day Dade City to Ocala to Gainesville. Before reaching Ocala provisions were used up and the army was reduced to eating boiled greens, unripe maize stalks, and palmetto cabbages. A relief party found some of their compatriots lost in a swamp eating herbs and roots, "and what was worse, not knowing what they were." The strayed soldiers must have feared their meal was poisonous, yet were too hungry to care. Sometimes wild chestnuts, "rich and of very good flavor," helped fill many stomachs.

At Ocala the Spaniards found "maize, beans, and small dogs, no small refreshment for people about to die of hunger." This was the first of several times the Spanish mentioned dining on canines. Even though these explorers must have rebelled at eating them, hunger drove them to it. They pronounced the flesh good.

Following the approximate route of today's Interstate 75, once a main native trail north and south, the expedition pushed on to the vicinity of Gainesville, another fertile spot. Around here the chestnut trees were much smaller than those seen further south. Possibly they weren't chestnuts at all, but chinkapins. Often, where Indians periodically burned the land, chinkapin trees grew in great numbers.

Continuing north, De Soto's expedition built a bridge over the Santa Fe River—the River of Discords, the men called it—and arrived at the pleasant village of Lake City on the edge of what is now Osceola National Forest. Now de Soto turned due west, following the general route of Narváez.

Near Live Oak, "a very pleasant village, in a pretty spot, with plenty of food," the Spaniards had their first serious encounter with the locals. The Indians, Timucuas again, received the worst of it. De Soto's troops captured about three hundred natives and put them in chain gangs to carry their equipment and supplies. It was the beginning of a system of intimidation and degradation that would last for the duration of De Soto's New World stay.

Continuing west, the Spanish crossed the River of Deer—the Suwannee—on a bridge made of pine trees. Afterward they settled into winter quarters at Apalachee, where Narváez had been. The area was "very fertile and abounded greatly in yield of much maize, beans, and squash. There were many fruits and deer and a great diversity of birds and fish."

Hearing of the Spaniards' approach, the natives fled and left both standing crops and full cribs. Soldiers harvested the Indians' crop and spent a pleasant five months in the region, except for occasional disturbances by the Indians who remained—the ones, of course, who had been dispossessed.

Spring came and De Soto headed north again, into Georgia. Despite the swollen rivers and the mud brought on by spring rains, they found Georgia, "picturesque and luxuriant." Forests were sometimes thick with undergrowth, at other times open and inviting. The men admired the long leaf pines—"taller than the tallest spire in Spain"—that dominated many forested areas. Mulberry trees were "quite like those of Spain, just as tall and larger, but the leaf is softer and better for silk."

Mulberries, the Spaniards had already discovered, were "of great advantage as food." Indians dried them into cakes and stewed them with cornmeal and oil. Southeastern Indians used the inner bark of the mulberry tree, beaten thin and dyed, to make remarkably beautiful and serviceable cloaks and shawls.

Along the trails were "countless roses growing wild like those in Spain, and although they do not have as many leaves, since they are in the woods, they are nonetheless fragrant and finer and sweeter." Wild strawberries were "very savoury, palatable, and fragrant . . . a fine, delicate fruit." The plants grew so thickly the Spaniards found it hard to believe. They made many a meal on strawberries, wild spinach, wild potatoes, and roots of the wild flag.

By now the Spanish were in Creek tribal lands, where they found something akin to their own civilization. The Creeks had well-developed agriculture, lived in comfortable houses, and wore well-made clothing. The Spaniards marveled at the abundant fields of maize, wild flax, and several other crops. A long growing season in this part of the country allowed for two harvests a year, perhaps even three.

As it was for most Indians, maize was the Creeks' principal crop. Yellow corn was for eating—often it was roasted and eaten green—while the white version was for making flour. These Spaniards, like other early comers, learned that it was more convenient to eat roasted maize in the Indian fashion than to take the time to turn it into flour.

Each Creek dwelling had its own small field, the other larger fields held in common. Planting time was announced by an aged warrior known as the "old beloved one," and storytellers and musicians playing on skin drums helped ease the tedium of sowing. Everyone went to work in the fields—even the highest chiefs—and stayed until the work was done.

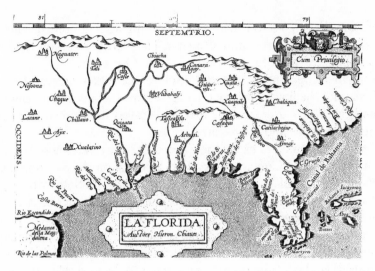

Planting was not skillfully done though, and old women supposed to do the weeding could not work up much enthusiasm for the task. Rich soil made up for any neglect.

Sturdy Creek homes, bright with a whitewash made from oyster shells, were constructed of cypress, pine, locust, or sassafras logs driven into the ground. Roofs were gabled with planks made of split tree trunks and covered with saplings and bark while walls were plastered inside and out with a tough mortar mixed with grass. Loopholes, through which to shoot in case of attack, were left in the walls, then covered with thin plaster and circled on the inside. From outside there did not appear to be any holes but, when it came time to defend the home, warriors punched out the plaster to shoot their arrows. It was a clever deception, one copied later by European frontier settlers.

The Creeks furnished their houses with cane couches covered with skins of deer, cougars, or bears—all skillfully tanned and soft. Hoping they would grow up with the virtues of these animals, little boys slept on cougar skins and little girls on fawn hides. The legs of couches rested in cups of water to discourage spiders or snakes from climbing in with the sleepers. Covering the floors were carpets of hemp or flax, woven in intricate designs.

In summer the Creeks wore as little as possible; when winter came they donned clothes made of deer, otter, and beaver skins. Hunters wore skin leggings underneath their long coats. Everyone went barefoot in summer, ignoring the plentiful snakes, and in cold weather wore moccasins of deer or elk skin. Women sewed skins together using horn or bone needles and thread made of hemp or animal sinews. They left the hair on the inside of garments for warmth, rather than outside for looks.

The chief Creek man sported a headdress of turkey or swan feathers. This was not the flowing war bonnet of western Indians, but a band worn around the head—a crown, the Spaniards called it. Women wore ornaments of seashells and fresh-water pearls.

The pearls seemed to excite the Europeans. They were most impressed when the queen of Cofitachequi, a Creek capital on the Savannah River at about the site of Augusta, Georgia, presented de Soto with a pearl necklace. The queen came out to meet the Spanish leader on a covered litter carried by men of rank.

Creeks here, "a very clean people of polished manners," offered the Spaniards presents of clothes, dried deer meat, "dry wafers" (probably cornbread), and salt from over the mountains to the west. Hospitably they turned over half their village to the strangers with the queen leaving town to avoid contact with the soldiers.

The Spaniards, as usual, helped themselves to the corn stored in granaries. Much of the rest of the time they spent gathering up over two hundred pounds of pearls, some of them snatched from corpses. The custom hereabouts was to store the dead above ground in mortuary temples with pearls in their eyes, ears, and noses, and in slits in their arms, legs, and stomachs. The Europeans were not aware of it yet, but these pearls were practically worthless. They came from mussels instead of oysters.

Some of the men found Cofitachequi such a fine place they wanted to stay and found a colony. But De Soto, eager to find gold, pushed on into South Carolina. He took with him a hostage the records call the Lady of Cofitachequi. It isn't clear whether this Lady was the queen or someone else. In any case, she gave the Spaniards the slip at the earliest opportunity.

Moving across the Piedmont of South Carolina, the expedition met natives of a less elegant culture. They had little corn, but provided the Spaniards with small dogs and turkeys. They probably were Cheraws.

Following the Savannah River north, De Soto found the ground sloping sharply upward; they were approaching the Blue Ridge Mountains. The journals say little about crossing this watershed except to mention that they passed over "a high range of rough and lofty ridges." Nights were bitterly cold and hailstorms battered them.

When they were crossing a corner of present-day North Carolina an

Indian chief presented De Soto seven hundred turkeys. They were hefty birds, later called "big chickens" by explorers. They flew from time to time, but would rather run. Some natives hunted wild turkeys for food, though it appears that many did not care for turkey meat. Yet all were fond of the beautiful raiment that could be made from turkey feathers. Gray-black feathers tinged with silver and copper made gorgeous cloaks for men and all sorts of imaginative millinery for women. If the Indians did not want to ruin the feathers with an arrow, they tried chasing them down, not always an easy task.

The expedition crossed a bit of present-day Tennessee and followed the Tennessee River southwest into northern Alabama, territory of the Upper Creek nation. (Later, the English named them Creeks because their towns were built on streams.) The Spaniards followed the Tennessee to its great bend around Guntersville and then made a short trip overland to the Coosa River.

De Soto was headed for Cosa, a town on the river he had been hearing much about for some time. Once there, the chief came out to meet De Soto, "borne in a litter on the shoulders of his principal men, seated on a cushion, and covered with a mantle of marten skins, the size and shape of a woman's shawl. On his head he wore a diadem of plumes. He was surrounded by many attendants playing upon flutes and singing."

As he had in other Creek lands, De Soto found that this area was not an aboriginal wilderness: "The country, thickly settled in numerous and large towns, with fields extending from one to another, was pleasant and had rich soil with fair river margins." Orchards were interspersed with fields of corn and beans and corncribs raised on posts made it difficult for rats and vermin to reach the grain. "In the woods were many plums . . . and wild grapes on vines growing up into the trees near the streams, and a kind that grew on low vines elsewhere. The berry was large and sweet, but for want of hoeing and dressing had large stones."

These were probably Chickasaw plums, as they are known today, and much relished by southern Indians. In later times, they were still found around old abandoned native villages. Some of these plums may have been persimmons, a fruit unknown to Europeans.

Cosa, believed to have been in present-day Talladega County, Alabama, was a center of the temple mound culture that was dying out. Mound building, borrowed from the more advanced cultures in Mexico, flourished from about 5000 B.C. to the beginning of the sixteenth century. Some mounds in this part of the southeast, though worn down by De Soto's time, had been as much as a hundred feet high. Originally they had temples on them.

The presence of these mounds made De Soto think he was close to another magnificent culture like those in South and Central America. But there were no riches in Cosa and the expedition continued south, following the Alabama River.

Lands along the lower Alabama River were the province of the great chief Tascaloosa, the Black Warrior who ruled over the Mabila branch of the Choctaw Indians. When De Soto arrived the chief received him in the central plaza of the village, seated atop a mound. The journals describe him as tall and noble, wearing a feather mantle reaching to his feet and with an attendant holding a sunshade over him. Tascaloosa did not rise when De Soto appeared, clearly meaning to establish his authority. The Spanish commander quickly settled the issue by having the chief

clapped in irons and ordering him to take the Spaniards to the town of Mabila.

Secretly Tascaloosa had sent runners to Mabila and when the Spaniards reached the town—near the confluence of the Alabama and Tombigbee rivers—hundreds of braves awaited. Accompanied by the captive chief, De Soto and an advance guard entered Mabila first. As the Spaniards passed through the gates of town a group of women apparently began dancing to divert the soldiers' attention. Suddenly warriors jumped out of hiding and the battle was on. After a short but fierce fight the little group of Spaniards backed out of town; De Soto had narrowly avoided death.

With their foes occupied, several hundred Indians began taking most of the Spanish expedition's equipment. When he heard of this, De Soto ordered his men to retake the town. Lasting all day, the battle proved the bloodiest this Spanish expedition would engage in during its New World wanderings.

After the fighting had ended, eighteen Spaniards were dead and 170 were wounded. De Soto took an arrow in his hind quarters. Now without medical supplies, the men dressed their wounds with the fat of dead Indians.

De Soto had been in North America now for almost two years and had nothing to show for it except a few bags of flawed pearls. Still he was so determined to find wealth like that of Mexico and Peru, he refused to give up searching. When he got word that his ships were waiting in Pensacola Bay, he kept the report from his men and ordered them to proceed north again.

A march through almost unbroken forest brought De Soto to the village of Chickasa in present-day Pontotoc County, Mississippi. It was fertile country, much of it under cultivation; the corn was in and it supplied the Spanish for the winter. The local chief gave them leather clothing, shawls, and 150 rabbits.

This was the country of the Chickasaws, closely related to the Choctaws and Creeks. The local Chickasaws developed a taste for the Spaniards' pork and early on there was an epidemic of pignapping. De Soto, in his usual direct manner, put a quick stop to this by executing two guilty Indians and cutting off the hands of a third.

For a couple of months relations were peaceful, although understandably strained, until one night when the Chickasaws slipped into De Soto's camp and set fire to everything that would burn. A sudden rainstorm

intervened, but desolation lay all about the Spanish. Their carefully hoarded food was ruined, much of their clothing was burned, their armor and weapons damaged. About three hundred pigs were turned into roast pork.

Two years in the wilderness had taught the Spaniards to fend for themselves. Setting up forges for retempering their swords and other weapons, they also refashioned pikes with shafts cut from the forest. In the Indian manner of making ropes, they twisted grass into reins and harnesses. For clothes some used "mats of dried grass sewed together, one to be placed below, and the other above." When a second attack came, the Spaniards were ready and put the Indians to flight.

Afterward the expedition threaded its way through the northwest corner of Mississippi, a thinly inhabited country full of thick forests and "pondy places." Its appearance was a sign that they were nearing the great river the Indians had been talking about for weeks, a river with oxbow lakes, bayous, and sluggish tributaries.

Somewhere between Memphis and the mouth of the Arkansas River this gaunt and tattered remnant of a once-proud expedition became the first Europeans to see the Mississippi River above its mouth. Although the Mississippi was indeed a magnificent sight, for the moment it was simply another obstacle to overcome.

A scouting party found a bend in the river with slack water and a sandbar, a good place to cross. The men started chopping down trees and fashioning them into barges using spikes and nails made by melting down some of their armor plate. No sooner had they begun work than a fleet of some two hundred dugout canoes approached swiftly across the river in their direction. A double row of paddlers, protected by wicker shields, propelled the boats. In the lead boat, under an awning, a chief sat self-importantly.

Though the Indians appeared to be friendly, De Soto decided to take no chances; he ordered his crossbowmen to shoot. Quickly the vessels swung about, the oarsmen never missing a stroke, and returned to the far shore. Every day at noon the native boats appeared, to be driven off in the same manner.

When everything was ready De Soto, fearing his men would not get safely across the river otherwise, ordered a dawn crossing. Taken by surprise, the Indians fled. By noon the Spanish commander had all his men, equipment, horses, and swine on the west side of the Mississippi. It's believed by most that the crossing was at or near Sunflower Landing just south of Helena, Arkansas.

Once on the other side, the expedition tried following the Mississippi but found the going slow and frustrating: "All one day we marched through water, in places coming up to the knees, in others as high as the waist." The expedition was now in the delta country of Arkansas, a bewildering maze of swamps, bogs, bayous, and oxbow lakes. It was "the

worst tract for swamp and water we have found since entering Florida."

For days the men floundered in wilderness mire, "where we did not find even trees and only some wide plains on which a plant grew so rank and high that even on horseback we could not break our way through." Apparently they were in one of the dense cane brakes that grew along streams in the primitive South. Flourishing in the rich alluvial soil, cane rose as high as forty feet, crowding out most other plant life. Canestalks might rear their tasseled heads for as many as a hundred miles in every direction. Indians used the tough, rigid stalks for making spears, arrows, and knives; cut off and hardened by fire, a cane tip was razor sharp, its wounds painful and long lasting.

A cane-and-reed jungle could be a prison for any man, yet it was a cozy refuge for different sorts of wildlife—ducks, minks, muskrats, beavers, bears, deer, and occasional cougar. And, of course, there were plenty of snakes.

Yet, curiously, the De Soto journals had nothing to say about snakes, especially while the expedition was in Arkansas. Cypress swamps against the background of the Ozark Mountains made the area a haven for many kinds of troublesome serpents. In few other places in the country, if any, could one find four varieties of poisonous snakes—water moccasin, copperhead, rattler, and coral.

Perhaps De Soto's chroniclers felt snakes were extraneous, not worth mentioning. Or maybe the expedition had no brushes with them because of its size. When it entered Arkansas, though considerably reduced by this time, the force was larger than most Indian hunting parties. There were about 350 men, some fifty horses, and an undetermined number of native porters.

Yet the expedition's clamor and confusion could have sent the vipers slithering away. The little coral snake, in particular, is a recluse preferring to hide under the debris of the forest floor. And don't forget the pigs, those adroit snake catchers.

Abandoning the Mississippi, the expedition emerged joyfully in northeast Arkansas. Here the country was higher and drier. Flooded annually, the land was black and rich and extensive cultivation came as no surprise to the Spaniards, who had not seen much good agriculture since leaving the Creeks. "In the fields were many walnut trees, bearing tender-shelled nuts in the shape of acorns, many being stored in the houses." Actually these were pecans, not walnuts. They were products of the ancient labors of a tree that grew to its full robustness in the Mississippi River valley.

It must have been the first time these Spaniards had seen pecans, without doubt the favorite food of many Indians in the valley.

Pacan is an Indian word, although it meant any kind of nut that had to be cracked. But only pecans cracked easily and had such sweet meat. Pounding the meat into paste, Indian women made flat cakes, or used it as thickening for stew. They also found many uses for its oil, "which they knew how to extract very well, which was good and contributed much to their diet."

The pecan, a member of the hickory family, was also used in making one of the Indians' favorite drinks, *powhicora*. Squaws pounded up the nuts and dropped them, shells and all, into water. After the shells sank, rich milk was skimmed off the top and served with cornbread hot from the fire. For a thicker version—a sort of gruel—they mixed the meat with cornmeal and flavored it with ashes or lye.

The natives living in northeast Arkansas were the Quapaws, staying in the alluvial lands between the Mississippi River and Crowley's Ridge, a natural levee left by the former course of the St. Francis River. De Soto thought the several towns in the area "the best situated of any we have seen in Florida." The biggest of them was Pacaha, "very well enclosed with towers on the walls and a moat around it." A canal connected the moat and the Mississippi, and the number and variety of fish that passed through it astonished the Spaniards.

Some of the fish were strange indeed to European eyes. There was one, "the third part of which was head, with gills from end to end, and along the sides were great spines. . . . In the river were some that weighed from a hundred to a hundred and fifty pounds."

Surely the explorers were getting their first look at the great Mississippi River catfish. Its size and fearsome appearance—jutting barbels, great mouth, pop eyes—must have startled anyone seeing it for the first time. Some early comers, to their dismay, discovered why the catfish was such

a formidable opponent. Le Moyne d'Iberville, later the first French governor of the Louisiana Territory, reported in 1699 that there were "fishes that have a sting." One of his men was so badly hurt by catfish spines that he was unable to stand for two months and almost lost a leg.

In 1986 a fisherman pulled a 140-pound catfish out of the Arkansas River near Little Rock. In De Soto's time it is likely the fish were much bigger—three hundred, four hundred, even five hundred pounds. In southern Arkansas in 1983 workers for the Arkansas Geology Commission uncovered the fossilized remains of a catfish skull two feet long. Judging from the skull, this catfish would have been about ten feet long and weighed close to fifteen hundred pounds when it lived in the shallow waters covering this part of Arkansas some forty million years ago.

With such a long time to slim down, it shouldn't be difficult to imagine mere five hundred pounders in the Mississippi four and a half centuries ago. One of these catfish may have been the one "as big as a hog" mentioned in the De Soto records.

Some fish mentioned in the journals, undoubtedly, were alligator gars. One of the gar's favorite habitats was the St. Francis River. Strong bonelike scales joined edge to edge instead of overlapping give it great natural protection. Indians used their scales as arrow points and their teeth for bleeding themselves.

When De Soto asked the Quapaws where they got hides for their shields and their wonderful woolly robes, he was told that in the north a certain large animal provided the natives of that country with everything they needed. Though happy to trade with them, the Quapaws were so

Barbue

Poisson Armé.

afraid of these warriors they did not go into the region to hunt for themselves. These boogermen were probably the Osages of Oklahoma and southern Missouri, who considered northern Arkansas their special hunting preserve.

The Spaniards had heard of buffalo before, but this seems to have been their first direct knowledge of what they called cattle or cows. The record isn't clear on whether they actually saw any buffalo. If any did they were probably members of a small scouting party De Soto sent north on a rumor of gold. The party came back telling of Indians that lived in skin tents who, when they went off to hunt, packed up the tents and took them along. The cattle there, said the report, "were in such plenty no maize could be protected from them and the inhabitants had to live upon the meat."

Instead of heading north where his army could have lived very well on the buffalo, de Soto turned south and reached the Arkansas River just upstream from where it runs into the Mississippi. It was a rough trip, the men passed through "an immense pathless thicket of desert for seven days where they slept continually in ponds and shallow puddles." This was the tangled, muddy wilderness of the White and L'Anguille rivers and numerous bayous. (In the sixteenth century desert meant a wilderness.)

Despite the uncomfortable surroundings, the country provided plenty of food. Much corn grew on the fertile levees and fish were plentiful. There were so many fish in shallow streams the Spaniards simply clubbed them to death.

After reaching the town of Coligua, about on the site of present-day Little Rock, the Spanish turned southwest and entered the Ouachita Mountains. Here they paused to rest and make salt. The horses drank so much from "a warm and brackish lake" their bellies swelled. Obviously this was Hot Springs.

Eventually the Spaniards fought with the natives of this region too, the Tulla. Tullans were the first Indians the men encountered who fought with "long staves like the pikes of the Spaniards." After capturing some of the natives, De Soto sent a half dozen back to their chief minus their hands and noses. Duly presenting himself, the chief made profuse apologies for his subjects' unruly behavior and gave De Soto gifts of buffalo hides. In these parts those skins were a highly prized article of trade.

Later the Spaniards set up winter quarters in southern Arkansas, around present-day Camden, and put a stout fence around their camp to keep the Indians from burning it. It turned out to be an exceptionally severe winter, nothing like the winters in southern Arkansas today. Not able to leave their quarters for a month because of deep snows, the men were not uncomfortable in their cabins. There was plenty of food—maize, beans, nuts, dried plums and mulberries, rabbits—and plenty of firewood. Some of the rabbits were little cottontails, others big ones "of the color, form, and size of the great hare, though even longer."

The Spanish had been given rabbits before, but didn't know how to capture them. Friendly Indians around camp, probably Caddoes, showed them how to make a rabbit trap. The contrivance "yanked them from the ground by a noose of stout cord around the neck that passed through rings of cane so that it could not be gnawed through."

De Soto broke up winter camp in the spring of 1542 and began following the Ouachita River into Louisiana. Along the way Juan Ortiz, the interpreter he had found in Tampa, died. It now took hours to understand what Ortiz could have translated in one sentence. Often the expedition wandered around for days, not knowing which direction to go and sometimes crossing the same river two or three times.

One time the Spaniards were held up by a snowstorm for four days, although it was late March and they were far south. Eventually they reached the Mississippi somewhere near Natchez, in a land of natural levees and many bayous. Travel was difficult "on account of the great bogs that come out of the river, and the canebrakes and thick scrubs that are along the margin."

Apparently De Soto had given up any hope of finding treasure and was planning to take the Mississippi to the gulf and then follow the coastline to Spanish settlements in Mexico. But here in the wilds of Louisiana he

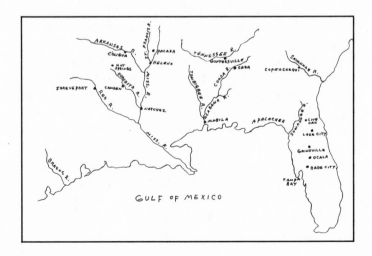

"sank into a despondency and took to his pallet." Soon he was dead of "a putrid fever."

The expedition's new leader, Luis Moscoso, ordered the general's belongings put up for auction: five Indian slaves, three horses, and his share of the pigs—seven hundred by this time. Hungry soldiers promptly slaughtered the pigs and feasted on them for days.

Moscoso decided on trying to reach Mexico by striking out overland to the West. The route was uncertain, information scanty. Apparently the expedition crossed the Red River near present-day Shreveport and plunged into Texas. In eastern Texas they saw lots of maize, plus turquoise and cotton mantles probably traded from the Pueblo peoples further west. Pushing southwest, Moscoso must have gone just beyond the Brazos River where the countryside afforded so little that his expedition came close to starving.

Moscoso decided to return to Louisiana and the Mississippi River. On the Mississippi's banks the men built several small vessels to take them downriver. The boats were caulked with Indian hemp and had cables made of mulberry bark; stirrups served as anchors. A convenient flood floated these little craft down the Mississippi to the gulf and eventually what was left of de Soto's expedition made it to Mexico.

The survivors had nothing to show for more than four years of travel and travail. They had no gold and their bags of fresh-water pearls had been lost long ago. The American wilderness had abjectedly humbled the first to venture into its interior vastnesses, and dreams of riches died early.

Out west, in a wholly different world, the Coronado expedition was in hard pursuit of the same dream at the same time.

PIERCING THE "NORTHERN MYSTERY"

Cabeza de Vaca, Estevan, Fray Marcos de Niza, Coronado

On a bright day in 1536 a band of Spanish slave hunters in northern Mexico stumbled upon quite a sight. Out of the desert wastes to the north, where no European had ever been, emerged four ghosts. These shaggy sun-scorched creatures—not ghosts but four Spanish soldiers given up for dead years before—had just completed one of the most amazing journeys in history. What a tale they had to tell.

These four men were the only survivors of the Narváez expedition—at least the only ones to make it back to civilization. When we last left it in Chapter 2, members of that ill-fated expedition were trying to sail makeshift boats along the shores of the Gulf of Mexico.

Storms had tossed that little fleet about and scattered it; most of the boats and men were never seen again. But a boat containing Alvar Nuñez Cabeza de Vaca, one of the four men cited above, washed ashore at or near Galveston Bay. It was November, 1528, and the weather was already cold, unusually so. The men from the ship disembarked and to stay alive made driftwood fires and drank water from puddles. Another craft had beached nearby and the two groups—about ninety men altogether—eventually found each other.

Friendly Indians of the Karankawas took in the Europeans and kept them alive. These natives and their neighbors to the east, the Attakapas, were mainly fishermen and collectors and lived on oysters, herbs, berries, nuts, cactus, fish, roots, and an occasional deer or antelope. In the leanest times they looked with favor on snakes, rats, spiders, and vermin.

"Then they kill a great quantity of fish and very good ones," wrote Cabeza later. "They dress many, but the greater part is lost because they have no salt." Their fish were caught by spearing, or by poisoning the water with roots and skimming off the dead ones.

For the Karankawas arrowhead was an important source of edible roots. The white-flowered plant—sometimes known as wapatoo or duck potato—was called arrowhead because of the shape of its leaf. A common vegetable in most of the country, it thrived in marshes and swamps. In winter, when the roots matured, the Karankawas waded into the water and dug out the tubers with their hands or feet. When Cabeza joined in, he was reported to have dug for days on end, until his hands were bloody masses of flesh.

The winter of 1529 proved rough for both the Spanish and the Karankawas. Many men died of "a sickness of the stomach," but more natives expired than Europeans. A few Spaniards were executed by the Indians, who were horrified because some of them ate their dead. Four Spaniards eventually headed off down the coast, hoping to walk to Mexico, and were never seen again.

Only a handful of Spaniards remained by spring, and these soon moved off with the Karankawas in search of more food. They left Cabeza de Vaca behind because he was too sick to travel. Before his illness Cabeza named his habitat *Malhado,* or Wretched Island. Presumably he was on present-day Galveston Island.

Eventually Cabeza recovered and spent the next few years moving between the coast and interior, trading with other Indian tribes. Taking shells and other matter from the coast, he brought back skins, flint, and red ochre for himself and the Karankawas. Hauling wood and water and tending the sick, Cabeza considered himself a slave, yet seemed to be able to move about and enjoyed a measure of acceptance. Five years later, in 1534, Cabeza again saw some of his former companions.

When cold weather came the husks dropped their nuts and Indian tribes, ignoring territorial rights, met at the annual pecan festival, probably along the Colorado River of Texas, to feast for a month or so. Among these tribes were some of Cabeza's Spanish mates. After getting together this handful of Spaniards made plans to meet again at an even bigger gathering when the prickly pears were ripe.

The pears ripened in summer and the Indian gathering lasted about three months. At the prickly pear convention in 1534, de Vaca and three comrades laid their plans and the following summer fled. After six years they had learned much about living in the wilderness—they expected to survive on prickly pears, acorns, and edible roots. They weren't sure which way to start out, but thought if they went west eventually they would find their way to Spanish settlements in Mexico. They began by following the upper Colorado River of Texas west.

The four men spent their first winter with the Avavares, believed to have been a Caddoan tribe. These natives "were very gentle and had some notice of Christians, though very little." Perhaps the Avavares had heard of white men appearing out of the sea on the coast. This was not a pleasant stay, however, for the Avavares had little food. A little game did sustain the men though, and they were able to make buckskin clothes and packs.

Continuing to move, Cabeza's party joined other Indians and shared mesquite pods and the cooked pads of prickly pears. The Spaniards bartered some of their buckskins for dogs to eat. Traveling north along the Colorado, the men changed their course to westward and shortly came to a village of forty to fifty houses. It was here the Spaniards ceased to be men and became gods.

In this locale the natives seemed to think the men had dropped out of the sky, children of the sun. "The Indians made a great feast in our behalf, and danced and celebrated all the time we were there," wrote de Vaca. "And at night six Indians to each one of us kept watch at the entrance to the lodge we slept in, not allowing anyone to enter before sunrise."

At their next stop, perhaps somewhere around Big Spring, the natives had already heard of the Europeans' approach and were waiting to honor them: "So great was their excitement and their eagerness to touch us that everyone wanted to be first. They nearly squeezed us to death, and without suffering our feet to touch the ground they carried us to their village."

There the townspeople turned out in swarms, bringing their sick, lame, and blind for a cure and their children to be touched by the men from heaven. The children of the sun touched the invalid, mumbled half-forgotten prayers, and made the sign of the cross. Amazingly many of the sick reportedly rose up and walked.

One of the four Spaniards, Estevàn, was singled out for special reverence. A Moor of black skin, Estevàn came to America as a slave of someone on the Narvàez expedition. Indians of the Texas interior had never seen white men before, but apparently reserved extra awe for a person of dark color.

From here on Cabeza de Vaca's journey was triumphant; the reputation of the holy men went before them. Awestruck crowds followed them everywhere and passed carefully from one tribe to another; the men were received everywhere with feasts and celebration. "The women brought us prickly pears, spiders, worms, and whatever else they could gather."

Of course this was not manna from heaven, but it must have held body and soul together. They also received gourds for carrying water and blankets of buffalo hide even though there were no such animals in the area. The Indians must have traded for the hides with natives further north.

According to Cabeza, the adoring hordes, who numbered in the thousands, eventually became a nuisance. But escape was impossible. If the men tried to run away they were pursued by natives who only wanted to touch them. "We received great inconvenience from the many persons following us," was Cabeza's understatement.

Following the Pecos River into present-day New Mexico, Cabeza and his companions crossed the Sacramento Mountains and headed south. This turned out to be the most enjoyable part of the journey, apparently not in typical desert surroundings. The local Indians provided the Spaniards with deer and jackrabbit meat and "a great quantity of nuts that had a thin shell that is eaten with the nut." These were pine nuts, or piñon nuts, from the small, bushy variety of the tree which grew in the southern Rocky Mountain region. Piñon nuts, eaten raw or roasted, were standard fare.

The prosperous times, however, did not last long. Cabeza de Vaca's men were struggling through "some desperate sierras, in great hunger by reason of the poverty of the country, which had neither prickly pears nor anything." When they left this barren region, though, hundreds of Indians were waiting for them, with piñon nuts and high expectations for deliverance from their ills.

A few days later guides brought the Spaniards to a great river—the Rio Grande near today's El Paso—where, for the first time, they saw cultivated crops, including maize. They came to an Indian village, but "there was little to eat, mainly beans and squash and a very little maize." The villagers "had nothing in which to cook but made stew in containers of calabashes." The men's hosts, later known as Mansos, gave the travelers numerous buffalo robes, though there were no buffalo around there either.

The Mansos told the Spaniards that if they traveled west there would be no food for thirty to forty days. Instead, they should follow the river north for eight or nine days before turning west again, where they would find more crops. The Spaniards did as they were advised, living at night in Indian villages. Their hosts fed them deer meat and some kind of tree fruit the travelers thought sadly lacking in nourishment. Since the Spaniards were acquainted with piñon nuts and mesquite, the mystery food may have been juniper berries.

The little party, it is believed, crossed the Rio Grande near present-day Rincon, New Mexico. By crossing that far south they missed the affluent Pueblo culture. But after the river, Cabeza turned and headed for Mexico. The Mansos had kept them well supplied with food, especially rabbits and, according to Cabeza, three kinds of deer. The young bulls he mentions must have been mule deer, the other two white-tail and antelope.

At last the four men reached Sonora, the northernmost province of Mexico. When they came upon an Indian wearing a belt buckle and a nail around his neck, they knew Spanish outposts could not be far away. Soon they met the slave owners and their long ordeal ended.

Since they had set foot in Florida eight years before, Cabeza de Vaca and his three companions had almost crossed the continent. Yet telling Spanish officials about their adventures fell on deaf ears. Enthralling them the most was what Cabeza had to say about the supposed great golden cities somewhere north of his route. The officials gasped when they heard about them—these must be the seven cities of legend.

Cabeza tried to reason with these important men, telling them he had not actually seen the cities himself. The Indians, he said, had tried to tell him of them in sign language and he could have misunderstood. The cities might not exist.

There was no reasoning with men thirsting for wealth. The officials ignored Cabeza's pleas and decided the cities must be there somewhere. They must be in the region Cabeza called Cíbola, and they intended to find them.

No one knew what lay north of Cabeza de Vaca's route; for that matter no one knew how far north went. It was all part of what became known as the Northern Mystery. The Seven Cities of Cíbola became the chief fantasy in this tale and it was thought there could be even more fabulous realms north of Cíbola. Francisco de Coronado, twenty-nine years old, would lead an expedition to find out.

First the region needed to be reconnoitered and Mexican viceroy, Don Antonio de Mendoza, sent out a small expedition under Fray Marcos de Niza. With Cabeza de Vaca gone home to Spain, Mendoza appointed Estev\án, celebrated but still a slave, to lead the friar. With a small escort of friendly Indians and two greyhounds, Estevań went ahead of the group to report what he found back to Fray Marcos. The friar's instructions were for Estevań to send back a cross for every important discovery: the bigger the find the larger the cross.

Since Indians thought gourd rattles possessed magic powers—all the big medicine men carried them—Estevań got a couple and posed as a great shaman. Trudging through the desert of Arizona, north of the route he had used to return to Mexico, he began picking up a large retinue of admiring Indians, especially women. Soon the crosses began to come back to Fray Marcos, a bigger one each time.

Estevań seemed to be finding finer and finer lands as he went along. He was also reportedly taking too many liberties with Indian women. By the time Estevań reached the region known as Cíbola, the Indians there had heard of his doings. Killing him, they distributed dried parts of his body to all chiefs in the area so they would know the black magician was no longer among the living. For good measure they dispatched his greyhounds.

As soon as he learned of Estevań's fate, Fray Marcos returned to Mexico. Though he had seen little of the country, he nevertheless added his bit to the seven cities legend. Admitting that he had not entered Cíbola, Fray Marcos nevertheless claimed he had seen the city shimmering in the distance: "I was told there is much gold there and that the natives make it into vessels and into jewels for their ears." The Cíbolans, he casually tossed in, even had small gold blades for wiping sweat from their brows.

Fray Marcos went on to say that there were camels, elephants, and other animals "with a single horn reaching to their feet." The friar may have been the victim of an Indian hoax, or perhaps he simply misunderstood the natives' sign language. Possibly the viceroy simply passed along these tales so more volunteers would sign up for Coronado's expedition.

Coming from a distinguished old Spanish family, Coronado left Spain to seek his fortune in the New World after his older brother had inherited all the family estates. In Mexico he had gained a reputation by putting down a native rebellion and then garnered a large country estate in Mexico City by marrying an heiress. He had just been appointed governor of New Galicia, a province of northern Mexico, when Fray Marcos returned.

Although the friar had little evidence, the Spanish believed there were gleaming cities out there in the desert just waiting to be found. So, in 1540, off went Coronado with about three hundred soldiers, some thirteen hundred friendly Indians, a thousand horses, and many pack mules. For meat on the hoof he took cattle and sheep and, like De Soto, at that moment struggling through the wilderness of the Southeast, a herd of pigs. Fray Marcos de Niza was Coronado's guide.

Riding in the vanguard was an officer named Melchor Díaz, whose party scouted ahead. Entering present-day Arizona his men went north through the San Pedro River valley. He found it "well populated, with flat-roofed houses and many people on the road." The people were Pima Indians, sedentary farmers who were "of interest only to be made Christians."

Yes, the Pimas said, they knew of a region called Cíbola, but their description of it was not remotely like Fray Marcos's. Díaz sent back to Coronado a disturbing report on what the Indians told him of the city:

> There are seven settlements each a short day's journey from the others, all called Cíbola. They have houses of stone and mud, rudely fashioned and made in this manner: A long wall, partitioned into rooms at both ends, the rooms about twenty feet square and roofed with unhewn beams. Most houses are entered by ladders reaching from the street to the flat roofs. The houses are of three or four stories—they say only a few are of one or two stories. Each story is one and a half *estados* [about the height of an average man] except the first, which is scarcely more than one *estado.* Ten to twelve houses are reached by one ladder. They keep stores on the ground floor and live in the upper ones. Beneath the houses they have chambers made at one side as in Spanish fortresses. The informants say that when attacked all the people gather in the houses, from which they fight. When they go to war they take shields and jackets made of dyed buffalo skins. They fight with stone arrows and mallets and with other arms of wood, the nature of which I have been unable to understand. They eat human flesh and those they take in war they keep as slaves.

Certainly the Pimas' report on fabulous Cíbola was hardly the kind of notice to stimulate a conquistador. But it was an accurate description of the pueblos of the American Southwest. The chambers were *kivas*, partly underground ceremonial rooms, and the buffalo skins must have been traded for. The remark about cannibalism was Díaz's only inaccuracy.

Leaving the Pima settlements the expedition, now including Díaz, moved up the Gila River to Chichilticalli, the Red House or Red Temple Coronado had been hearing about. In ruins, it must have been a devastating disappointment to the Spaniards. Not much of the building remained, and what they saw was covered with sagebrush: "The house was built of brown and red earth, and it must have been despoiled by the natives of the region, who are the most barbarous people so far encountered."

At one time Chichilticalli must have been a fortress or sacred building of some renown. It is worth mentioning because it was the first archeological ruin Europeans came upon in the desert Southwest. And it was a landmark of sorts, for here the scrubby grasslands ended and the higher country of the Colorado plateau began.

The region was virtually uninhabited, clothed in squat pines that produced piñon nuts and in oaks that dropped sweet acorns. An unidentified plant yielded a fruit "like that from which coriander preserves are made." There were plants the Spaniards were familiar with like watercress, grapes, penny royal, and marjoram. The Spaniards reported seeing mountain goats (Bighorn sheep), bears, gray lions and leopards, the last probably being cougars and wildcats. In the streams were otters and barbels and picones. The barbels of course were catfish, the picones may have been Gila River trout.

Coronado went up the Gila River, then traveled along the San Carlos River. After crossing the Black River, the expedition followed the White River past the future site of Fort Apache to somewhere near present-day McNary, Arizona. This was the *despoblado*, uninhabited area, now the present San Carlos and Fort Apache Indian reservations. It was indeed barren country, yet it boasted some of the most picturesque mountains and forests in the land. Food was hard to come by, though, and around McNary three famished soldiers died after eating a strange plant, perhaps green locoweed. The Apaches would later claim this land as their own.

The Spanish expedition soon crossed the Little Colorado River, and came to a cool resting place with nut and mulberry trees, flax, and grass. After feeding their horses and skirting a petrified forest, they crossed today's Arizona-New Mexico border near the present town of Zuni. Here they found the first of the seven cities, Hawikuh, the place of Estevan's demise.

The Zuñi Indians living here were warlike. Pulling up their ladders, they turned the pueblo into a fortress and fired their arrows from their roofs and through openings in the walls. Coronado's golden armor, glistening in the desert sun, made him a conspicuous target; an arrow struck him in his only vulnerable spot, his foot. Twice the Zuñis knocked him down with large stones, and the second time he was unconscious for an hour. Eventually the Spaniards prevailed and captured the town's large store of maize.

When the Spaniards learned that Hawikuh—just a few houses "all crumpled together"—was the first of the seven glorious cities of Cíbola they were, to put it mildly, irate. They had nothing but curses for Fray Marcos—he was sent back to Mexico in disgrace—and, of course, Coronado was livid. He fired off a message to the viceroy about the mendacious friar: "I can assure you that he has not told the truth in a single thing he has said, for everything is the opposite of what he related except the names of the cities and the large houses. The Seven Cities of Cíbola are seven little villages." Actually the friar was wrong about the number—there were only six.

It didn't take long to discover the whole of Cíbola. Afterward Coronado described the region to the viceroy:

> The climate and temperature of this country are almost like those of Mexico, for it is hot now and there are rains. . . . According to what the natives of the country say, the snow and cold are excessive, and this is very probably true, judging by the nature of the country. . . . The country is all level and is nowwhere shut in by high mountains, although there are some hills and rough places. There are not many birds, probably on account of the cold and because there are no mountains nearby, nor are there many trees for firewood. . . . The food they eat in this country consists of maize, which they have in great abundance, beans, and game which they must eat (although they say they do not), for we found here many skins of deer, hare, and rabbits. They make the best tortillas I have ever tasted anywhere, and this is what everybody ordinarily eats.

Coronado thought the Zuñi people intelligent and "so far as I can make out these Indians worship water because they say it makes the maize grow and sustains their lives. . . . They wear long robes of feathers and the skins of hares." They also had buffalo skins, certainly traded from Indians further north.

"We found fowls here," continued Corondo, "but only a few. The Indians tell me they do not eat them in any of the seven villages, but keep them merely for the sake of the feathers. But I do not believe this because the fowls are very good, and larger than those of Mexico." The fowl must have been domesticated turkeys, and it may be true that they were not raised for eating. Zuñis used the feathers to make beautiful cloaks that doubled as blankets.

"There are many animals here," Coronado went on, "bears, tigers, lions, porcupines . . . wild goats, whose heads I have also seen, as well as . . . the skins of wild boars." The tigers and lions were surely cougars or bobcats. The goats were mountain sheep and the wild boars peccaries.

Peccaries were the New World's version of swine, savage little wild hogs giving off an odor like a polecat's. Few Indians considered eating them, yet some thought the peccary's meat to be the best of all flesh. These Indians cooked the animal in a pit while drawing off the offensive odor with a cane tube.

News of a great river to the west prompted Coronado to send out a small investigating party. Twenty days of travel brought these men to a region "high and covered with low and twisted pine trees." Soon they found themselves gazing down into the Grand Canyon of the Colorado River. How awe inspired these Spaniards were is hard to say, but the leader's report was short and laconic. The Spaniards hadn't come sightseeing—they were looking for water and the water in this river was a long way down.

For three days the men tried to find a way down the jagged canyon walls. Finally three eager young men, "being the most agile," discovered a likely looking spot. Shortly after they disappeared from sight, and after a few anxious hours appeared again, scrambling up the rocks. The going had been "rough and difficult," and they went only a third of the way to the bottom. They reported that some of the boulders they had seen from the top of canyon, which seemed to be about the height of a man, "were taller than the great tower of Seville."

After realizing they couldn't get to the bottom and in need of water, the little group of Spaniards, the first Europeans to see the greatest natural wonder of the North American wilderness, turned about and headed for Hawikuh. When the news of this discovery was reported to Coronado, he showed little interest in this enormous hole in the ground. He had come after gold, and despite the disappointment of Cíbola, still intended to find some.

Turning due east, Coronado's expedition entered the stark but spectacular mesa country of present-day New Mexico. Here great flat-topped piles of rock, wide vistas between them, rose up out of the red desert sands like the remains of ancient cities. Perched on the most immense of the mesas was the fortress city of Acoma. The mesa was "out of reach, having steep sides in every direction, and so high that it was a very good musket that could throw a ball so high. There was only one entrance, a stairway built by hand that began at the top of a slope around the foot of the rock."

This stairway had about two hundred steps, followed by a hundred or so narrower ones. But the stairs didn't go all the way to the top. To reach it one had to scale the mesa's wall using small holes cut in the rock. Amazed Spaniards watched as natives moved up the steps and holes "so freely that they carry loads of provisions, and the women carry water, and they do not seem to touch the walls with their hands." Maize grew on top of the mesa, wells caught rainwater and snow.

After staying at Acoma awhile, Coronado's party moved on. Three days after passing present-day Laguna Lake, they arrived at a good-sized river they named the Nuestra Señora because they discovered it on the eve of the Feast of Our Lady. Today it is known as the Rio Grande, the great river of the Southwest.

The Spaniards moved up the Rio Grande to Tiguex, a large region of many settlements around present-day Albuquerque and Bernalillo. People of the pueblos, dressed in holiday regalia, came out and received the visitors cordially. They had heard of the Europeans and the fearsome beasts they rode, and were eager to make friends. According to Coronado, "The people appear to be gentle, more like farmers than warriors. . . . They dress in the skins of buffalo and wear turkey feathers. They cut their hair short."

The upper Rio Grande was fertile country, a welcome sight to the travel-weary Spanish. Groves of cottonwood and willow trees, those staunch river companions, dotted the broad valley. Beyond were the Indians' fields of corn, beans, and melons. Natives of Tiguex and other tribes along the river cultivated the land through irrigation and control of flood waters.

"The country is so fertile," remarked Coronado, "they do not have to break up the ground, but only plant the seed." Planting was at night, for the natives believed crops grew as the moon did. Plants set out under a waning moon would die.

As with most Indians, maize was their principal crop. It was prepared in several ways, the simplest being to toast the cob over a fire. The corn also was mashed into thin wafers, mixed with ashes, and baked into tortillas.

Pumpkins, another main crop, were eaten raw, stewed, or in pies. Indians saved pumpkins for later use by scraping out the seeds, trimming the rind, and cutting the rest into strips for drying.

Meat came from the wilds—mountain sheep, deer, squirrels, badgers, prairie dogs, field mice, and ducks. Fat and bone marrow were considered the best parts of an animal. Meat might be stewed with milkweed, wild onions, or roots.

The residents of Tiguex lived in houses typical of these parts—rough rectangular structures of baked clay over a wooden frame. Putting up dwellings was a community venture:

> They all work together to build these villages, the women being engaged in making the mixture and the walls, the men bringing the wood and putting it in place. They have no lime, but they make a mixture of ashes, coals, and dirt which is almost as good as mortar, for when the house is to have four stories they do not make the walls more than half a yard thick. They gather a great pile of thyme [probably sagebrush] and sedge grass and set it on fire. When it is half coals and ashes they throw a quantity of dirt and water on it and mix it together. This plaster the Spaniards called *adobe*, meaning mud.

In the beginning the Tiguex Indians were friendly, but when the "hairy mouths" set up winter quarters here, the natives hospitality wore thin. Eventually fighting erupted. Nearly a hundred Spanish soldiers were struck with arrows, some of them poisoned. The poisons were two kinds: sap from an unidentified tree and rattlesnake venom.

To get venom Indians would put rattlesnakes into cages and poke them with arrows so that they would bite the points, making them poisonous. These were desert rattlers, fat and sassy and not hard to find. Thirty or forty might be curled up in one rocky den.

Among the Hopi Indians, visited by one of Coronado's scouting parties, the rattlesnake was revered. In snake dances—pleas for rain—the Hopi would hold the rattler in their mouths, their teeth packed with clay so the snake would not be harmed. After the dance was over, the snakes were flung into a writhing heap and sprinkled with holy cornmeal. Then each dancer grabbed one of these now thoroughly confused reptiles and raced off to set it free. The Hopis believed the snakes went straight to the Great Spirit and told it what worthy people they were.

At nearby Cicuye—modern Pecos, New Mexico—the Spanish surely met one of history's most accomplished liars. He was an Indian they called the Turk "because he looked like one." *El Turco* apparently was a slave of the Pecos Indians, probably a Pawnee or Wichita taken captive in a raid on the Plains natives. At first *El Turco* told only of the great herds of buffalo back home, an animal the Spaniards were becoming more and more curious about. Of course they had seen buffalo hides and a few pictures of buffalo painted by Indians, but so far they had not encountered any of the animals alive.

Soon the Turk was weaving fantastic tales of a place called Quivira, his homeland to the northeast. In Quivira, he said, rivers were four miles wide and contained fish as big as horses. Sailing on the rivers were enormous canoes with golden oarlocks and golden eagles on the prows. The king of Quivira, the great Tatarrax, dined with gold and silver table service. After eating he slept under a tree hung with tinkling silver bells.

Surely the Spaniards were suspicious of the Turk and yet wanted desperately to believe him; he told them what they wanted to hear. Some came to believe he was some sort of witch doctor, one claiming to have heard him talking to the devil in a water jug. Soon off the expedition went on another golden goose chase.

Keeping the Pecos River on his left, Coronado journeyed past the future site of San Miguel, New Mexico, one day to be an important station on the Santa Fe Trail, and the impressive Starvation Peak. Building a bridge across the Pecos—"a medium-sized river with exquisite water"— they marched across a broad landscape sprinkled with scrub juniper and cactus and broken by scarped mesas. Soon in the distance they could see an imposing line of rampartlike cliffs with a vast expanse of grass in front of them. It appeared that the cliffs enclosed the plains, so the Spaniards named this region *Llano Estacado,* the Stockaded Plains. The words were mistranslated as Staked Plains, and by that name the region is known today.

This area was in eastern New Mexico and western Texas, a great sea of grass about four-inches high: "The earth was so round that whenever a man stood it seemed as if he were on the top and saw the sky around him within a crossbow shot. . . . There are no trees except along the streams found in some barrancas [gorges], which are so concealed that one does not see them until he is at their very edge." There was no way to make a trail, for when the grass was trampled "it stood up again as clean and as straight as before." Even the many men and horses left no trace of their passage through these plains. It was "as if no one had passed over them, so that it became necessary to stack up piles of bones and buffalo chips at various distances in order that the rear guard might follow the army and not get lost."

When some individuals did become lost, the men of the expedition blew horns and started bonfires to give them their bearings. Perhaps the Turk was in league with the Pecos to get rid of the Spaniards by leading them here and abandoning them. If so, their ploy did not work.

On the edge of the *Llano Estacado,* somewhere near the present-day New Mexico–Texas line, Europeans and Plains Indians met for the first time. These new Indians seemed different, people "living like Arabs and called Querechos." Probably they were Apaches, at the time not a large tribe but already a pugnacious one. (The name itself, Apache, is a Zuñi word meaning enemy.) The Apaches showed no fear of the Spanish, coming out of their tents as if merely to satisfy their curiosity. They neither cultivated the earth nor produced anything, but picked up their tents and moved with the buffalo.

Their tents were poles fastened together at the top and laid over with tanned and greased buffalo hides. When ready to move the Querechos loaded their belongings on dogs in a pack saddle arrangement French voyageurs later called a *travois*: "These dogs transport their houses for them. In addition to what they carry on their backs, they transport the poles for the tents, dragging them fastened to their bodies. The load may be from thirty to fifty pounds, depending on the dog. . . . The dogs go about with sores on their backs like pack animals." Remarkably the dog was the only beast of burden North American natives had.

In the Texas panhandle the Spaniards next met the Teyas Indians, "a large people of very fine appearance." The Teyas, who gave their name to Texas, were also buffalo hunters but not exclusively like the Querechos. They also lived on turkeys, mulberries, wild grapes, plums, and nuts, but they practiced no agriculture.

They were friendly and, the Spaniards thought, very intelligent. An old blind man indicated by signs that some years before he had met, further south, four Spaniards and one of them was black. Perhaps he had seen the Cabeza de Vaca party before he lost his sight.

The expedition had come upon the Teyas in a great barranca, apparently Tule Canyon which cuts a deep gash in the eastern escarpment of the *Llano Estacado.* Here the Spanish had their first experience with the sudden, vicious hailstorms so common in the prairie country. The "great cyclone" rained down hailstones "as large as bowls"—ripping tents to shreds, denting helmets, shattering pottery and gourds. Most of the terri-fied horses broke lose, but none got away because they were packed so tightly into the gorge.

Soon Coronado came to an even greater barranca—the rugged canyons of Palo Duro. Here the Prairie Dog Town branch of the Red River cut out a colorful arrangement of gorges sixty miles long and a thousand feet deep. "There was a small valley covered with trees and with plenty of grapes, mulberries, and rose bushes. . . . There were nuts and also turkeys of the variety found in New Spain and great quantities of plums like those of Castile." The trees were wild China (western soapberry), cottonwood, hackberry, and mulberry.

It was here that Coronado changed his line of march to the north, heading for Quivira. Crossing the Texas panhandle the expedition first saw humpbacked cattle, the buffalo. Astonished by the impossibly large herds that made the prairie black for as far as the eye could see, the Spaniards could think of nothing to compare these numbers with "unless it was fish from the sea. . . . There was not a single day from then until our return from the plains that we did not see them."

Though the Spanish had heard of these woolly beasts in Mexico, their first sight of them is memorable:

Their faces are short and narrow between the eyes, the forehead two [hand] spans wide. Their eyes bulge on the side so that when they run they can see those that follow them. They are bearded like very large he-goats. When they run they carry their heads low, their beards touching the ground. From

the middle of the body back they are covered with very fine woolly hair like that of a choice sheep. From the belly forward they have thick hair like the mane of a wild lion. They have a hump larger than that of a camel. The horns, which barely show through the hair, are short and thick. During May they shed the hair on the rear half of the body and then they look exactly like lions. To remove the hair they lean against small trees found in some of the gorges and rub against them until they shed the wool, as a snake sheds its skin. They have a short tail with a small bunch of hair at the end, and when they run they carry it like a scorpion. One peculiar thing is that when they are calves they are reddish like ours but in time, as they become older, they change in color and appearance. . . . The bulls are large and fierce, although they do not attack very often. But they have wicked horns and they thrust very savagely. They killed several of our horses and wounded many others.

Plains Indians called the buffalo uncle, considering the animal all-wise and all-powerful. On the other hand, the buffalo seemed the dumbest of animals to the Spaniards; they seemed to stand around unconcernedly while other members of their herd were hunted and killed.

Yet it is easy to see why Plains Indians revered the buffalo; the shaggy fellow meant life itself to them: "With the skins they build their houses, with the skins they clothe themselves, from the skins they make ropes and obtain wool. With the sinews they make thread, with which they sew their clothes and tents. From the bones they shape awls."

This was not all of the buffalos' usefulness. Their horns made ladles, crushed hooves their glue, and their blood paint. The thick folds of their neck, dried and flattened, made tough shields. Even the magnificent sinews along the back became fine bowstrings and their long black hair decorated clothes. Neither was their tail wasted—it made an admirable fly whisk. Buffalo chips served as fuel.

It was remarkable how quickly Indians could skin a buffalo: "They open the cow at the back and pull off the hide at the joints, using a flint the size of a finger, tied to a small stick. They do this as handily as if they used a fine large knife. They sharpen the flints on their teeth." Of course the buffalo's flesh was the main thing: "They sustain themselves on the meat, eating it slightly roasted and heated over the dung. Some they eat raw. Taking it in their teeth, they pull with one hand and in the other they hold a large flint knife and cut off mouthfuls, swallowing it half chewed like birds." The meat tasted like beef, the buffalo chips fire giving it something of a peppery quality. Tongue and fleece—meat on either side of the backbone, including the hump—were considered the best parts.

Buffalo flesh was said to be tastiest in the fall after the animals had feasted all summer on high sweet grass and succulent herbs. A big bull buffalo represented a ton or so of meat, though the flesh of cows was thought to be more tender and their hides more pliable. Meat not eaten right away was made into a travel ration called *pemmican*—cut into strips, dried, and pounded almost into powder. Berries were added for flavor.

The Indians hunted without horses. The horses they rode three hundred years later are generally believed to be descendants of some of Coronado's strays, but this is disputed by some scholars. The records of the expedition list only two mares in Coronado's complement, and all mounts were strictly guarded to keep the Indians from stealing them. In other Spanish expeditions, on into the seventeenth century, there was no mention of Indians riding horses. It seems more likely that their horses were strayed or stolen from later Spanish settlements.

Soon *El Turco* told Coronado that Quivira was not far to the northeast. Coronado sent the rest of his expedition back to the Pecos River and struck out for the fabled land with a band of carefully chosen men. The little group crossed the Cimarron River into southwestern Kansas and then crossed the Arkansas River at the future site of Ford, Kansas, where many a later Texas cattle drive would follow. Coronado followed the Arkansas to Great Bend and probably got as far as Salina.

The Spaniards had reached the magnificent land of Quivira. But they found no great cities, no gold or silver, no precious jewels. Nothing was here but the empty grasslands of central Kansas, dotted here and there with grass houses. The Turk, that unmitigated liar and reprobate, was rewarded by being strangled.

This was the land of the Wichitas and Pawnees. The Wichitas were easily identified—no other tribe built the same kind of beehive-shaped grass huts. They set forked posts in a circle, lashed logs to them, and covered this framework by weaving the tough bunch grass of the Kansas prairie "in and out in such a manner that each bunch overlaps the one below." Wichitas and Pawnees lived mainly on the buffalo, but they also grew maize, beans, and squash. They had no cotton or turkeys, "nor do they bake bread on griddles, but under the ashes."

Apparently Quivirans were impressive physical specimens. Said Coronado, "I had some Indians measured and found they were ten [hand] spans tall (about six feet, eight inches)." Tatarrax—what was assumed to be his name turned out to be the Wichita word for headman—though aged was "a huge Indian with a large body and limbs in proportion." He was accompanied by two bodyguards wearing "I don't know what over

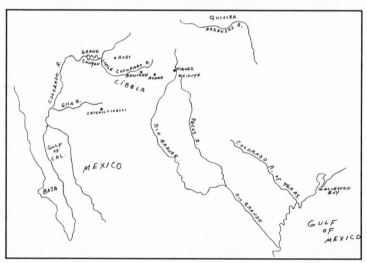

their heads." Probably the bodyguards were Pawnees, close relatives of the Wichitas, and the headdresses may have been the high roach of hair affected by Pawnee warriors.

Though Quivira must have been a disappointment, some Spaniards were smitten with the beauty and fertility of the land. One wrote: "This country has a fine appearance, the like of which I have never seen anywhere in our Spain, in Italy, or any part of France. . . . It is not a hilly country, but has table lands, plains, and charming rivers with fine waters. It greatly pleased me and I am of the belief that it will be very productive of all sorts of commodities." Of course this man was talking about some of the finest farmland in the world.

Eventually the Spaniards turned and retraced their weary steps, arriving in Mexico with nothing to show for their pains except stone bruises.

As Coronado trudged through the Southwest, Hernando de Alarcón was sailing up the Gulf of California. Rumor had it there was a great river flowing into this gulf, one that might run through Cíbola. Viceroy Mendoza sent Alarcón to further pierce the Northern Mystery by exploring the river as a possible route for getting supplies to Coronado. No one realized the river did not come anywhere close to Cíbola.

When he reached the head of the gulf, Alarcón found that indeed there was a large river flowing into it, one the Spanish would name the Colorado because the water was reddish. Entering its mouth Alarcón found "a mighty river with so furious a current we could not sail against it." Leaving his three ships there he set off upstream in two small launches.

Soon the expedition met its first Indians, the unusually tall and powerfully built Cocopas, a Yuman people. Both sides were excited—and both afraid. Some Cocopas stood on the bank and made threatening gestures while others hurried off to hide their belongings.

Alarcón tried to reassure the Indians by turning his launch into midstream and ordering the men to sit quietly and put aside their weapons. Soon about 250 warriors had assembled on the beach with bows and arrows and "some banners like those [of the Indians] of New Spain."

Again approaching the shore, Alarcón stood in the stern of his launch and tried to reason with the Cocopas. They answered with angry shouts and by gestures warned the strangers away. To prevent a landing they placed logs along the shore.

"Looking at them I began to make signs of peace," wrote Alarcón. "Taking my sword and my shield, I threw them on the deck . . . trying to make them understand by this and other signs that I did not want to fight them. . . . Taking some of the things I carried for barter, I called to the natives and offered them as presents."

The Cocopas held a hasty conference and, apparently influenced by the presents, decided on peace. Bearing a staff decorated with shells, a chief boarded Alarcón's launch and presented him with this token. Alarcón embraced the chief, gave him some trinkets, and sent him back to shore. Apparently it was all the reassurance the Cocopas needed; they came piling on board to receive their own gifts. Thus friendship was established, and word spread quickly upstream to other natives.

At the next village on the Colorado River "more than a thousand Indians," including women and children, came out to view the new arrivals. Here Alarcón wrote the first description of the Cocopas:

These Indians were adorned in different ways. Some had streaks almost entirely covering their faces, each one painted according to his fancy. Others had their faces covered with black soot, and still others wore masks of the same color. On their heads each one had a deerskin two [hand] spans high, like a helmet, and on it a crest of feathers. . . . Some have their noses pierced, and from them hang pendants, while others wear shells. They also have their ears pierced with many holes in which they place shells and beads. All of them, big and little, wear a multi-colored sash around the waist and a round bundle of feathers hanging down behind like a tail. . . . They carry small blades of deer bone with which they scrape off the sweat. . . . Their bodies are branded by fire [tattooed]. Their hair is banged in front, but in back it hangs to the waist.

Realizing that the Cocopas were sun worshippers, Alarcón passed himself off as son of the sun, a supernatural being and the most powerful of medicine men: "From then on whenever they brought me anything they first cast some of it toward the sun, then turned to me and gave me the rest. They . . . wanted to carry me bodily to their homes and did not refuse anything I asked of them."

Mainly what Alarcón asked of them was to pull his boats upstream; the Indians jostled one another in their eagerness to serve. Further upstream the Spaniards found other Indians who accepted them as men from heaven.

The Spanish learned that most of these tribes were monogamous and cremated their dead. Some Indians "emitted blood through the mouth," probably tuberculosis victims; local medicine men tried to heal them by blowing their sacred breath on the men. The natives also carried hollow reeds "with which they perfume themselves," obviously tobacco pipes. They raised maize, beans, squash, and a little cotton.

Alarcón did not go far up the Colorado, only to its junction with the Gila River near present-day Yuma, Arizona. After erecting a large cross there, the expedition retraced its journey. In the meantime Coronado, knowing of Alarcón's trek, sent out a small party under Melchor Díaz to search for Alarcón. This expedition would add a little more to the Spaniard's information about Arizona and the lower Colorado River region.

Díaz went overland through extreme southern Arizona until he struck the Colorado River just south of where Alarcón had turned back. Here he and his men, in their turn, were properly impressed by "a people like giants, exceedingly tall and muscular.... When transporting burdens they carried on their heads more than three or four hundred pounds. It once happened that when our men wished to bring a log for the fire and six of them were unable to carry it, one of the Indians picked it up in his arms, put it on his head all by himself, and carried it with great ease."

Díaz was so impressed by these people he wanted to send one of them home to display to the viceroy. But the young man he chose was so strong several soldiers couldn't tie him up. He "yelled so lustily" they let him go for fear his cries would set the others on them.

Crossing to the west side of the Colorado River, Díaz and his party went south for five or six days. Here in Baja California, they came upon beds of burning lava. When they walked the ground "resounded like a kettle drum, as if there were lakes underneath. It was amazing to see the cinders boil in some places, for it looked like something infernal." Frightened, the Spaniards turned their backs on this infernal place, sought out the river again, and returned to Coronado.

Although the Spaniards found nothing they were looking for—or were interested in—at least the Northern Mystery was less of a mystery now. It would be three centuries before anyone took a serious interest in the rock-and-desert wilderness of the Southwest, other than a few traders up from Mexico and the ubiquitous Spanish priests come to save the souls of aborigines.

Before the sixteenth century was out the Spaniards' mortal enemies, the English, were thrashing about on the East Coast, even as far north as the land of the midnight sun.

5

ENGLISH BEGINNINGS
Frobisher, Davis, Roanoke, Jamestown

Cruising the coast of Nova Scotia in 1569, a French sea captain was startled to find three white men standing on a rock and waving frantically. They seemed like specters: long beards, flowing hair, dressed in animal skins. The captain picked up the men, all young and English, and took them to France. When they reached home the trio created a sensation with their bleak tale of survival in the forbidding New World wilderness.

The youths were sailors claiming they had been set ashore in the Gulf of Mexico by the English freebooter John Hawkins. They had started north on foot, they said, and had walked across a great deal of the North American continent.

Records show that John Hawkins, after losing one of his ships to the Spanish, had indeed put 114 men ashore at the gulf just north of present-day Tampico, Mexico. Most of these castaways, in fear of the wilderness, decided to go south and throw themselves on the mercy of the Spanish. All were tortured to death by the Inquisition.

The remaining twenty-three headed north, hoping to reach the coast above Mexico, to be picked up by someone friendly. Unfortunately this did not happen. On the men traveled, crossing the Mississippi River, skirting the great swamps of Georgia, then following the Atlantic coast-line. But the bayous and marshes forced them to go inland, following Indian and animal trails.

Once back in England the spokesman for the three, David Ingram, said that during their long trek the other twenty crewmen perished—killed by Indians, drowned crossing streams, or starved to death. On the days they didn't travel, the party nursed sore feet, trapped animals for food and clothes, or figured out how to get across streams and around impenetrable tangles of undergrowth.

The Relation of David Ingram, his account to the government, certainly contains misrepresentations, but essentially is factual. The falsehoods surely come from the fact that he spent an awfully long time in a confusing wilderness.

The "elipantes" Ingram claims to have seen may have been noticed on an earlier trip to Africa—he is known to have made one. His "buffes" (buff, buffle, and boeuf were early names for the buffalo) were not as big as he described and did not have "longe eares like a Blood Hound." Yet the buffalo did have long shaggy hair and it is possible Ingram thought part of its mane was "eares." Probably he never got close enough to be sure.

Ingram also described a "Monstrous Beaste twice as big as an Horse, and in proportion like to an Horse . . . saying it was small towards the hinder parts like a Grey Hound. These beastes hath two teeth or hornes of a foot long growing straight foorth by their nose-thrilles." Could this have been the mammoth? Remember two centuries later the Indians assured Thomas Jefferson that the great woolly mammoth still lived deep in the interior wilderness (see Introduction).

According to Ingram, "There is also a greate plentie of Deare both red, white, and speckled"—ordinary red deer, ones in their grayish winter coat, and fawns. There were "Beares both black and white." Black bears might have been seen anywhere; the white ones may have been polar bears seen when the Englishmen reached the north country.

Or perhaps the white bears were grizzlies: a "strange Beaste bigger than a Beare, he had neither head nor neck, his eyes and mouth were in his breast." Ingram must have seen the animal in its defensive pose, with the head sunk below the shoulders so that it did indeed seem to be growing out of its breast. Grizzlies must have struck newcomers as something more than a mere bear.

"There are also Birds of all sortes," reported Ingram, "as we have here [in England] and many strange Birds. . . . There is a Bird called a

Flamingo, whose feathers are verie red, and is bigger than a Goose, billed like a Shovell." Of course he found the flamingo along the southern coasts. Offshore, in the north, were birds "of the shape and bignesse of a Goose but their wings are covered with small feathers and [they cannot] fly: You may drive them before you like Sheepe. They are exceeding fat and have verie delicate meate." These were auks, no doubt.

As for the topography, Ingram described it thusly: "The ground and Countrey is most excellent, fertile, and pleasant, especially towards the River of May [the St. Johns, Florida]. For the grasse of the rest is not so greene, as it is in these parts, for the other is burnt away with the heate of the Sunne. And as all the Countrey is good and most delicate, having great Plaines, as large and as fayre in many places as may be seene."

Ingram also claimed to have seen "greate plentie" of iron, pieces of gold "as big as a mans fist," and on some houses pillars of silver "as big as a boyes leg of fifteene yeeres of age." There were also rubies four inches long and two inches wide, he said, and chairs of chiefs made of silver or crystal and "garnished with divers sortes of precious stones."

More than likely Ingram was just telling his listeners what he thought they wanted to hear. Regardless, English interest in the New World, already stirred by other accounts, began to quicken. So did their interest in getting to China by finding the Northwest Passage.

To search for the mythical strait Queen Elizabeth sent an expedition headed by Martin Frobisher. A typical English "sea dogge" of the period, Frobisher was a dour Yorkshireman of little education but had a profound knowledge of seafaring. He was one of the few survivors of an African expedition he had been on when he was only fourteen. On a later African voyage his captain left him as a hostage with the Portuguese, who finally shipped him home.

As an adult Frobisher became a professional sea rover, accepting commissions from anyone at home or on the continent. He was, it is believed, involved in a large number of maritime activities of questionable legality. Yet all this made him eminently qualified for the job Queen Elizabeth wanted him to do—the task would require a man of courage and sublety. Martin Frobisher made three voyages to the New World between 1576 and 1578, landing first at what is now Frobisher Bay on Baffin Island. He was not impressed with what he saw: "There is verie little plain grounde and no grasse. . . . There is no woode at all. To be brief there is nothynge fitte or profitable for the use of man."

Nevertheless Frobisher thought he was entering the Northwest Passage, and was disappointed when the bay ended. Then he sailed up

Hudson Bay a bit, but turned back because of ice. Overall the expedition spent a great deal of time trying to avoid this "monstrous and huge yce." One of the smaller ships, picking its way through the ice, "received suche a blowe with a rock of yce that she sunk down therewith in the sighte of the whole fleete." All hands were saved.

At the time large schools of whales, including the white beluga, sported in these waters. Once one whale rammed into a ship with such force the vessel "stood still, and stirred neither forward or backward. The whale thereat made a greate and uglie noyse, and cast up his boddie and tayle, and so went under water, and within two days after there was founde a greate whale dead swimming above water."

More interesting than these big mammals must have been a narwhale found dead onshore. The sailors called it a "sea unicorn" because it had "a horne two yards longe, growing out of the snout or nostrels . . . wreathed and strayte, like in fashion to a taper made of wax." The "horne" was the long, spiraling extension of a canine tooth, growing up to six feet. The whale itself normally grew to about eighteen feet; this one, according to the report, was about twelve.

The Englishmen met their first Eskimos when they spied "a number of small things fleeting in the sea afarre off, whyche we supposed to be Porposes or Ceals, or some kinde of strange Fishe." The fleeting things turned out to be Eskimos in their sealskin boats or *kayaks*. They were "like Tartars, with longe black hair, broad faces, flatte noses, and tawnie in color. . . . The women are marked in the face with blewe streakes down the cheekes, and round about the eies." A distinctive fold of skin in the corners of their eyes, giving the eyes a deceiving slanted appearance, perhaps revealed the natives' Mongoloid ancestry.

Of course they weren't called Eskimos yet. The natives around here called themselves *Inuits*, the people. Englishmen called them simply the savages or "the countrey people." The word *Eskimo* is a corruption of the Algonquin word for raw meat eaters, and was picked up by Europeans in the next century.

The *Inuits* were wholly carnivorous people, eating flesh, fish, and fowl. "They eat their meat raw . . . or parboiled [partly cooked] with blood and

a little water. . . . They neither use table, stoole, nor table clothe for comelinesse: but when they are imbrued with blood knuckle deepe, and their knives are in like sorte, they use their tongues as apt instrumente to lick them clean: in doing whereof they are assured to lose none of their victuals."

Seal was the native's staple. They stalked the creatures by crawling along ice floes on their bellies, seal-like themselves, or harpooned them from their kayaks. When the Inuits took a seal, or any other animal, they enacted the following ritual: They offered the victim a drink of water, kept thawed in a mitten, and then opened a cut on the head to let its spirit escape.

The Inuits caught whales with harpoons attached to buoys, making it difficult for the mammals to dive, and then stabbed them repeatedly with spears. They also speared fish through ice holes or caught them on hooks of bone or ivory. They killed wildfowl with blunt arrows or tripped them up with the *bola,* a clever little device of three cords knotted together and weighted on the ends with stones.

Despite being in a subartic region, there were many land-based animals, including caribou, polar bears, musk oxen, hares, mountain sheep, beavers, ground squirrels, foxes, wolves, and wolverines. As for the foxes and wolves, they were disposed of in a decidedly unsportsmanlike manner. Inuit hunters scattered about balls of fat containing pointed strips of whalebone, dried and folded up. After the fox or wolf ate the fat, the whalebone would straighten out in the animal's stomach bringing death through internal bleeding.

According to Frobisher, "These beastes, fishes, and fowles, which they kill, are their meate, drinke, apparell, houses, beddynge, hose [trousers],

shoes, threade, and sailes for their Boats, withe many other necessaries whereof they stande in neede, and almost all their riches. . . . They dress their skins softe and supple with the hair on." The Inuits wore two or three layers of clothing, the inside layers with the fur inside and the outer clothing with it outside, trapping warm air between the layers. Everyone wore a fur-lined hood, women carrying babies in theirs.

Frobisher's men eventually captured two Eskimo women, one of whom they were sure was a witch. The captain "had her buckskins plucked off to see if she were cloven-footed," then let her go because of her "uglie hue and deformitie." He took the other woman, plus a man and child, to England to show the homefolk what natives of the icy northern wilderness looked like. Though the Inuits were fed raw meat and allowed to wear their sealskin clothes, all three died within a month.

Frobisher also brought home tons of worthless rocks, including a strange black one "which by the weight seems to have been some kinde of metall." Perhaps it was a meteorite. Some assayists at home claimed there was gold in the rocks, others that they were just everyday stones. Before leaving the New World for good Frobisher stopped at Newfoundland and was astonished by the multitude of sea life. By this time the English were policing the Grand Banks, charging other nations for fishing there.

Though Frobisher abandoned the search for a Northwest Passage, Queen Elizabeth did not. After her first explorer came home, she sent over master mariner John Davis, who was allied by marriage to Humphrey Gilbert, half brother to Sir Walter Raleigh. In 1583 the queen sent

Gilbert to take formal possession of Newfoundland and plant a settlement. In short order the colony failed and on the way home to England, Gilbert's ship sank.

John Davis made three voyages to the New World between 1585 and 1587, yet he too never found the strait, never made any money, and for the most part has been forgotten by history.

Davis landed first on Baffin Island, where there were low-growing withes and flowers resembling primroses. The men killed four white bears "of monstrous bignesse." Further south the Englishmen entered a "greate Baye," Cumberland Sound.

On his second voyage Davis coasted down from Baffin Island to the Labrador coast, with "verie fayre woodes on both sydes." Off Labrador he made an incredible haul of "the largest and beste Fish that ever I saw." Preparing to end this second trip, and wanting to save some of the fish for the homeward journey, the captain sent some men ashore to split and salt the remainder of the catch. The five young sailors were suddenly set upon by "the brutish people of the countrey, who laye secretly lurking in the woode."

Davis moved one of his ships in closer and fired off several volleys of musketry, scaring the natives. Two seamen were killed and a third swam to the ship with an arrow in his arm. Having seen the Inuits, Davis thought these natives were a different people. They may have been Naskapis, an Algonquin group known to have occupied southern Labrador.

Davis did not go on up Hudson Strait, probably because of ice. It would be some years before anyone found the giant bay in the frozen land the strait led to. Henry Hudson would do it in 1610-1611, and the bay and strait would be named for him.

Around this time the English were also thinking of settling in Virginia, a name they used for the East Coast north of Florida. Colonizing the New World was the great dream of Sir Walter Raleigh, who fervently hoped to plant the flag of his beloved England on some fertile North American shore.

In the summer of 1584, just after his half brother's abortive colonizing attempt in Newfoundland, Raleigh sent to America a small exploring expedition. The party landed on Hatarask Island on present-day North Carolina's Outer Banks. Before landing the explorers said the land smelled like "a delicate garden abounding with all kindes of oderiferous flowers."

Upon reaching the shore the men saluted the occasion by firing off a musket. The sudden loud noise raised a flock of whooping cranes that gave out "such a crye redoubled with many Ecchoes, as if an armie of men had showted all together." The party also found the marshy ground overrun with woodcock, plover, and snipe. The streams were full of all kinds of fish, beaver, otter, muskrat, and mink.

Grapes were abundant "on the green soil of the hills, over the plains, climbing on every little shrub and towards the tops of high cedars." The men thought the cedars "the highest and reddest of the world." Along with these trees the land was well forested with pine, tupelo, oak, cypress, and sassafras. Because of its reputed healing powers, sassafras was valuable and selling at a premium in London bazaars. All the trees had "an excellent smell," and most were so tall they could not be put aboard a ship unless they were halved.

On the third day of the Englishmen's stay on the Outer Banks, three Indians in a canoe appeared. They seemed afraid of the big boat and the strange beings in it, but the Englishmen persuaded one to come aboard. They gave the fellow a shirt and hat, and a couple drinks of wine. The native got back in his canoe and soon returned with a load of fish for the Europeans.

The next day the chief's brother appeared, with some forty attendants. All were "verie handsome and goodly people, and in their Behaviour as mannerly and civill as any of Europe." The English gave the chief's brother, Granganimeo, a tin dish and he was most delighted. Right away he punched a hole in it and hung it around his neck, saying it would protect him from all his enemies.

A few days later Granganimeo reappeared, this time with his wife and two or three children. The wife was "verie well favoured, of mean [average] stature, and verie bashful: she had on her back a long cloak of leather, with the fur side nexte to her boddie. . . . Aboute her Forehead she had a bande of white Coral, and so had her husband many times; in her eares she had Braceletts of Pearls hanging down to her middle, and those were the bignesse of good Pease." Pendants of copper dangled from the wife's ears too, and even more from her husband's. On his head Granganimeo wore "a broade plate of Gold," probably gathered from some shipwreck.

These Indians were Roanokes, of Algonquin stock. Remaining friendly, every day they sent the English all the fish they could eat, fat deer, maize, cucumbers, pumpkins, and nuts. The natives lived on Roanoke Island— about twenty-miles north—in a palisaded village of cedar houses.

After the Roanokes had been to the ship several times, eight Englishmen decided to pay them a visit. Granganimeo was not there but his wife greeted the visitors with courtesy and fed them fish, venison, melons, boiled roots, and ginger tea. Village women removed the Englishmen's clothes and socks, and washed and dried them; other women cleansed their feet. When a few braves gathered outside in a threatening mood, Granganimeo's wife sent some other natives out to break their bows and arrows and and make them leave.

Roanoke Island was too sandy for growing much, yet on the mainland the soil was "the most plentifull, sweete, fruitfull, and wholesome in the world." Between May and September it produced three crops.

When the Englishmen asked the name of this fair land they were told Windgandacon, or something similar. Later it was learned the Indians did not understand the question, merely responding with "What pretty clothes you are wearing." Members of the expedition told Raleigh the Roanoke Indians were genial souls, "gentle, loving, faithfull, and lacking all guile and trickery."

After the glowing accounts of this Eden, Raleigh sent out a colonizing expedition to Roanoke Island in 1585. But this time the Indians were not so friendly, probably because it looked as if these Englishmen had come to stay. Soon there were disagreements and a little fighting; food ran short and some settlers were reduced to eating dogs "boyled with Saxefras leaves." Colonists had to make a trip to the mainland every now and then to gather edible roots and oysters. Though they loved oysters at home, these colonists seemed to think it a chore to have to go out looking for them. Just as matters were becoming desperate Sir Francis Drake came along and took the would-be colonists home.

In 1587 Raleigh sent over another group of colonists. The colony's governor, John White, went home for supplies and was delayed because war had broken out with Spain. When he returned three years later, all his colonists had vanished, including little Virginia Dare, first child born of English parents in the New World.

No one knows what became of the Lost Colony. There was no sign of violence at the hands of Indians: no dead bodies, the fort and homes still intact. The only clue was CROATAN carved into one tree and CRO into another.

The best explanation seems to be that the settlers abandoned the place and went to live with the nearby Croatan tribe and were eventually assimilated by them.

Fortunately John White, an artist by profession, and another early settler, the scientist Thomas Hariot, left us in text and pictures our first good look at the East Coast wilderness of what is now the United States. They noticed that the fine pine trees on Roanoke Island would be a good source of naval stores—pitch, tar, turpentine—and that red cedar, "a verie sweete woode and fine timber" would make glorious cabinets. Sassafras, White and Hariot believed, was "of most rare virtues in physic for the cure of many diseases."

The waters were full of sturgeon, herring, trout, rays, mullet, "and many other varieties of excellente Fishe." Natives caught them in weirs or stabbed them with sharp canes. There were also giant tortoises, "some of them so large that sixteen Men were exhausted by carrying one a short distance from the Shoar to our Cabbins." Apparently they measured more than a yard across the back and although their heads, feet, and tails looked like a venomous serpent's, "They are verie goode to eat, as are their Eggs."

Like everyone else, the two men were impressed by the size and "aboundance" of grapes. There were two kinds, Hariot said. One was "small and sour and of the ordinary bignesse of ours in England." The other was "farre greater and of himself luscious sweete." The large luscious one probably was a muscadine, native to these parts.

Maize, beans, and squash—as usual—were the principal crops. Maize was white, red, yellow, or blue—all of it yielding a fine white flour. "There is another greate herb, in form of a Marigold, about six feet high," wrote Hariot. This was undoubtedly the cultivated sunflower, a common garden dweller in eastern woodlands. Indians also grew a tall plant of some kind that they boiled as a potherb and apparently used to make salt. From Hariot's description it must have been lamb's quarters, alias pigweed. Today a nuisance weed, the Indians made great use of it. They boiled the tops into a dish resembling spinach and ground the seeds into a flour that when cooked tasted like buckwheat.

The natives lived in villages of up to thirty dwellings. These were frame structures made of bent poles tied together at the top "after the manner as is used in many Arbors in our Gardens in England." Rush and grass mats, made to roll up for light and ventilation, covered the framework with sleeping benches around the walls. One large building was set aside for the care of the dead, another for feasts and religious festivals.

Like Indians everywhere, these natives spent most of their time hunting, fishing, tending to crops, and warring with other tribes. They spent winter months in the woods, with the women building shelters and the men hunting.

Hariot's words and White's paintings gave us a good look at the Roanokes and their neighbors. White shows the men to be tall, graceful, and dignified. They shaved their heads except for a coxcomb, a narrow strip of hair from the forehead to the nape of the neck that indeed looked like

a comb; it was decorated with feathers. In their ears were rings, pearls, or bird claws, around their arms pearl bracelets, and around their necks pearl or copper beads. They dressed in finely cured animal skins, mostly of deer, and left the tail hanging down in the rear as if it were their own.

Werowances, or chief men, wore the coxcomb as well, but let their hair grow long in the back and tied it in a knot. From a *werowance's* neck hung a large square of copper—probably traded from the Lake Superior region—as a symbol of authority. Old men had large cloaks, worn like togas, and let their scraggly beards grow rather than pluck out the hairs as the young men did.

Women had "small eies, plaine, flatte noses, narrow foreheads, and large mouthes." Their hair was worn in bangs, shoulder length or tied in a knot while their foreheads, cheeks, and chins were "chalked," or pol-

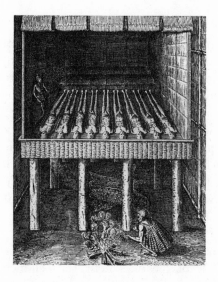

ished, and other parts of their skin were tattooed. They wore necklaces of pearls or polished bones, and sometimes small green snakes lapped around their heads. Mostly they wore fringed buckskin dresses. Noble women signified their rank with a headband and by carrying one arm in a bead necklace used like a sling.

The Roanokes were taught from infancy to obey their chiefs and honor their priests. After a notable died even his corpse was treated with great respect and solemnity. The body was disemboweled, the skin removed, and the flesh cut from the bones. Then the skeleton, still held together by ligaments, was covered with skin again so it would appear that the skin had never been removed.

This mortuary work done, the skeleton was placed on a high scaffolding covered with rush mats. Beneath the scaffold lived a priest, constantly tending these sacred remains.

Despite the misfortunes of Roanoke, the English did not give up plans for settling Virginia. In 1607 the Virginia Company of merchant adventurers sent over three boatloads of colonists who, when reaching the New World, sailed up a river they named the James and founded Jamestown. Their settlement was supposed to be on an island, the better to protect themselves from England's rivals, the Spanish. Instead they chose a malarial swamp on a peninsula and had to fight mosquitoes instead of Spaniards.

The new colonists were delighted with "the mildness of the ayre, the fertilitie of the soyle, and the situation of the ryvers." Most of the shore-line was marshland, yet further inland were "thicke sett woodes where the mould and sword of the earth" was two feet thick. Anything put into the ground in the spring and summer grew quickly, sometimes to an astonishing size. Sweet potatoes for example were "as big as a Boy's Leg, and sometimes about as longe and as big as boath the Leg and the Thigh of a yong Childe, and very much resembling it in shape."

Settlers were quickly introduced to the American wilderness's giant oysters when they found a spot where the Indians had been roasting them. Some had been left in the ashes and the Englishmen found "within the Shoares of our ryvers whole Bancks of Oysters and Scallopps, which lye unopened and thicke together, as if there had bene their naturall Bed before the Sea left them."

Used to the small oysters of their island home, the Englishmen were amazed by the size of the ones here: thirteen-inch oysters were not uncommon. (William Makepeace Thackeray, visiting America in much later days, felt after eating an oyster that he had "swallowed the baby.") Indians boiled them with mussels and thickened the mixture with corn-meal, making a delicious "spoone meate." Until well into the 1800s oysters were the hotdogs of America. They were eaten raw, boiled, broiled,

creamed, scalloped, stewed, or pickled, as well as added to soups and omelettes.

Wildfowl of all kinds haunted these marshlands. In the woods wild turkeys "of an incridible Bigness," pigeons, deer, rabbits, foxes, raccoons, panthers, wildcats, opossums, and bears. Natives hunted black bears, found in plenty along the coast, "most greedily, for indeed they love them above all other [than] their flesh," and often refused to sell bear meat to settlers. English taste buds agreed: bear meat "was verie toothsome sweete venison, as good to be eaten as the Fleshe of a calfe of two years old."

Berries and fruits, high in vitamins A and C, grew wild around the little settlement. The fruits in general were more sour than modern varieties, a problem the Indians remedied by opening them and filling them with honey. As usual, grapes were everywhere. "Behold the goodly Vines burthening every neighbor Bushe, and clymbing the toppes of highest Trees, and those full of clusters of Grapes in their kinde, however dreeped and shadowed soever from the Sun. . . . I can saie that we have eaten there as full and lushious a Grape as in the villages between Paris and Amiens."

Some fields were also full of "fine and beautifull Strawberries, four-times bigger and better than ours in England." They were "much fairer and more sweete." In the moist valleys was a berry "verie much like unto Capers" that without boiling "differed not much from poyson." Probably

it was the wild cranberry, flourishing as far south as Virginia, which the Indians used as a sauce for meat. The colonists' "raspies" were native wild raspberries and also may have included blackberries and dewberries. Their "hurts" were the blueberries growing in profusion.

There also were beach plums, but no doubt the "little plums" Jamestowners mentioned were persimmons. Technically this delicious fruit is known as *diospyros*—food for the gods. Indeed the persimmons tasted good, and they were rich in vitamins. The Powhatan Indians of the vicinity made the persimmon an important part of their diet.

In the fall, after a frost, the persimmons turned a rosy orange and the sweet golden pulp became custardy. Native cooks then mashed them and spread them out to dry. Later the pulp was stewed with venison fat or bear oil and made into cakes with some of it pounded into loaves of bread and put away for the winter. Persimmon bread is mentioned often in early writings, especially as an Indian gift or peace offering.

Jamestowners learned the hard way that the persimmon's appearance was deceiving. It was not ready to eat when it seemed to be, the tannin in it making it "harsh and choakie and furre in a man's mouth." Later settlers had to learn the lesson for themselves. Said one, "The putchamin . . . if it be not ripe, it will draw a man's mouth awrie with much torment."

American nuts met with instant favor—chestnuts, black walnuts, acorns, chinkapins. Jamestown's most famous colonist, John Smith, first described the Allegheny chinkapin as "a small Fruit growing on little Trees, husked like a chestnut, but the Fruit most like a verie small Acorn." Indians, he said, called them *checkinquamins* and "esteemed them as a greate daintie."

In the streams fish abounded—herring, trout, bass, flounder, shad, sturgeon—"lying so thicke with their Heads above the Water." Shad especially were "in greate store, of a yard longe, and for sweetnes and fatnes a reasonable goode Fish." Sturgeon were so large, up to nine feet, "all the World could not be compared to them." After one fishing trip Smith reported netting "more Sturgeon than could be devoured by Dogg and Man"—sixty-two of them.

Despite the largess of land and sea, Jamestowners had food problems. In the early days of settlement many colonists seemed unable to live off the land as the Indians did. Unable or perhaps unwilling. The Jamestowners may have been transplanted on an alien shore, but they were still Englishmen. They wanted to live, and eat, as they did back home.

Some of the colonists were "gentlemen," belonging to a class unused to work. It was beneath their dignity to do common labor, and sometimes that even included fishing. When they did fish they had trouble catching anything—the hooks they had brought were not the right size. They seemed to be too fumble-fingered to make good weirs, those enormous reed traps Indians stretched across streams, or even to repair weirs Indians made for them.

Soon the green colonists lost the support of the "salvages"; they refused to give them any more food. Then the discovery that rats had been in the Englishmen's corn supply brought more trouble. Colonists now had to fend for themselves—and they weren't much good at fending. As John Smith said, "Though there bee Fish in the Sea, Fowles in the Ayre, and Beastes in the Woods their boundes are so large, they so wilde, and wee so weake and ignorant, wee cannot much trouble them."

Before long the Englishmen were reduced to eating eagles, hawks, dogs, cats, toadstools, and "what nott." Some of the "poorer sorte" crept out of the stockade, dug up an Indian recently buried, and ate the body. One man is said to have "powdered" (salted) his wife, just deceased, and devoured her.

For a time the little colony teetered on the brink of extinction. But eventually the settlers learned to partake—to some extent at least—of nature's bounty the way the natives did. They ate what had earlier appeared to be inedible wild plants or plain old weeds. Poke, purslane, plantain, and Virginia waterleaf were made into "Brothes and Sallets." Wild onions and the tuberous roots of iris, hyacinth, smilax, and arrowarum—sometime called Virginia tuckahoe and having a root weighing three or four pounds—were eaten raw or pounded into meal.

But sometimes these culinary experiments backfired. Several soldiers were said to have been stricken with amnesia and temporary insanity after boiling jimson weed for a salad.

Particularly interesting to the Englishmen was the Indians' use of wild plants for medicine. Tobacco, the natives said, was good for any ailment. As the English understood it, tobacco fumes "purged superfluous Phlegm and grosse Humours from the Boddie by opening all the Pores and Passages." Not illogical for European medical theory of the day held that there were four humours and that they needed to be in delicate balance. For that reason much of the medical practice of that day concerned bleeding and purging. American Indians seem to have had similar ideas about the cause and cure of disease.

Convinced that a sickness entered the body by the digestive tract, the Indians' usual treatment was giving the sufferer an emetic or purgative or both. Bark of the slippery elm was a common emetic, but none was as

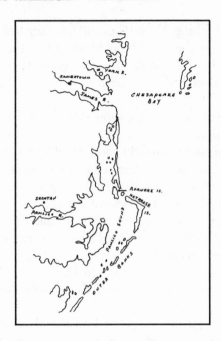

effective as the black drink mentioned in Chapter 2. Calamus (sweet flag), purslane, and senna were good laxatives.

"Drinking" tobacco soon became the latest fad among the English upper classes, who seemed to take its curative powers for granted. After all, weren't the natives of America the picture of good health? The freebooter John Hawkins had already brought tobacco to England and Hariot and Raleigh, both heavy smokers, introduced the clay pipe there. Hariot, incidentally, apparently died of nose cancer.

After John Rolfe, the Jamestown planter who married Pocahontas, began the sysematic cultivation of the tobacco plant it became the chief export of the Virginia colony. Soon it took its place beside sassafras tea as an all-purpose "apothecary drugg."

Like most tribes in America, Virginia Indians made frequent use of the hot house. This was a primitive version of a sauna, a place where patients sweated out the poisons that were making them sick. There were various kinds of hot houses, some were small huts holding no more than two occupants, others were large ceremonial buildings where steam baths were part of a regular ritual. Patients, their heads and shoulders wrapped in blankets, huddled around a hole filled with hot stones, breathing in the steam generated by pouring water on the rocks. Afterward a patient plunged into the cold river, dried off, and went to bed.

Certain plants, particularly boneset and yarrow, helped induce sweating. Boneset was so universally used it might be called the aspirin of aboriginal Americans. Medicine men used yarrow and boneset poultices for wounds and sores, sometimes covering them with peat moss. Ginger drinks supposedly aided digestion and eased gastritis. Teas of dandelion and goldenseal were taken as tonics, to detoxify the body and improve health generally.

In 1676 Virginia planters revolted against the rule of Governor William Berkeley, a conflict known as Bacon's Rebellion. During the fighting Jamestown was burned and in 1699 the government moved to Williamsburg.

In the meantime, though still clinging to the Atlantic seaboard, the English continued to colonize. Fearful of the unknown, they were unwilling to strike out any great distance inland for almost 150 years. Instead they consolidated their foothold by building other colonies along the coast, beginning with a celebrated one at Plymouth, Massachusetts.

EXPLORING AND SETTLING
NEW ENGLAND
Sassafras, Champlain, and the
Pilgrims

In 1602 sassafras led the English sea captain Bartholomew Gosnold to New England, the first European of record to visit these shores since Giovanni da Verrazano briefly blew by in 1524.

By this time the most fantastic virtues had been attributed to the roots and bark of the sassafras tree. European doctors claimed sassafras mixtures cured "griefes of the breast . . . and griefes of the head," that they "comforteth the liver and stomacke," and that they restored locomotion to "them that bee lame and creepelles and them that are not able to goe." Sassafras was considered a specific for French poxe, or syphilis, believed to have been brought to Europe by sailors of Columbus.

Sailing down from Maine, Gosnold apparently went ashore first on Cape Cod, "a white sandie and very bolde shore." The tall trees, and the long vistas among them unobstructed by undergrowth, impressed him. This lack of undergrowth was not nature's doing—it was the habit of Indians. They burned undergrowth in spring and fall, creating a habitat likely to attract the animals they most liked to hunt—deer, elk, beaver, porcupine, turkey, and quail.

After making a preposterously large haul of codfish there, Gosnold gave Cape Cod its name:

There is upon this coast better fishing, and in as great plentie, as in Newfound-land: for the sculles [schools] of Mackerell, Herrings, Cod, and other fish, as we daily saw as we went and came from the shore, were wonderfull; and besides, the places where we tooke these Cods (and might in a few daies have laden our ship) were but in seven fadome water . . . where in Newfound-land they fish in fortie or fiftie fadome water.

In 1605, three years later, an English crew caught cod there three to five feet long "so fast as the hooke came down." And in 1607 another crew "tooke great stor of cod fyshes the bigeste & largest that I ever saw or any man in our Ship."

Flounder were also everywhere in the sea and even close to land: "They do almost come ashore, so that one may stepp but halfe a foote deepe, and pick them up on the sands." All fish, the Englishmen noticed, were "well fed, fatte, and sweete in taste."

Here and in other parts of New England shellfish, often enormous, were plentiful, especially lobsters. One European found them "greate, and fatte, and lussious." Several reports mentioned twenty, even twenty-five-pound lobsters. The crew of one boat took fifty large ones in an hour, in three feet of water using a large hook fastened to a stick. All were "so large, so full of meate, and so plentifull in number, as no man will believe that hath not seene."

Rounding Cape Cod, Gosnold's ship put in at Martha's Vineyard,

Sassafras

which he named for his wife. He was astonished by the "incredible store of vynes, as well in the woodie part of the island, where they runne upon every tree, as on the outward partes, that we could not goe for treading on them."

He was also taken with the berry bushes of the region, especially the red and the white strawberries "as sweete and much bigger than ours in England." Most Europeans, in fact, had kind if not ecstatic words for the giant American strawberry. Raspberries, blueberries, and gooseberries also grew there in great profusion.

On Martha's Vineyard the Englishmen saw "Cranes, Stearnes, Shoulers, Geese, and divers other Birds which there at that time upon the Cliffs being sandie with some rockie Stones, did breed and had yonge." Although historians are not sure what some of these birds were, one was probably the heath hen, a pretty little chickenlike creature once seen in great numbers on the island.

The heath hen at first was called a heathcock or sometimes "pheysant," and was later known in the West as the prairie chicken. They were so numerous around Boston in the middle of the seventeenth century that a wealthy diarist instructed his servants "not to have Heath Hen brought to the table oftener than a few times a week." By the eighteenth century they were already growing scarce, and by the early nineteenth century the only survivors lived on Martha's Vineyard. The last one disappeared in 1932.

Traveling west to nearby Cuttyhunk Island, the English stayed there awhile and found sassafras trees in abundance. The soil was so "fatte and lustie" the wheat, barley, oats, and peas they planted were up nine inches in only fourteen days. In the middle of the island was a freshwater lake full of small tortoises and fowl. In short, Cuttyhunk was a fine place "in comparison whereof the most fertil part of al England is (of it selfe) but barren."

Yet Cuttyhunk did not compare with Buzzards Bay where the explorers "stood like men ravished at the beautie and delicacie of this sweet soil," and the clear freshwater lakes and great green meadows never seemed to end. It was a dream land, a spot where nature "showed herselfe above her power."

As for the natives living here they were probably Sakonnets. Their complexion was "much like a dark Olive, their eie-browes and hair blacke, which they weare long, tied up behinde in knots, whereon they pricke feathers of fowles, in fashion of a crownet." Probably the olive hue was caused by something the Indians rubbed on their skin.

Gosnold's men accounted these Indians "exceeding courteous, gentle of disposition, and well conditioned." They concluded it must be "the wholesomnesse and temperature of the Climate" that gave these natives "a perfect constitution of body, active, strong, healthfull, and very wittie." Obviously the Englishmen were not there during a New England winter.

Much encouraged by the Gosnold voyage, English merchants the next year sent over Martin Pring for more sassafras. Unlike Gosnold, Pring did not overshoot Massachusetts Bay; he coasted along until he reached beautiful Plymouth Harbor. There his men built a small stockade and lived for seven weeks.

Pring remarked on the fruitfulness of the soil and the tall good looks of the Massachuset Indians; the natives loved music, he found: "We had a youthe in our companie that could play upon a Zither, in whose homely music they tooke great delight, and would give manie things, as Tabaco, Tabaco-Pipes, snakes skins of six foote long, which they used for Gurdles, Fawn skins, and such like, and danced twentie in a Ringe, and the Zither in the midst of them, using manie Salvage gestures, singing lo, la, lo, la, la, lo."

The Massachusets, Pring went on, were "inclined to a swart, tawnie, or Chestnut color, not by nature but accidentally, and doe weare their haire brayded in foure parts, and trussed up about their heads with a small knot behind: in which haire of theirs they sticke many feathers and toyes for bravery and pleasure." The visitors were also impressed by the Indians' birchbark canoes. Though not weighing more than sixty pounds, they would hold nine riders standing upright.

Besides sassafras, the woods were full of birches, beeches, oaks, cedars, walnuts, maples, and "wich-hasels." Pring collected his sassafras and sailed for home.

The year 1604 saw the appearance in New England of Samuel de Champlain, a fine soldier and seaman and one of the great figures in the exploration and colonization of North America. Happily, he was perfectly fitted by character, temperament, and experience to carry the French banner into the wilderness; he had a curious mixture of the religious zeal of the Middle Ages and the daring and initiative of more modern times.

Between 1604 and 1608 the man, soon to be known as the Father of New France, made three trips down the New England coast. Sailing down New England on his 1604 voyage, Champlain passed many islands and rounded point after point where Maine's many fingers reached out into the sea. He came to an island "very high, with notches here and there, so that it appears when one is at sea like seven or eight mountains rising close together. The tops of most of them are without trees, because they are nothing but rock. The only trees are pines, firs, and birches. I called it *Ile des Monts Deserts.*" There may not have been many kinds of trees, but some of them were enormous. Meadow grass was tall as a man.

After he had won them over with tobacco and biscuits, some natives guided Champlain up the "beautiful and delightful" Penobscot River, getting as far as Bangor before the rocky walls closed in. He found the country "pleasant and agreeable." Oaks looked as if they had been planted there by design.

Here the Frenchmen met about fifty natives and their chief Bessabez: "As soon as the Indians on shore saw Bessabez arrive they all began to sing, dance, and leap until he landed, after which they all seated themselves on the ground in a circle, according to their custom. . . . They were much pleased to see us, inasmuch as it was the first time they had ever beheld Christians." A meeting went on for some time, Champlain managing to convince the Indians the French meant to be their friends. He sealed the bargain with presents—hatchets, rosaries, caps, and knives.

Champlain worked his way through the bewildering assortment of islands in Penobscot Bay and crossed Muscongus Bay before turning back. He vowed to make a more thorough accounting of the territory on the next trip.

Returning to that point in 1605 on his next voyage, Champlain found the mouth of the Kennebec River and sailed north. Returning to the ocean, the Frenchmen went on south, passing Casco Bay where Portland would one day rise, rounding Cape Elizabeth, then going on down the coast to Saco Bay.

Until that point the Maine coast was unprepossessing, but at Saco Bay the land was different. Trees, grapevines, and glittering sands on present-day Old Orchard Beach made it "very pleasant and as agreeable as anyone can see." Thirsty Frenchmen crushed grapes and made "a very good verjuice."

Going up the Saco River on the tide, the expedition was greeted by Indians. These natives shaved the front part of their hair and wore the back long, plaited, and stuck through with feathers; their faces were painted a startling black and red. These were the first farming Indians Champlain had seen, growing maize, beans, pumpkins, squash, grapes, and tobacco. Sometimes they mixed willow bark with tobacco, calling the result *kinikinik*.

Rounding the cape at Kennebunkport, the Frenchmen found seals and porpoises in such numbers that they became a nuisance. The French called seals *loups marin*, sea wolves, because of the baying sound they made. A middle-aged male might be eight-feet long and weigh about eight hundred pounds.

"There was not a day or night," wrote Champlain, "that we did not see and hear pass our boat more than a thousand porpoises, which were chasing the smaller fish." The fish, in magnificent numbers, were herring, salmon, bass, halibut and, of course, cod. This area is now called Cape Porpoise.

Soon the expedition was cruising down the Massachusetts coast. With obvious relish, Champlain mentioned eating oysters here. Oyster banks along the Massachusetts shore ran for as much as a mile, and some of the oysters were a foot long. The tide also brought in countless lobsters and clams with many clams the size of a penny loaf of bread. The Frenchmen drew the line at eating them though. There, too, were large ducks, brants, and passenger pigeons. The migrating piegeons appeared "in infinte numbers, of which we took a great quantity."

From Cape Ann to present-day Boston, excited Indians ran along the shore following Champlain's ship, lighting fires to show the strangers the site of their villages. Occasionally the French leader went ashore and gave the natives knives, rosaries, and biscuits. The Indians seemed pleased.

Champlain's ship carefully slid into Boston Harbor. Much land along these shores had been cleared for cornfields and was surrounded by oaks, "walnuts" (possibly hickories), and "very beautiful cypresses which are reddish and have a very good odor," obviously red cedars.

Modern Boston then was a forest of pine, fir, spruce, oak, maple, and elm. The travelers spotted what must have been the mouth of the Charles River, but didn't enter it. Many swamps were around the harbor, but elsewhere the soil was "as fat black earth as can be seen anywhere."

Many of the trees had been felled to make the Indians' dugout boats—the explorers were too far south now to see the birchbark canoe. The natives created these heavy, durable boats from tree trunks, hollowing them out with fire and scraping the insides with clam shells or some other implement. The bow and stern were rounded and blunt. Some boats were big enough for forty men, though most carried ten to fifteen.

The explorers continued along the coast to a point just north of Plymouth where a number of Indians and their chief, Honabetha, came out to meet them in dugouts. Coming aboard Champlain's ship, Honabetha was treated royally; the French gave him presents and "something of good cheer" to drink. The Indians—these were Massachusets—gave the Europeans "little squashes as big as your fist, which we ate as salad like cucumbers, and they were very good. They brought us also some purslane, which grows abundantly among the Indian corn."

Pulling into Plymouth Bay, fast becoming the best-known harbor in New England, Champlain found the Indians fishing for cod with hooks of bone barbs and lines made of milkweed fiber known as "Indian hemp." Natives here were already familiar with Europeans. They remembered the visit of Martin Pring two years earlier and had frequently seen fishermen put in. Champlain, cordially received, carefully charted this important bay.

After rounding the tip of Cape Cod and sailing down the seaward side, Champlain put in at green, sleepy Nauset Harbor. The region was delight-

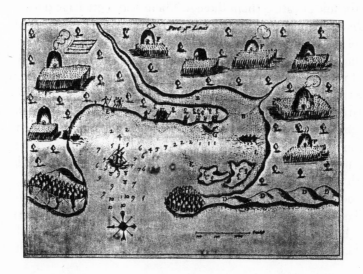

fully wooded, though little of the forest remains today. Indians in large numbers lived around the harbor, residing in dome-shaped houses erected over a sapling framework and covered with grass or reed mats. Natives here, Champlain noted, had few furs. Mostly they dressed in clothes of grass and hemp and painted their faces red, black, and yellow.

Going ashore to inspect an Indian village, Champlain admired the tall corn, beans, squash, tobacco, and tasty Jerusalem artichokes. The Jerusalem artichoke—not an artichoke at all—was a cousin to the sunflower with several fingerlike tubers similar to potatoes. It was to become an important food in much of the United States and Canada.

The Frenchmen did not think highly of the Indians here. Champlain wrote, "In appearance they seem to be of good disposition, and better than those to the northward. But the whole of them, to tell the truth, are not worth much . . . . They are great thieves, and if they cannot lay hold of a thing with their hands they try to do it with their feet."

Apparently the natives, having no metal themselves, were eager to get their hands—or feet—on one of the Frenchmen's metal cooking pots. A sailor, gone ashore to bring back water, was killed just for the pot he was carrying. This was to be the first recorded death of a European in New England.

At Nauset the Frenchmen saw their first turkeys, passenger pigeons, and an astonishing creature—Champlain called it a fish—now known as the horseshoe crab. A horseshoe crab's tail was perfect for tipping arrows, the Indians believed.

With storms coming up and provisions short, the French captain decided to return to Canada after only a month of exploration. On a later trip Champlain returned to continue his exploration south of Cape Cod.

On this journey the French explorer stopped at some different places than on his previous trip. One layover was present-day Gloucester, Massachusetts, where the tumbling rocks and green forest rim delighted Champlain so much he named it *Le Beau Port.* The chart of the harbor he made was so accurate that it probably could be used today.

From Gloucester the party continued south into new territory, past sand dunes, scrubby trees, and Nauset Beach. Turning the elbow of Cape Cod they pulled in at Stage Harbor at present-day Chatham, a pleasant place with beach plums, wild roses, bayberry, and flies. Here they stayed two weeks, making repairs to the ship and laying in supplies. Game was plentiful, especially plover. An officer claimed he brought down twenty-eight of these birds with a single shot.

Indians around Stage Harbor, Champlain noted, had a different language and economy from those farther north on Cape Cod. They also weren't as accommodating.

The Frenchmen had built an oven on shore and five of them were sitting around it eating biscuits when Indians sprang from the woods, killing three. One was found face down with a little dog on his back, both pierced by the same arrow. A fourth sailor died later of his wounds.

Soon the other Frenchmen came ashore, scattered the attackers, and buried their comrades. Three hours later, after the Europeans had returned to their ship with their guns, the Indians reappeared. The horrified Frenchmen watched as the natives dug up the corpses and scattered them around the beach. One Indian put on the shirt of a victim and danced around in it.

It would do no good to go ashore again, the Frenchmen knew. The Indians would simply vanish into the forest. Sad and angry, the Europeans sailed out of what they had so inaptly named Good Luck Harbor.

The expedition continued south, noticed a large island that may have been Martha's Vineyard, and then ran into contrary winds. Champlain decided to turn back for Canada even though this expedition had gone only a little farther than the last one.

If the Frenchmen had continued down the coast and found Narragansett Bay and New York Harbor—and the more cordial and appealing natives living in those parts—much of North American history might have been different. Some of us in the United States might have been speaking French.

Next up in New England was the redoubtable Captain John Smith of Virginia fame. Smith had gone home to England for medical attention after an accidental gunpowder explosion and never returned to Jamestown.

John Smith's life reads like a book of adventure fiction. Indeed, some of it may be fiction, though parts of it are corroborated by his contemporaries. According to his own account, he fought against the Turks in eastern Europe, on one occasion dispatching three of them at the same time in bloody hand-to-hand combat. After that he was the slave and then the lover of a Turkish princess. In America his career was no less remarkable.

In the two books that were written after returning to England, Smith told of his arrival in the New World under arrest for disobedience, of soon becoming a leader at Jamestown, and of being sentenced to hang.

The tale of Smith's rescue by Pocahontas may or may not be true, for no one mentions it except Smith himself. It is a typical wilderness tale, one first told by Juan Ortiz of the Narváez expedition to Florida almost a hundred years before.

There are two schools of thought on Smith's character. One is that he was a boastful and vainglorious troublemaker the struggling colony of Virginia could have done without. The other believes he was a courageous man who saved the little settlement from extinction in its first year. Both schools are probably right: There is no doubt he was brave and resourceful, and no less doubt that he was an egotist and braggart.

In 1614, six years after he departed Jamestown, John Smith was back in America, this time as a member of a New England whaling expedition. Whale fishing, Smith said, was "a costly conclusion." Although the expedition saw many whales and chased them, they were not able to kill any. Instead the members turned to fishing, taking in almost fifty thousand. On the side—"for trifles," Smith said—they got about thirteen hundred beaver, otter, and marten skins.

Smith spent much of his time mapping the New England coast, giving

New England, Massachusetts, and Plymouth their names. He saw the same sights Champlain had, but with his small boat he got a closer look. To him the coast was "all Mountainous and Iles of huge Rockes."

Ending his excursion at the Penobscot River in Maine, Smith looked east and saw only more "high craggy clifty Rockes and stony Iles." Since there was so little soil Smith was amazed that "such greate Trees could grow upon so hard foundations."

This was not the kind of report the good captain brought home for public consumption. His published accounts read more like a real estate agent's brochure, praising the land and everything about the country. His backers, London merchants, were eager to attract capital and settlers.

But Smith was sincere when he wrote about the fishing. Cod and hake were twice the size of those in Canadian waters and Smith believed "Hee is a very bad Fisher [who] cannot kille in one day with his hooke and line one, two, or three hundred Cods." He was especially impressed with the bass, "an excellent Fish, both fresh and salt . . . . They are so large the head of one will give a good Eater a Dinner . . . . At the turning of the Tyde I have seen such multitudes passe out of a pounde [net] that it seemed to me one might goe over their backes drishod." Also, mullet were two to four feet long and there were enormous amounts of smelt, flounder, salmon, and sturgeon.

Captain Smith was in New England only six months, then spent the rest of his life trying to persuade fellow Englishmen to settle there. He concluded that if a man could not make a good living in the region he deserved to starve. Thirty or forty men, properly equipped, should be able to provide two or three hundred people "with as goode Corn, Fish, and Flesh as the earth has of those kindes, and yet make that labour but their pleasure."

Later on Smith negotiated with those religious dissenters known later as the Pilgrims to return to New England as their adviser, but was turned down. They thought him too headstrong, potentially troublesome. So the famous Pilgrims came over without any expert help, arriving late in 1620. They did not step right off onto that celebrated rock, if they ever set foot on it. First they rounded the tip of Cape Cod and anchored in the fine wide bay of modern Provincetown.

The landscape did not look promising. Summer had faded and everything, according to William Bradford, the later governor of Plymouth Colony: bore "a weather-beaten face, and ye whole countrie full of woods & thickets, representing a willd & savage heiw." Disembarking, the

women got off to wash clothes and some of the men started off on their first reconnoitering expedition.

Even though Bradford pictured the landscape as bleak, it was not. The whole bay was "encompassed aboute to the Sea with oak, pine, sassafras, and other sweete woode." Other trees included walnut, ash, birch, cedar, and maple. A little distance inland the exploring party noticed that beneath the sand was "excellent blacke earth" of about a spade's thickness. Apparently, the party spent the first afternoon ashore cutting juniper trees, and when they returned to store a handsome load of this sweet-smelling wood, the rangy old *Mayflower* began to smell more like its name.

Later on everyone became excited when a school of whales came up close to shore, spouting off and lolling around. One of the whales came near enough to be shot at, but when one sailor tried to fire his musket it blew up in his face. No one else was willing to fire now, so the whale remained close by until he "gave a snuff, and away!" The crew thought this must be a better place for catching whales than Greenland and were sorry they did not have the proper equipment for doing it. Indeed this part of Cape Cod seems to be a favorite haunt of these leviathans. On a single day in 1984 nineteen beached themselves at Wellfleet Harbor, a few miles down the coast. Nine of them died.

Eventually the Pilgrims tired of the meager and monotonous ship's supplies and looked about for something fresh to eat. The fishing was not good—it was the wrong time of the year: "For Cod we assayed, but found none. There is goode store, no doubt, in their season. Neither gott we any Fish all the time we lay here but some little ones on the Shore."

But there were plenty of tender, soft-shell clams and the succulent quahogs now known as cherrystones, littlenecks, or brights. To their great regret though, some of the company stuffed themselves with the large mussels, "very fatt and full of Sea Pearl," which made them "to cast and scour." In other words, they became ill.

An exploring party commanded by Captain Miles Standish saw the first Indians, five or six of them. When approached, the natives dashed into the woods with the Pilgrims following; they wanted to find out if there were any more of them. The Pilgrims never saw those natives again.

The next morning the English did some more exploring, wandering around the hills and valleys near what is now Truro. Soon they were hopelessly lost, falling into "shuch thickets as were ready to tear their cloaths & armore in peeces." They were fiercely thirsty and had with them only a little "aqua vitae," probably Holland gin.

Suddenly they stumbled out of the tangled woods into a spacious clearing. The sight of deer excited them as did flocks of partridges, ducks, and wild geese that took flight upon their approach. Then they saw a stream and found the clear spring that fed it and quenched their "greate thirstie" with long sweet draughts. It was the first fresh water they had tasted since boarding the Mayflower, and it tasted "as pleasante as wine or beer had in for-times."

The Pilgrims felt no qualms about opening a nearby mound that seemed too small to be a grave. In it they found "a little old Basket full of fayre Indian corne," and farther down a new basket of recently harvested corn. Farther still was another corn cache and a bottle of corn oil. These were "very goodlie sights."

The settlers had brought wheat and barley seeds, yet they knew from the experience of the Jamestown settlers that corn grew best in this new country. So the party took all the corn—about ten bushels—with them. They promised themselves they would reimburse the Indians as soon as they could, a promise fulfilled when their first harvest was in. The site is still known as Corn Hill.

It was near Corn Hill that William Bradford was caught in an Indian deer trap. At one spot on a pathway in the woods the Indians had scattered corn to attract the deer, and had attached a rope to a sapling arched over the place. Bradford, unaware of the trap, stepped on the rope and was suddenly swung upward by one leg. After being cut down, Bradford and his saviors had a good laugh.

Bradford was intrigued by the ingenious trap. "It was a prettie Device, made with a rope of their own making, and having a Noose as artificially [artfully] made as any roper in England can make and as like ours as can be."

The Pilgrims were not satisfied with Provincetown Harbor as a place to settle. While the *Mayflower* remained at anchor there, an exploring party in a small boat made its way along the landward curve of Cape Cod. Rounding a point, they found themselves in cozy Wellfleet Harbor.

Here, there was another encounter with the natives. The Indians were on the beach, "very busy about a blacke thing." No one could make out what the thing was and it was too close to dark to find out. The party put up for the night and next morning the Indians were gone.

What the natives had been working over was a great black fish about fifteen feet long, covered "some 2 inches thicke in fatt, like a hogg . . . and fleshed like a swine." This was a grampus, a member of the dolphin family that looked like a small whale. Two more were in the shallow water nearby, both dead. The Englishmen knew there was valuable oil in a grampus and regretted having neither the time nor the tools to extract it.

Time was growing short. Already it was December and a bitter New England winter was upon them. The Pilgrims needed to find a suitable place to settle and build and also had to do something about food as quickly as possible. "Our victuals were much spent, especially our Beer," lamented Bradford.

The exploring party continued up the Massachusetts coast, looking for an inlet that one of the ship's officers called Thievish Harbor. He had been

there on a whaling expedition and his crew had named the place after some Indians had stolen a harpoon. Thievish Harbor turned out to be Plymouth Bay, already mapped and named by John Smith.

The leaders decided on Plymouth without much debate—they simply liked its looks. It was, in the quaint expression of the day, "a place fitt for situation." The bay was large and well sheltered, ringed with woods, and alive with waterfowl. The soil was "excellent black mold, and fatte in some places," and fine trees, wild fruits, herbs, and berries abounded. There was also good clay, "excellent for Pots and Pans and will wash like soap."

A "sweete Brooke" ran into the harbor. On the high ground behind the brook the Pilgrims at last decided to establish their settlement on the lower part of the bay just behind Plymouth Rock. There was: "a great deale of land cleared, and hath been planted with Corne three or four years agoe . . . . On the further side of the river also, much Corne ground cleared. In one field is a greate hill on which we poynt to make a platform & plant our ordinance, which will command all round about."

Cleared fields showed the area had once been occupied by numbers of Indians; now it was deserted. The Pilgrims had seen such as this before and had wondered about it, especially about the mass graveyards along the coast. Not long before these shores must have been visited by some calamitous event, they concluded.

While still living on the *Mayflower*, Pilgrim men got off every day and worked on the wattle and daub structures that would be their new homes. From time to time they saw smoke from distant campfires, yet no natives appeared. Captain Standish took a few men off to see if they could find out what the Indians were up to, but the party found no one, only coming upon an abandoned village. The Pilgrims did return with an "eagle—"it may have been a fish hawk—they shot. Ravenous for fresh food, the men cooked the bird and ate it, declaring it good and "hardly to be discerned from Mutton."

A fourteen-year-old adventurer, Francis Billington, exploring alone one day, discovered the nearby lakes, a large and small one. The boy felt

certain he had discovered the Western Ocean. The company, perhaps in jest, named the large lake Billington Sea, a name it still bears. Full of fish, the lakes' banks abounded in waterfowl and the water itself was full of fish. The growing season was long past when the Pilgrims moved into Plymouth. Of course there were no fresh fruits or greens and though game and waterfowl were abundant, the settlers' guns were clumsy matchlock muskets hard to load and slow to fire. To kill anything with one of these a hunter had to fire "hayle shott" into a large flock of fowl and hope for the best; there was no second chance. As for fishing the Pilgrims, like the Jamestowners, had brought the wrong kind of hooks.

During the winter almost half the colonists died. Bitter weather, hard work, and a diet of bread, butter, and cheese from the ship's meager larder had weakened them. Many fell victim to scurvy or an influenza-type virus that swept through the little settlement.

At one time the Pilgrims were reduced to living almost entirely on groundnuts. First described by Thomas Hariot at Roanoke, the groundnut was a twining vine often found in moist ground or marshes. It is a member of the pea family and, as Hariot said, "grows together as if in ropes or as though fastened by a string."Although they looked like peas, the small tubers tasted like potatoes.

With spring came renewed hope. The surviving colonists planted the barley and peas they had brought from home and the Indian maize they had stolen. By this time they had cultivated the friendship of the local natives and had made an impression on Chief Massasoit by curing him of constipation. Then the mystery of the graves and abandoned cornfields was solved. Four years earlier a strange and debilitating plague, perhaps typhus, brought by rats escaping from a ship, or maybe smallpox or measles brought by some Europeans, had struck the area. Much of the Indian population was killed but Massasoit and other survivors retreated about forty miles into the interior.

The Patuxet tribe, living around Plymouth, was wiped out except for one young brave. His name was Tisquantum and he had been lucky enough—as it turned out—to have been kidnapped before the plague struck and taken to Europe. When John Smith brought him back several years later he found all his relatives dead and buried in mass graves.

Tisquantum—the Englishmen called him "Squanto"—attached himself to the Pilgrims as a sort of county agent, instructing them in wilderness farming techniques. Corn should be planted "when the leaves of the white oak are as large as a mouse's ear." He also advised them to fertilize corn by putting in each hillock three alewives (a kind of herring), placed spokewise. Perhaps he learned this technique not in the wilderness but in Europe where much farmland had long since been exhausted. Few if any Indians were likely to have used the method. They had no way of transporting large quantities of fish from stream to field. There was plenty of land and instead of trying to revitalize the soil they were more likely to simply move on to other land.

Squanto taught the newcomers how to build weirs for catching alewives and other fish that made spawning runs in the spring. He also showed them how to catch eels. During cold weather eels buried themselves in the bottoms of streams, "being bedded in gravell not above two or three foote deep." The Pilgrims were astonished as they watched their Indian mentor feel for the squiggly things with his toes and then work them out of the mud with his feet.

Later settlers learned the trick too. Governor John Winthrop of Massachusetts Bay Colony told of how two or three boys "brought in a bushell of greate Eels at a time, and sixtie greate Lobsters." Another settler said eels were "as greate as ever I saw anie" and they were "passing sweete, fatt, and wholesome, haveing no taste at all of the Mudde." Settlers also learned to make eel pudding, an Indian delicacy.

The Pilgrims' first harvest, the following fall, was a good one. The barley and peas from England did not amount to much, but there were twenty acres of succulent corn. Feeling appreciative, the settlers invited Massasoit to a harvest feast. The Plymouth settlers may have thought this celebration something new to the natives, yet it was an immemorial custom in the eastern part of the continent to celebrate the ripening of crops with a "green corn dance." Besides feasting for several days, Indians cleaned their homes inside and out, threw away old clothes, lit new fires—all this to symbolize a new year, a new beginning.

Imagine the Pilgrims' consternation when Massasoit arrived with ninety hungry braves. They needn't have been alarmed—the Indians knew what was expected of them. Some went into the woods and killed five deer, others probably brought in a lot of shellfish and fat eels.

There was a variety of luscious wilderness food at that first Thanksgiving. For three days settlers and Indians ate venison, duck, goose, partridge, clams, lobsters, oysters, and tasty eels. Turkeys? No one mentioned turkeys, but that doesn't mean there were none. Massasoit's braves might have been among the Indians who didn't like turkey and could have brought the birds to the feast just to get rid of them.

Every householder in Plymouth had his own private garden. From these

came "sallet herbes": parsnips, carrots, turnips, onions, cucumbers, beets, and cabbages. Wild fruits of the summer—strawberries, gooseberries, plums, cherries—had been dried under Squanto's expert direction and some cooked into "dough cases." These were the ancestors of New England's celebrated pies.

Newly harvested corn was served parched, in hoecakes, or as cornmeal boiled in a bag with molasses and called "Indian pudding." They may have cooked some of it in earthern jars over an open fire until it burst and became popcorn. Indians had been eating popcorn for generations and sometimes poured maple syrup over it until it stuck together into balls.

Later settlers made regular use of pumpkins in pies, bread, and sauces, yet no pumpkin dish seems to have appeared on that first Thanksgiving table. There is no mention of cranberries either, though nearby bogs crawled with them. These were what the English called "quaking boggs," for those walking on them felt as if the earth moved. In them grew plants that thrived in a highly acidic environment: cranberries, pitcher plants, and orchids.

Probably because Pilgrims had not yet found out how to prepare them, there were no cranberries at the original Thanksgiving feast. A few years later though, they were to be used in "steamed puddings" made of chopped cranberries, flour, and molasses.

Although they had one bad winter, the Pilgrims quickly adapted to their new circumstances. They profited from the experience of the Jamestown settlers, who suffered from ignorance and an unwillingness to learn.

The fact is, the population of the entire continent of Europe could have been set down in the North American wilderness and there would have been more than enough food for all.

Newcomers to this land had to learn where to find food, how to get it, and what to do with it after they got it. These were not easy lessons to learn, and many later settlers had to learn them over and over again.

Meanwhile the Spanish, slowly and gingerly, were investigating the West Coast from Mexico up to the present state of Washington. And in time the English, Russians, and Americans would be interested in this region as well.

7

~~~~~~

THE WEST COAST: "BLESSINGS FITT FOR THE USE OF MAN"
Spanish, English, Russians, and Americans

In sixteenth century Spain a favorite book retooled the hoary legend of the Amazons, those warlike women who, according to this tome, "lived at the right hand of the Indies, very close to the Terrestrial Paradise, abounding in gold."

According to legend Queen Calafia ruled these brazen ladies on her island of California. Some early comers to this continent thought the land now known as Baja California was this fabulous island. They were bitterly disappointed when Baja proved to be a peninsula. But the name California stuck.

Alarcón and Díaz, on the Coronado expedition, were bound to have seen a bit of California from the Colorado River near Yuma, Arizona, but we can't tell whether they set foot on California soil. History books give the honor of discovering California to Juan Cabrillo, a Portuguese seaman in the employ of Spain who sailed up the coast in 1542.

Sailing north from Mexico, Cabrillo paused first at San Diego Bay. Filling the bay waters were sturgeon and sole "of delicate taste." The sturgeon weighed only fifteen to twenty pounds—small compared to the East Coast variety—but reportedly tasted quite good.

As for other sealife sardines here were as plentiful as they were in the

Mediterranean, and there were numerous large mackerellike fish called bonito. The Pacific oyster was also smaller than its eastern counterpart, but it tasted fine.

Around the bay the country was mostly meadowland with a lot of shrubs and grapevines and almost without stones. The meadows boasted few trees, yet the San Diego River was lined with willows, alders, poplars, and cottonwoods. Like much of the rest of California, the countryside was overrun with wild roses.

From San Diego, Cabrillo sailed through the Gulf of Santa Catalina, past the future site of Los Angeles, across Santa Monica Bay, and up to Point Mugu where there was a large Indian town. From Malibu to Point Conception, and on the adjacent Santa Barbara Islands, there were many native settlements. Of course the climate was nearly perfect.

Somewhere around here, probably at or near Santa Barbara, the Spaniards met the most advanced of California Indians, the Chumash. For travel these natives built seagoing boats of planks lashed together and made watertight with an asphalt caulking. Using antler wedges, they split the boards from cedar trees and smoothed them with seashells or rough stones. The boats carried up to twenty riders, and strong rowers propelled them with double-bladed paddles. Such paddles were not used by anyone else except Eskimos, so it makes one wonder if the Chumash, or their northern cousins, had contact with civilizations far across the Pacific.

The Chumash lived in large round houses, some of them harboring several families. Small houses congregated around large ones and in front of them were thick timbers covered with paintings, apparently totem poles.

Cabrillo found most California tribesmen sleeping on the ground—especially in the Santa Barbara Islands—but the Chumash were one of a few tribes that had real beds; they were platforms raised from the ground and covered with rush mats. Other mats hung about the beds for warmth and privacy. A rolled-up mat served as a pillow.

Cabrillo may have sailed north as far as Washington, but he did not think much of the northern country. He arrived at a bad time—November, 1542—to be impressed by the glories of the northwestern wilderness. Storms and mountainous waves buffeted the frail little ships and fog blinded the pilots. On the return trip Cabrillo sailed around what probably was Monterey Bay; fear of the surf may have kept him from going ashore.

About this time Cabrillo died of a fall and command of the ships passed to Bartolomé Ferrelo. The new captain decided to go north again—

although he probably did not go any farther than his late commander had—and heard from some local natives that a great river flowed nearby. This probably was the Columbia, but instead of trying to find it Ferrelo sailed back down the coast for Mexico. After he returned the Spanish lost interest in the West Coast for a time.

The next explorer to visit California was one of the most famous English seaman of that or any other day: the celebrated buccaneer Francis Drake (not yet a Sir). Drake disliked the Spanish intensely, especially their threat to the budding prospect of England as mistress of the seas.

Earlier Queen Elizabeth had given Drake a privateering commission, a polite way of saying, Go raid all the Spanish treasure ships you can find. Drake did that for a number of years, making his name as hated among the Spanish as Satan.

So the Englishman wasn't exploring—there was no profit in that— when he came to California. He had just plundered Spanish treasures on the West Coast of South America and was looking for a good place to fix the leaks in his famous raider, the *Golden Hind.*

He appeared off the California coast in 1579, where his men complained of the "extreame and nipping colde." Because of contrary winds they had to "runne in with the Shoare, which we then first descried, and to cast anchor in a bad bay, the best roads we could for the present meet with."

Probably this unfavorable spot was the cove just south of Cape Arago on the Oregon coast, where they suffered "extreame gusts and flawes." This was no place to careen a ship, so Drake headed south through "most vile, thicke, and stinking fogges." For fourteen days he did not see the sun.

Sailing south, the mariners complained of more "nipping colde." When they could see land at all it appeared "to bee but low and reasonable plaine. Every hill (whereof we saw many, but none verie high), though it were June, and the sunne in its neerest approach unto them, being covered with snow." Apparently these were the Coast Ranges.

Drake finally found a comfortable harbor at the latitude of present-day Point Reyes. The spot had white cliffs like those of Dover—reminding the sailors of home—and a hard beach just right for repairs. Where this bay was is still disputed, but most researchers agree that it must have been the inlet now known as Drake's Bay, thirty-six miles north of San Francisco.

Wherever it was, the treasure seekers spent five lovely spring weeks there. Back from the coast the fog dissipated and the Englishmen roamed about thirty miles inland. They found the country "farre different from the Shoare, a goodly countrie, and fruitfull soyle, stored with many blessing fitt for the use of man."

The whole country was "a warren of a strange kinde of conies." In old English writings a "coney" was a rabbit, but if these mystery animals were "a strange kinde" they may have been pocket gophers. They were present in such multitudes that early California settlers poisoned them to keep down their numbers.

There were also many fat deer and antelope, as well as hordes of waterfowl. The natives hunted wild geese and ducks from rafts made of bundled reeds, using stuffed geese as decoys. With their bone-pointed reed spears, Indians brought in such an abundance of fish that much of the catch spoiled before it could be eaten. A great pile of mussel shells marked many an abandoned campsite.

One day area natives—some of the Coast Miwoks living between present-day Mendocino and San Francisco Bay—came to visit. It apparently was a custom of these Indians to dramatically greet newcomers by rolling on the ground while slashing their chests and cheeks with their fingernails until their blood ran, all the time screeching. Of course Drake's men did not understand their declamations. Drake himself broke up a screaming-and-scratching spell by having his on-board chaplain conduct a church service complete with psalm singing. Abruptly ceasing their fits, the Miwoks listened attentively and wonderingly to the gospel and joined in on the psalms with a chorus of unmelodious shouts.

Soon a chief appeared. This king, as the English called him, "had on his Head a Knit Cawl [cowl] wrought somewhat like a Crown, and on his Shoulders a Coat of Rabbet Skins reaching to the waste." The cawl was the net cap filled with eagle down commonly worn by Indian dignitaries in central California.

This chief placed a "rustic Crown" on Drake's head, perhaps a headdress of woodpecker or vulture feathers with a band that might have been
studded with abalone or seashells. The Miwoks afforded Drake and the
other English the greatest respect, even veneration. After all, these
bearded strangers may have been spirits returned from the dead. That at
least would account for their pale color.

The Miwoks supplemented their honorable visitors' meager shipboard
rations with gifts of boiled fish, acorn bread, and a dish called *petah* made
from bulbs of the mariposa lily. Growing wild in the West, the plant was
an important food for the natives who ground the bulbs into meal, or ate
them boiled, steamed, or roasted. Early Mormons would sustain themselves on the plant through many a food crisis, and were so thankful they
made the mariposa lily the state flower of Utah.

Acorns were another important food. When they were ripe Indian boys
climbed oak trees and knocked the nuts down, while old women gathered
the catch in baskets. Later the women shelled and dried the acorns and
pounded them into meal that became gruel, porridge, or bread.

The Miwoks also made gruel and bread from cattail roots. The cattail,
easily identified by its green shoots with sausage-like shapes on them, was
an important source of food. The root was nourishing and the pulp inside
the shoots was edible. The shoots themselves were edible when boiled as
greens. Although the sausage-like part could not be eaten, the pollen
inside it made good flour.

The Miwoks lived in semisubterranean houses typical of other north
central California natives. Houses were

> dug round into the Earth, and have from the Surface of the Ground, Poles
> of wood set up and joined together at the top like a Spired Steeple, which
> being covered with Earth, no Water can enter and are very warm, the Door
> being also the Chimney to let out the Smoak . . . . Their beds are on the
> hard Ground strewed with Rushes, with a fire in the midst round which
> they lye, and the Roof being low round and close, gives a very great
> Reflection of Heat to their Boddies.

Very soon Drake took formal possession of the country and named it
Nova Albion "for two causes; the one in respect of the white Banckes and
Cliffes . . . the other that it might have some affinity, even in name also,
with our own Countrey, which was sometimes so called." (Albion was an
old name for England.)

The captain "set up a monument of our being there, as also of Her

Majesties right and title to the same, namely a Plate, nailed upon a faire greate Post, whereupon was engraven Her Majesties name and the Day and Yeere of our arrival there." A plate has been found in modern times, but experts cannot decide whether it is genuine. Most think it is counterfeit.

The Indians remained friendly throughout Drake's stay. As the day neared for the Englishmen's departure "the Sorrows and Miseries of this People" grew worse and worse. There were new fits and lacerations, many "wofull Complaints and Moans." When the *Golden Hind* sailed away the Indians "tooke a sorowfull farewell of us, but being loath to leave us they presently ranne to the top of the Hills to keep us in their sight as longe as they could, making fires before and behinde, and on each side of them."

Certainly the first Englishmen in this part of the New World had made a good impression on its inhabitants and so had the Indians on Drake and his men.

When the Spaniards heard that the English were planning to make another trip to California, Spanish interest in the West Coast was renewed. In 1584 Francisco Gali sailed part of the coast, beginning somewhere near Santa Cruz.

A couple of years later Pedro de Unamuno, sent out to look for some islands that didn't exist, sailed into what may have been Monterey Bay, but more likely was Morro Bay. He went a short distance inland, impressed by the tall trees, fragrant plants, and an "infinite number of fish of various kinds." Next came Sebastian Cermeño.

Striking the coast near Cape Mendocino, Cermeño coasted south until he discovered—as far as the Spanish were concerned—Drake's Bay. His men allowed the ship to run aground and they had to sail carefully on down the coast to Mexico in a smaller vessel they made themselves. On the way Cermeño met the Chumash of the Santa Barbara Channel and paused to look around in San Diego Bay.

In 1602 Sebastian Vizcaíno visited the West Coast, ordered by the Spanish government of Mexico to take possession of the "Kingdom of California" for Spain. With him came a handful of monks who were to estimate the chances of saving heathen souls there. Probably Vizcaíno was also searching for that elusive figment, the Strait of Anian, a supposed waterway through the continent similar to the Northwest Passage. The Spanish suspected some English seadog had already found the strait and that the English were making use of it.

Vizcaíno's ships put in at San Diego Bay, the first of many spots along the coast the captain named for saints. He and his sailors were impressed by "the mildness of the climate and the goodness of the soil." The trees, shrubs, and numerous kinds of plants must have indeed been lovely. There were also "a great variety of fish, oysters, mussels, lobsters, sole, &c., and up in the country were found geese, ducks, quails." Rabbits roamed in rambunctious hordes.

Somewhere in the Santa Barbara Channel Vizcaíno met the Chumash. These Indians, by now familiar with Spaniards, hailed them as "Christianos" and asked them to stay. The Spaniards were especially impressed by the Chumash's adroit handling of their large plank boats.

Fighting headwinds, fog, and scurvy, Vizaíno continued north until he reached Monterey Bay—"the best harbor that could be desired." The country teemed with bears, rabbits, and deer "larger than cows." Like all early comers to this site, the Spaniards thought highly of the trees—oaks, white oaks, firs, willows, pines, poplars, and chestnuts—as well as the many lovely vines and the ever-present roses.

The oak trees were "of a prodigious size" and the tall pines straight and smooth, just right for ships' masts. Among the sea life the sailors were especially captivated by the marvelous abalone, "a large shell fish with conches equal to the finest mother of pearl." Natives used abalone for decoration and food.

Eventually an exceptionally severe storm blew Vizcaíno's ships perhaps as far north as Cape Blanco in southern Oregon, preventing the voyagers from possibly seeing San Francisco Bay. So far all explorers had missed what would become the great harbor of the western United States.

After Vizcaíno brought his scurvy-ridden crew home, more than a century and a half would pass before someone would make an expedition on foot into California. Only then did many Europeans become truly aware of a country, as Drake put it, "stored with many blessings fitt for the use of man." The land expedition began in 1769.

The expedition, commanded by the new governor of California, Gaspar de Portolá, began slowly working its way up the California coast. To convert the heathen natives, Portolá took along the Franciscan missionary Junípero Serra, who had a gimpy leg resulting from a scorpion bite in the Mexican desert. One day Father Serra's name would be a household word in California, after he founded a string of missions up and down the coast.

The expedition found the going rugged much of the time. Often the party had to use picks and axes to open a path for the pack train and their horses started at every strange noise. Especially disturbing to the men were the ominous rumblings in the earth—in one five-day stretch there were nine of them. Then, as now, California was threatened by earthquakes.

On the site of present-day Los Angeles, Portolá stumbled upon the La Brea tarpits, where fossils of prehistoric animals trapped in tar and oil

would later be found. In some places there were "large swamps of a certain material like pitch that was bubbling up." This was crude oil, used by the Indians for caulking boats.

Wild geese, ducks, pelicans, and cormorants covered the area's lakes and bays. Geese were easy to kill; one Spaniard reportedly brought down nine with three shots. Natives caught ducks by putting seaweed on their heads and corkwood under their arms so that they would float. Disguised in this manner they moved quietly on the water and pulled birds under "as one might pick figs from a tree."

Some sandy beaches were hidden under infinite quantities of tiny fish left by the tide. "The fish overflowed onto the land as a brimming bucket sheds its burden. We ate until we were completely full, but envied whales those vast bellies they filled with this delightful fish." This may be the first mention of the mysterious grunions that appear by the millions today on California beaches, riding up on the tide to lay their eggs in the sand. Friendly Indians brought the Spaniards so many fish "we had to tell them not to bring us any more because they would spoil."

Further inland were herds of antelope and large deer. Along the way up California the Spanish saw "troops of bears," or the torn-up ground where the animals had searched for roots. Like many other Indians, California natives raised bear cubs and fattened them up for the table.

Although there was plenty to eat in this country, at times Indians had to supplement their fish-and-meat diet with grass seeds, caterpillars, grasshoppers, maggots, wasps, ants, bee larvae, beetles, and the secretion of aphids. They whipped grass seeds into baskets with seed beaters and cooked them into bread or gruel or toasted them. Toasted, the Spaniards

thought, grass seeds tasted like almonds. The natives smoked caterpillars in trees, usually yellow pines, until they fell into waiting baskets. Boiled in salt water, the woolly things were said to be passable eating.

Grasshoppers were trapped in "surrounds"—driven by an ever-constricting circle into a pit. Then they were eaten on the spot or roasted later.

The little plant lice called aphids left an edible residue on reeds that one Spaniard described as "a kind of sweet paste and sugar." Plant lice in the desert of the Sinai Peninsula deposit a similar secretion during the night, one Old Testament writers called "manna." The residue is exported from that region today under the name "mannite."

Indian children did not count their age—they numbered the years according to what creatures they were able to catch and eat. At three years old they were bug age, at four mouse age, at six snake age, and, at about twelve, deer age.

Missed by explorers for two hundred years, San Francisco Bay was found at last by Portolá—but only by accident. Some of his soldiers chasing a deer reached the crest of a hill and there, spread out in all its pristine glory, was the bay. Blue waters stretched away into distant hills and bays—"a very pleasing view"—and stretches of sand and green flats bordered the shore. The tableland where the Presidio of San Francisco stands today was green and covered with flowers, especially violets.

In other places around the bay it was different—they were "muddy, miry, and full of sloughs." San Pablo Bay to the north seemed to have cleaner beaches while the Oakland side of the bay had forests and open country, thickly settled with Indians. Mariposa lilies were everywhere.

Much of the countryside was furnished with laurel, ash, oaks, and live oaks. While exploring north of San Francisco Bay, the Spaniards came upon "some tall trees of reddish-colored wood of a species unknown to us, having leaves very unlike those of cedar, and without a cedar odor. As we knew not the names of the trees we gave them that of the color of the wood, *palo colorado.*" They are still known by that name—redwoods.

The size of these great trees stunned the Spaniards—"Eight men all holding hands could not span one of them." They were of the genus *Sequoia sempervirens,* the "everlasting Sequoia," some of them over two thousand years old. Commonly known as coast redwoods, they appeared in dank valleys and fog-shrouded areas.

Of course, there was no way to tell the age of a tree in those days, but no doubt Father Serra would have been intrigued to know that some redwoods were alive and growing at the time of his savior. He told the expedition's carpenter he wanted a redwood coffin when he died.

When Portolá's party pushed on and saw the white cliffs and white sands of Drake's Bay and Point Reyes—they recognized them from mariners' reports—the governor realized he had gone farther north than he intended. He had missed the main object of his mission, Vizcaíno's Monterey Bay. On the return trip Portolá missed the bay again, and after that decided it didn't exist. But a few months later Portolá tried again and finally found it.

It was a grand sight: "Looking south, one sees the Sierra de Santa Lucia, sending out its foothills which grow lower as they approach the shore and whose ridges, crowned with pines and covered with pasturage, form a magnificent amphitheater. Its beauty is enhanced by the verdure of the different canyons which intersect the country, presenting an admirable variety and harmony to the eye." Tall reeds and very high grasses grew in many places, "proof of the fertility of the soil."

Portolá's investigations ended speculation that California was an island. It also helped to squelch rumors that there was gold there because of the gold-colored flowers. There was gold of course, yet it would be a long time before anyone discovered it.

The Russians meanwhile were moving south down the coast of Alaska. First to come, in 1741, was Vitus Bering, a Dane in the employ of the czars. His first glimpse of North America was that of a monstrous high peak covered with snow and overlooking a wilderness of islands, forests, and gleaming icebergs. He gave the peak the name it still bears, Mount St. Elias. His ship anchored briefly there.

As Bering headed back for Siberia, a storm blew up and a great breaker hurled his ship into a cove on a small island off the tip of the Aleutians. By this time many of his crew had died of scurvy and others were quite ill with it. Because of this predicament Bering decided to build huts and winter there.

Blue foxes seemed to rule the little island; they were ubiquitous, showed no fear of the sailors, and were a nuisance. They had to be chased away from the corpses of scurvy victims, they bit sick men, and scurried off with provisions. On the first day at work on the huts, the Russians killed sixty foxes with their axes.

Bering's men were understandably dispirited, but the long stopover was a fine opportunity for the expedition's naturalist, German-born Georg

Wilhelm Steller. "Along the shore of the island," Steller wrote in his journal, "especially where streams flow into the sea and all kinds of seaweed are abundant, the sea cow, so called by our Russians, occurs at all seasons of the year in great numbers and in herds."

Sea cows, natives of the island, were huge, wrinkled relatives of the manatees. They may have weighed as much as three tons, though no one can be sure because they became extinct not long after Stellar first described them.

Outwardly sea cows didn't seem very advanced, but they had an instinct for survival "which extended so far that when one of them was hooked all the others were intent upon saving him." This familial devotion, making sea cows easy to capture, is believed to be the main reason for their sudden disappearance.

Steller was also the first man to study the sea lions that lived in the thick kelp beds offshore. The lions, members of the seal clan, raised families on the wet rocks around the Alaskan and Canadian shores. A restless bunch, they rode far out to sea on swells, dove off rocks and ledges, and scrambled around after one another.

These male sea lions weighed in at a ton or more. They feared nothing except the killer whale—until man came. Thirty years after their discovery by Steller they had almost become extinct.

Eventually Bering died on this island, now named for him, and Steller perished crossing Siberia on his return home. But the remaining members of the crew brought something new to Russia: nine hundred sea otter pelts.

Bobri morski, or sea beaver as the Russians called the sea otter, haunted the Pacific Coast from the Aleutians to Baja California, living in thick kelp beds around rocky islands. The kelp was a sort of hideaway that saved the sea otter from its main enemies—killer whales, sharks, and sea lions.

The sea otters were four to five feet long with a loose folded skin that

stretched to six or seven feet. Their pelts were black with white markings and had white underfur that took on a silvery sheen when stroked. One Russian sailor thought "Nothing can be more beautiful than one of these animals when seen swimming, especially when on the lookout for any object. At such times it raises its head quite above the surface, and the contrast between the shining black and the white, together with the sharp ears and long tuft of hair rising from the middle of its forehead, which look like three small horns, render it quite a novel and attractive object."

The luxury-loving Chinese upper classes thought sea otter pelts the perfect accompaniment to their silk garments. Soon a brisk trade sprang up between Russian hunters and Chinese fur merchants. When they discovered that a single shipload of otter furs could make a man rich, the British entered the field. Pelts did not mean much to the natives—they eagerly sold hundreds for a few old chisels.

In a few years time the beautifully sleek sea otter was hounded almost to extinction. Since 1911 the small numbers remaining have been protected by international law.

The sea otter's valuable fur opened Alaska to commercial exploitation and led to its first European settlements. Gregory Shelikhov, head of the Russian American Company, founded the first permanent base, on Kodiak Island, in 1784. But this wasn't done without a great deal of resistance from Eskimos living there. "The savages came down from their rocks in great numbers and fell upon us with fury," wrote Shelikhov. But in this, and later encounters, Eskimo arrows were no match for European muskets.

After founding a base far down the Alaskan coastline at Sitka, Shelikhov felt he had the bargaining power he needed in convincing the Russian government to give the Russian American Company a monopoly in Alaskan fur trading. He had tried for years to convince the czar's officials that

rival fur traders made the business wasteful as well as detrimental to both Russians and the native peoples. In 1799 the czar finally granted the Russian American Company an exclusive charter, though Shelikhov was dead by this time.

Nikolai Rezanov became the new head of the Russian American Company and appointed Alexander Baranov, who became Alaska's first conservationist, as residential manager. It was too late for him to save Steller's sea cows, but he put limits on trapping sea otters and seals.

Baranov tried to extend Russian hegemony south along the coast, building an outpost just north of San Francisco in 1812. Russian settlers raised crops and cattle, which Baranov hoped would help sustain the colonies in Alaska. But things did not work out as Baranov hoped.

Poor soil and primitive farming methods at the California ranch resulted in an output mediocre at best. The Russian American Company kept up the post for a few years before selling it to John Sutter, the northern California entrepreneur. When Baranov died the new manager, Baron Ferdinand von Wrangel, sought to buy more land in California to support the Alaskan enterprise, but never actually did so.

The Russian population of Alaska was never more than eight hundred. It did not seem able to support itself, and because the government feared such far-flung colonies could be taken from them by the British or the Americans, Russia sold its Alaskan territories to the United States in 1867.

Thanks to Drake's tentative probe two centuries earlier, the English considered that they had a claim to the West Coast of North America. So in 1777 the famous sea captain James Cook left for Oregon. Cook, of course, was one of the most brilliant explorers of all time, charting Australia, New Zealand, Easter Island, and rediscovering Hawaii, then known as the Sandwich Islands.

Cook also found a way to keep his crewmen from getting scurvy, the great scourge of seafarers in those days. He had them drink quantities of an orange extract and eat watercress and sauerkraut, providing them with the vitamin C they needed.

Striking the coast of Oregon in March 1778, Cook found that the land there had "an uncomfortable appearance." He moved on up to Canada and thought it "differed much" from the land seen so far, mainly because the mountains descended close to the sea.

A storm soon blew Cook's ships into Nootka Sound on Vancouver Island, which he thought was part of the mainland. About thirty dugout canoes loaded with natives came out to meet the ships, the occupants

throwing out feathers and red dust as a friendly greeting. As Cook would learn, these natives had never seen Europeans or a sailing vessel before.

The natives were short and stocky with broad faces and peering eyes. Some wore metal pendants in their ears or noses, and many wore blankets of dogs' hair woven with cedar bark and skillfully decorated with paintings. Over the blankets they wore beautiful robes of fox or sea otter skins. The natives' hair was long, soaked in fish oil, and sprinkled with the white down of birds.

On shore stood a village of communal houses, several families living in each. Entering one of these, Cook found elevated platforms for sleeping and furniture consisting mostly of boxes. Everything else—wooden dishes, weapons, fishing gear—lay scattered about in confusion. "The houses are as filthy as hogsties," said the captain.

These natives were Nootkas, typical coast dwellers along here. For food they depended mostly on fish—cod, herring, halibut, candlefish, and salmon. Weirs across streams channeled the annual fish runs with halibut and cod taken on bone hooks with kelp lines. Herring coming ashore to spawn were so closely packed that Indians with herring rakes—poles with a row of bone teeth—swept up several at once and shook them into their canoes.

In the spawning grounds natives took herring eggs with branches concealed under bouys. Candlefish, a salmonid so full of oil natives strung them up and burned them for light, were taken in bag nets and the oil boiled out of them.

Cook stayed nearly a month in Nootka Sound, trading for "the skins of various animals, such as bears, wolves, foxes, deer, pole-cats, racoons, martiens and, in particular, that of the sea-otter." The Nootkas were especially eager to trade for anything made of brass: "Whole suits of clothes were stripped of every button . . . and copper kettles, tin cannisters, candlesticks and the like, all went to wreck." After more trading near Prince William's Sound and a look into present-day Cook's Inlet—he thought the inlet might be the Strait of Anian—Cook departed for the Sandwich Islands.

Four years later another British expedition, this one under Captain George Vancouver, came to the upper coast of California and headed north. To the captain, California had "a very pleasing appearance, high and covered to the top with tall pines with here and there some rich verdant lawns." Close to the sea the land was "beautifully green, with a luxuriant herbage." The next morning Vancouver's two ships were covered in fog, whales playing around them.

Continuing north, Vancouver saw the mountains rising inland: "A high, steep mass which does not break into perpendicular cliffs, but is composed of various hills that rise abruptly, and are divided by chasms." Along the Oregon coast woods came down to the sea and ended in white sand—what Cook thought was snow.

When Vancouver approached the coastal area west of modern Portland he found the sea had "river coloured water, the probable consequence of some streams falling into the bay." It was "a luxuriant landscape," the high country inland "agreeably diversified with hills, from which it gradually descended to the shore, and terminated in a sandy beach. The whole had the appearance of a continued forest extending as far north as the eye could reach."

Vancouver took a look around the island and spent some time in Nootka Sound. In the sound he met Captain Robert Gray of the American ship *Columbia,* and to his dismay learned that the "river coloured water" he had seen was the result of the discharge into the sea of the great river of the West. Gray had just discovered the river and had named it after his ship.

While traveling the coast Gray had stopped at the Queen Charlotte Islands north of Vancouver Island. Here the Americans found some curious folk, or at least the women were. They cut the insides of their underlips and into the slits placed pieces of wood that caused the lower lip to protrude about two inches. Despite their appearance the women were so lascivious—"enough to disgust any civilized being"—some of the crew romanced them anyway. Perhaps it was because the females were used to having their own way for, on these islands, women ruled over men.

After a stay in Clayoquot Sound just north of Nootka Sound, and another stop at what he named Bullfinch Harbor (now Gray's Harbor), Captain Gray steered onto a large river of fresh water. This was the huge estuary of the Columbia, the great river of the West that most had decided did not exist. The river's banks were covered "with forests of the very finest pine timber, fir, and spruce." These trees did not rival the giant California redwoods, but some were very tall, especially the Sitka spruce and Douglas fir.

Sitka spruce, with its swollen and buttressed base and boldly sweeping branches, is one of the stateliest trees in North America. It may rise three hundred feet or more. The Douglas fir soared to two hundred feet—sometimes for a hundred feet before the branches began—and reached its fullest splendor in present-day Washington and Oregon.

Salmon came up the Columbia River to their spring spawning grounds, while bears stood on the banks and flipped the fish out with their paws. Seals and otters came far inland and wild geese, ducks, and cranes covered the river as well as the coast. Sometimes flocks of geese would fill the sky. The natives took these birds on the water, fifty or sixty at a time, by flipping out a bark net.

When Gray docked alongside the Columbia hordes of natives came out to see him. The Indians "appear'd civill (not even offering to steal)." Of course they were interested in trading. The sailors collected many furs, trading for them with copper sheets, spikes, and nails.

After eight days and a push upstream of thirty-five miles, Gray departed the Columbia. He left the new United States its claim—along with the claims of Britain, Spain, and Russia—to the region from California to Alaska known as the Oregon Country.

Spain gave up its claim in 1819, in the same arrangement that made Florida part of the United States. A few years later Russia agreed to settle

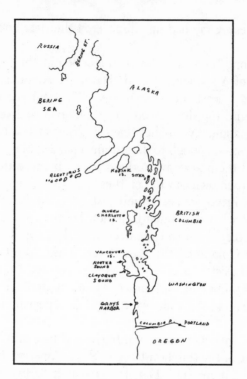

for Alaska and the U. S. bought the land from her in 1867. Britain and the United States held joint occupancy of the Oregon Country until 1846 when it was split at the present-day boundary between Washington and British Columbia.

The de Portolá expedition and northwest exploration are a long jump ahead. Returning to the East and the seventeenth century, we find the French taking a close look at New York and the Great Lakes country.

France, more than any other European nation, seemed predisposed to chase after distant frontiers—part of the national temperament, it appears. As the decades wore on the French attitude changed from one of exploitation to one of exploration. Seeing what was over the next hill became for many Frenchmen a grand adventure to be savored for itself, not merely for its results.

Yet New York exploration began not with the French, but with an Englishman named Henry Hudson.

NEW YORK AND THE GREAT LAKES

The Sojourns of Hudson, Champlain, and Radisson

Indians fishing in the Lower Bay of New York in 1609 glimpsed something large and strangely shaped moving slowly across the water. It was a floating house, they thought at first. As the object came closer it appeared more like an enormous canoe with great white wings. Whatever it was, the natives had never seen such a sight before.

The apparition—no moving house or winged canoe—was Henry Hudson's little sailing ship, the *Half Moon*. Hudson, an Englishman, was making a trip to America for the Dutch East India Company, searching for the elusive Northwest Passage. He had sailed down the coast from Newfoundland to somewhere around Virginia and now was following the coastline north again, having a closer look.

So far all explorers of the East Coast had missed New York Harbor except for Verrazano's brief appearance eighty-five years before. Out to sea the entrance to the harbor, shut in by Staten Island and Long Island, looked like just another indentation.

Legend has it that Hudson came ashore first at Coney Island, which got its name because of the enormous numbers of rabbits overrunning the place. At the time Coney Island was a tangle of brush and almost without trees.

Long Island, on the other hand, was well forested with maple, elm, oak, cedar, sassafras, beech, birch, hazelnut, and chestnut trees. In the middle of the island were fine valleys and an open, grassy plain.

As for Staten Island it was well wooded in the middle, with the south shore and western part mostly flat and marshy. The woods, so thick in places that one caught only an occasional glimpse of the sky, were overrun with deer, turkeys, snipe, and ruffed grouse. The shore was a playground for all kinds of waterbirds. On the beaches the tiny fish known as menhaden rotted by the thousands.

Cautiously the tiny *Half Moon* inched its way further into the Upper Bay and passed present-day Governors Island, mostly just a gigantic grove of nut trees that originally caused it to be named Nut Island.

The island the Indians called *Manna-hata*, more pointed than it is today, was indented with coves and bays and much of it covered with good

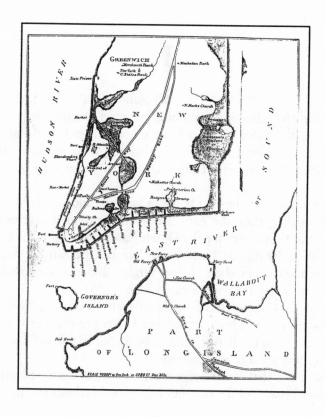

woodlands. Trees were not as thick as in some nearby locales and there were freshwater brooks "pleasant and proper for Man and Beast to drink, as well as agreeable to beholde, affording cool and pleasant resting Plaices." Many of these streams still run under the steel and concrete that is Manhattan today.

There was a stream and marsh along present-day Canal Street and most of the land from Fifth to Eighth avenue was under water. On the West Side the waters of the Hudson reached to Greenwich Street, and on the East Side there was a meadow of some 150 acres before the forest closed in again farther up the East River. From the tip of Manhattan a great trail ran north, probably pretty much the same route as Broadway today.

Hudson's ship entered "a greate Stream that came out of the Baye." It was the lovely river named for this explorer, one that he thought was a passage to the Indies. In the Hudson's waters were "manie Salmon, Mullets, and Rayes, verie greate." A short way up the river Hudson's crew first set foot on the island of *Manna-hata,* probably near the foot of what is now West Forty-Second Street. Here they caught mullet and a ray "so greate four men could barely haul it into the ship."

Indians hereabouts, probably Mahicans, were friendly and soon came aboard ship. They seemed "verie glad of our coming and brought green Tobaco and gave us of it for Knives and Beades." After some trading— and, reportedly, a little pilfering by the natives—a small fracas broke out and one seaman was lost with an arrow through his throat.

The Hudson was a tidal river (to the Indians it flowed both ways) and the explorers used the tide to move upstream. The woods along the way were full of deer, black bears, and an occasional moose while the many streams and marshes were populated by muskrats and beavers. Some Indians relished muskrat meat and beaver skins made excellent robes. The large flat tail of the beaver made for some fine eating. "The tail boyled proves exceeding good Meat, being all Fatt, and sweete as Marrow," wrote one of Hudson's crew.

A Beaver 26 inches long from the head to the tail

Indeed the beaver was not only good eating, but its pelt became highly prized both in America and Europe. A lively trade would spring up that sent Indians scurrying to the beaver ponds to catch the animals under water with their bare hands.

The Hudson, like other American rivers, teemed with fish—huge sturgeon especially—that would bite at almost any kind of bait. Natives spread nets of swamp milkweed across the river and weighted them down with stones. A carved wooden figure, "resembling the Devil," bobbed up and down to indicate a catch.

Hudson went as far as present-day Albany, but when the river began to narrow he decided this could not be the Northwest Passage. The captain, in a brilliant red coat trimmed in gold lace, stopped off here to chat with the natives. They thought such a magnificently attired man must be a god come by for a visit. There was feasting and the wine flowed.

The story goes that Hudson took a swig of wine and handed the bottle to some of the Indians gathered around. After sniffing the bottle, all the warriors except one declined the offer. This one took a long draught, staggered around for a moment, and then collapsed. Soon he was up again, assuring the others that never in his life had he tasted anything that made him feel so good. The other Indians then took their turns at the bottle and before long the entire company was drunk.

In some versions of the story the occasion took place on Manhattan and gave the island its name—Place of the Big Drunk. In any case it is a questionable tale since the island had its name before Hudson arrived.

The *Half Moon* then retraced its route. Hudson mentioned in his log that this river valley was "as pleasant a land as can be tread upon." Of course since his time, millions have found it to be true.

On a second trip the next year, this time into the frozen north, Hudson slipped past the ice of Hudson Strait and entered Hudson Bay, the first explorer to do so. He worked his way carefully along the shore of James Bay until his ship was frozen in the water there during the winter of 1610–1611. The men stayed alive by eating birds that wintered there and, after the ice began to break in early spring, by a little fishing.

By spring the Englishmen were in poor shape and unruly. Trying to enforce discipline, Hudson had not endeared himself to them. When the captain suggested making further investigations before going home, the crew mutinied. They put Hudson, his young son, and seven others in a small boat and cast them on the inhospitable waters of Hudson Bay. Nothing is known of what became of them.

Thanks in part to Hudson's earlier voyage, the Dutch claimed the

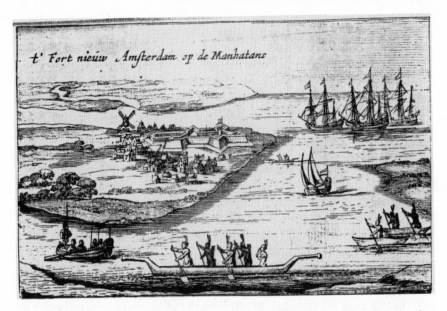

Hudson valley. As we all know they bought Manhattan Island from the Indians for about twenty-four dollars worth of trinkets. This came out to be about one-tenth of a cent per acre.

New Amsterdam—later New York City—was a company town. It was run by and for the Dutch East India Company, backers of the enterprise. The colony of New Netherland was a stronghold of the aristocracy and

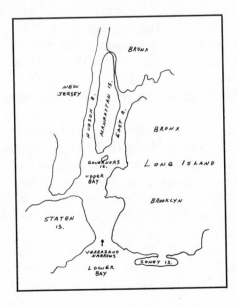

vast feudal estates grew up along the Hudson, one of them larger than the entire state of Rhode Island.

The directors-general of New Netherland were mostly incompetents. The best of them was Peter Stuyvesant, or Old Wooden Leg as the Indians called him. In 1664 Stuyvesant was forced to surrender New Netherland to the English without firing a shot. The English renamed the colony New York.

In 1609, three years after his exploration of the New England coast, Samuel de Champlain was back in what is now the United States trying to make sense of the river and lake systems of Canada and New York. He had with him a few Frenchmen and a goodly assemblage of Indians, mostly Hurons, who hoped for a chance to take a few whacks at their dreaded enemies the Iroquois.

Champlain started out on the beautiful Richelieu River in Canada, following it across the present New York state boundary. Soon the Richelieu disappeared into a great lake, a lake the explorer named in honor of himself. By this time his Frenchmen had grown faint of heart and, except for two volunteers, Champlain continued on with his Indian allies.

The expedition was compelled to give up its heavy boats in favor of the light, frail birchbark canoes that had been the staple transportation in this part of the American wilderness for centuries. In the great north woods, where birch trees flourished, the natives made these canoes by stripping the bark in sheets and shaping them to frames, keeping the white side of the bark on the inside. Overlapping edges were caulked with pine resin. These light skiffs were the finest canoes ever made, and could be carried on the back of one man. A single stroke of the paddle sent them skimming through the water; a native could make a canoe move twice as far with one stroke as an inexperienced European could make with the same exertion.

Champlain was soon in territory no other European had ever known, though at that very moment Henry Hudson was only a couple of hundred miles away on the Hudson River. The French leader was enamoured of the wild, primitive landscape along the shores of Lake Champlain, and of the islands in the lake. The woods came down to the shoreline and included chestnut trees that he had never seen before; forest vines were the prettiest he had ever beheld.

Champlain wrote that he liked to sit on the shore of the lake and cogitate. One day his musings were suddenly interrupted by the appearance of a huge fish "five feet long, as big as a man's thigh, with a head as large as two fists, a snout two and a half feet long." It was silvery gray and "armed with scales so strong that a dagger could not pierce them." Apparently this was a gar fish of some sort—the Indians said they often grew to be eight or ten feet long.

For an experienced explorer Champlain was still a little credulous. He seems to have believed the natives' tale that when this fish "wishes to catch birds it goes in amongst the rushes and reeds that lie along the shore of the lake and puts its snout out of the water without moving. The result is that when the birds come to light on its snout, mistaking it for a stump, the fish is so cunning that, shutting its half-open mouth, it pulls them by their feet into the water."

Looking across the lake, Champlain saw high mountains on the east side, probably the Green Mountains of Vermont, and to the south even higher ones, undoubtedly the Adirondacks. Directly south was another lake, now called Lake George. It was at the northern tip of Lake George, where the famous Fort Ticonderoga would one day stand, that Champlain kept his promise to his Indian allies. He and the two French soldiers took part in an attack on an Iroquois war party and, thanks to the terror their muskets instilled, won the day.

After their three chiefs were struck down by musket balls, the Iroquois fled in dismay. Champlain's Hurons came in with a dozen or so captives and shortly the explorer and the other two Frenchmen got their first taste of how cruel American Indians could be. Champlain described the ordeal of the first victim:

Our Indians kindled a fire, and when it was well lighted each took a brand and burned this poor wretch a little at a time in order to make him suffer the greater torment. . . . Then they tore out his nails and applied fire to the ends of his fingers and his privy member. Afterwards they scalped him and caused a certain kind of gum to drip very hot upon the crown of his head. Then they pierced his arms near the wrists and with sticks pulled and tore at his sinews by main force, and when they could not get them out they cut them off.

Horrible though it was, this was the typical treatment of captured enemies. The captive knew what was in store for him and in a way welcomed it; torture was the greatest test of a warrior's mettle, a chance to show what stern stuff he was made of. Some prisoners went off singing to the place of their undoing.

The sight nevertheless sickened Champlain, and he let his swarthy friends know he was exceedingly displeased. They then allowed him to put the victim out of his misery with a well-placed musket ball. Later, when the French explorer was more inured to the realities of Indian life, he merely looked the other way when captives were brought out for torture.

In 1613 Champlain set out from Montreal to explore what is now Ontario and to find the western end of Hudson Bay. The party of seven Frenchmen and two Indians portaged the violent Lachine Rapids below Montreal—"no small labor"—and paddled out into the broad reaches of Lac St. Louis where the St. Lawrence and Ottawa Rivers meet. The lake was "filled with fine large islands like meadows, where it is a pleasure to hunt, venison being found there in abundance."

In the lower Ottawa were other treacherous rapids. Champlain fell out of his canoe at one of them and, if he had not been caught between two large rocks, would have lost his life.

The little band pushed on through "a clean, attractive country" until it reached the superb falls of the Rideau River that flowed into the Ottawa River from the south as the Gatineau did from the north. Champlain thought it a beautiful spot, this future site of the city of Ottawa.

When the party entered long Lac des Chats the river began to narrow and flow swiftly over granite boulders. For several miles, the Indians said, the Ottawa was sprinkled with dangerous rapids. Champlain took their advice and portaged around this hazard.

In boggy country now, the Frenchmen were pretty well worked over by the vicious "mushgetters," or muskeg mosquitoes. "It was wonderful how cruelly they persecuted us," says Champlain. "Their importunity is so remarkable that it is impossible to give any description of it." Yet no one fell sick because of these onslaughts. Scholars believe the malarial parasite was not indigenous to America but brought by the first Europeans, and had not yet worked its way this far north.

Champlain's journey continued to Muskrat Lake through "more difficult country than we had seen, on account of the wind having blown down pine trees one on top of the other, which is no small inconvenience because one must go now over and now under these trees." Around here somewhere Champlain lost his bronze astrolabe, found two and a half centuries later by a fourteen-year-old boy and now in a museum.

The rest of the portage, from Muskrat Lake to Lake Allumette, was relatively easy. The Allumette Algonquins, the Frenchmen found, were "the best clothed and most prettily bedecked" of any Indians they had seen in some time. They worshipped the dead and buried them in elaborate tombs painted red and yellow and decorated with wood carvings, including a carving of the deceased. Here Champlain learned he was nowhere near Hudson Bay, and after setting up a white cedar post decorated with the French *fleur-de-lis*, returned to Montreal.

In 1615 Champlain returned to the Ottawa River country. Passing on from Lake Allumette he entered a new and "unattractive country full of firs, birches and some oaks, a great many rocks." The natives did not seem to care for the region either, for it was uninhabited except for a few fishermen. Nevertheless, says Champlain, "It is true that God appears to have been pleased to give this frightful and abandoned region some things in their season for the refreshment of man. . . . For I can assure you that along the streams there are such a great quantity of blueberries, small fruit very good to eat, and many raspberries and other small fruits, that it is marvelous. The people who live here dry these fruits for their winter supply, as we in France do prunes for Lent." On more than one occasion the Frenchmen might have starved had it not been for the abundance of these small fruits, especially blueberries.

The expedition soon left the Ottawa and followed the Mattawa River to Lake Nipissing. This was a lovely land of water and meadow, the most beautiful place on earth according to the Indians living there. From Lake Nipissing the party took the French River to Lake Huron, named by Champlain the Freshwater Sea. Along the French River the travelers again saw a wasteland of rocks where only the most hardy trees grew in cracks and crevices. "I did not find in all its length ten acres of arable land," wrote Champlain.

Near the mouth of the French River, Champlain met a party of about three hundred Indians he called the *Cheveux Relevées*, or High Hairs, "because they have their hair elevated and arranged very high and better combed than our courtiers." Their bodies were elaborately tattoed, with faces painted green and red. These natives were known as Ottawas, and they had come to this place to dry the blueberries that would "serve them as manna in the winter when they can no longer find anything."

Turning southeast, Champlain followed the east coast of Georgian Bay. He found a drowned country with over ninety-five thousand islands, some large and others mere whalebacks. When the French explorer entered "Huronia," the land around Lake Simcoe, he found a fine country of soft rolling hills and rich forests of maple, elm, and oak. Some thirty thousand Hurons lived here in agricultural plenty, cultivating squash, corn, beans, and the French peas given them by their foreign friends in Quebec. In this soil the peas grew twice as big as they did in France.

Also growing wild were sunflowers, strawberries, plums, and "a kind of fruit that has the form and shape of a small lemon, about the size of an egg." There is no mystery about this plant—it was the May apple, known to early settlers as wild lemon. It bore gorgeous white blossoms and the fruit was edible if taken in moderation, though some thought its taste mawkish. Indians sometimes used it as a purgative.

Many fish inhabited Lake Simcoe. On the shores were "many cranes, as white as swans," which may have been the little blue herons that were almost pure white in their youth. Forests—"the common resort" of partridges and rabbits—hid bears and deer. Driving these animals before them with beaters, until the bears and deer reached some point of land projecting into the water, native hunters closed in on them. Other hunters in canoes dispatched those trying to escape by swimming.

The French priest Gabriel Sagard, shortly following Champlain into Huronia, wrote of turkeys, geese, black foxes, and beavers. Black fox peltries were highly prized, and so many beavers were taken that the good father thought the animal surely on the edge of extinction. Doves (passenger pigeons) appeared in immense flocks and stripped the trees of acorns, swallowing them whole.

The beautiful little ruby-throated hummingbird particularly captivated Father Sagard with its grace and size. Calling it the "fly-bird," it was in his opinion "one of the great rarities of this country, and a little prodigy of nature." Indeed it was a veritable flying machine as compact as a watch, having a range of several hundred miles. It could fly, invisible to the human eye, at speeds of seventy miles an hour and could cross a body of water as big as the Gulf of Mexico without stopping. Its only fuel was the sweet nectar of flowers, extracted with its needle-like bill.

Eventually Champlain agreed to aid his Huron allies in an invasion of Iroquois lands to the east. The war party worked its way along the northern shore of Lake Ontario, living off the land. It was lovely country, Champlain thought—"Along the shores one would think the trees had been planted for ornament in most places."

The region was uninhabited, the natives having left for fear of their dreaded Iroquois neighbors. The Frenchmen wasted ammunition shooting deer for sport—and wounding a Huron into the bargain. "At this a great clamor rose among them, which nevertheless subsided upon the gift of some presents to the wounded man, the ordinary method of allaying and ending quarrels."

The war party crossed the eastern end of Lake Ontario, probably landing under the high bluff at present-day Stony Point. They were in New York now, in the tribal lands of the Onondagas, one of the five nations known as Iroquois. Following the approximate route of today's Interstate Highway 81, the party found "very agreeable and beautiful country . . . where there was an unlimited amount of game, many vines, beautiful woods, and a great number of chestnut trees." The chestnuts were smaller than the European variety, but the Frenchmen thought them sweeter, tastier.

Somewhere along the way Champlain was joined by a war party of Algonquins under Chief Iroquet, who had been with Champlain on his earlier New York expedition. One day the allies attacked an Onondaga fort on Lake Onondaga, at or near present-day Syracuse. After a siege of

several days they had to admit defeat. Champlain, wounded in the knee, was carried from the field. His party started back to Huronia.

For the first few days of the return trip Champlain traveled in a wooden seat on the back of a sturdy warrior, trussed up with his back against the Indian's. His legs, hunched up under his chin, were tied in place. "Never did I find myself in such a hell as during this time. The pain I suffered from the wound in my knee was nothing in comparison with what I endured."

On their trek back to Huronia the Frenchmen and their allies lived on geese, ducks, small birds, trout, pike "of immense size," and the ever-present deer. The Indians caught deer by frightening them with noises until the animals were driven into the apex of a triangular stockade the natives had constructed. Once inside the deer were easily disposed of with bow and arrow. In a few days the party captured 120 deer "with which they made good cheer, saving the fat for the winter and using it as we do butter."

On his expeditions Champlain was often astonished—and amused—by Indian superstitions about killing game. The important thing, the natives thought, was disposition of the bones after the animal was eaten—this decided the success or failure of future hunts. Hurons considered it bad luck to let bones fall into the fire, except in the case of fish. The fish, they believed, did not object to having their bones cast into the flames and didn't even object to being caught if the fishermen assured them they wouldn't be.

Some natives thought it bad luck to let dogs chew the bones of animals.

Some tribes believed the ghosts of beavers visited camps to find out what humans had done with their remains. The ghosts didn't mind seeing their bones thrown into the fire or the river, but if they found dogs gnawing on them they reported the outrage to living beavers. Indians also apologized to animals for the necessity of taking their lives.

During the unsporting but effective deer hunts, Champlain wandered off and was lost in the woods for two days. He claims he was lured into the forest by a bizarre creature as big as a hen, with a yellow body, red head, blue wings, and a beak like a parrot. It made short flights like a partridge, but apparently was fast enough to escape him. Its like, obviously, was never seen again.

By now it was December, the lakes and marshlands frozen over. The Hurons made snowshoes for themselves and toboggans for their meat supplies and deer hides. Travel was easier now except for the thaws that "gave us much trouble and discomfort, for we had to pass through fir woods full of streams, ponds, marshes, and swamps, with many fallen trees lying one upon another, giving us a thousand troubles, with obstacles that brought us great discomfort on account of always being wet even above the knee."

At length Champlain's party reached the Hurons' main village on Lake Simcoe. There the Frenchmen spent the winter months, Champlain recuperating from his knee wound in one of the longhouses. The place swarmed with mice, lice, and fleas and twelve fires lit the eighty-foot-long structure, with no outlet for the smoke. To escape the wretchedness of the longhouse, Champlain wandered about the village learning what he could of Huron life. He was followed by children and by fat little dogs unknowingly awaiting their time in the cooking pot. Outside, in a strong cage, several bears were being fattened up for the same fate.

Unlike most Indians, the Hurons stored up a winter provender. Corn was their staple. It was pounded into meal, mixed with berries or deer fat, and baked into loaves in ashes. Some of it was "chewed bread," women and girls having gnawed the kernels off the cob with their teeth.

Corn still on the cob might be buried in the mud of a stream and left there until it rotted. "I assure you that nothing smells so bad as this corn when it comes out of the water," Champlain said, "yet the women and children take it and suck it like sugar-cane, there being nothing they like better."

During the winter there was little meat save for an occasional dog. The Frenchmen, once they recovered from their initial disgust, learned that roast dog was not bad at all. There were plenty of fish, caught in nets through holes in the ice. If everything else was exhausted there were still cornstalks and lily bulbs.

When illness arose Champlain had occasion to watch the doctor-priests, the *okis*, at work. These self-styled healers worked themselves into a frenzy, dancing wildly around the patient while other people sang and beat sticks on bark. "They become like lunatics or madmen, throwing fire about the cabin from one side to the other, swallowing red-hot coals, holding them for a time in their hands, also throwing red-hot ashes into the eyes of the other onlookers, and on seeing them in this state one would say that the Devil . . . possesses them and torments them in this manner."

Nevertheless some of the sick became well, but according to Champlain "rather by happy accident and chance than by science . . . bearing in mind that for two who get cured ten others die from the noise and great din and the blowings they make, which are more fitted to kill than to cure a sick person."

A popular cure for a sick or demented woman was to surround her bed with male and female youths of the village who spent the night in love-making while an *oki* sat at each end of the house, singing and rattling a tortoise shell. No statistics are available on the recovery rate.

Virtue was constantly compromised, as it was in most Indian societies. Both boys and girls went from one lodge to another after dark, taking their pleasure as they saw fit. This was an age-old custom, and no shame or blame was attached to it. But when a girl produced a baby she was obliged to move in with the father of the child—by this token she had become a wife, he a husband. When more than one young man claimed to be the father, the mother would choose the disputant she preferred.

Afterward both could continue their lodge-hopping, but they must always return to the mutual hearth for appearances' sake and to confer legitimacy on any babies born to them. Because of the uncertainty over paternity, inheritances were passed down on the mother's side of the family.

Two favorite pastimes of the Hurons were lacrosse and a gambling game called *dish*. Sometimes an *oki* ordered a game of lacrosse as the cure for a sick person. Indians played the sport with such a will it often resulted in broken bones and occasionally death. Dish, similar to dice, involved six plum stones painted black and white. Ambitious players might wager everything they owned. One Huron, already stripped of his worldly possessions, bet his hair and little finger while a woman offered herself, and after losing went into slavery. A chief's son hanged himself over a game.

Champlain found much to praise among the Hurons: their courage, uncomplaining endurance, disregard of pain, and their acute sense of smell and hearing. The men were splendidly built, the women beautiful. On the other hand, the French explorer reported the Hurons to be cruel, vainglorious, filthy in their habits, and much given to thievery.

In the spring Champlain finally retraced his route back to Montreal and his days of active exploration ended.

Champlain had not gone very far inland either time he visited New York. The first explorer of record to see the interior of the state was another Frenchman, this one an unlettered child of the wilderness named Pierre Esprit Radisson. He also penetrated far into Great Lakes country and may have gone beyond the juncture of the Mississippi and Missouri rivers.

Radisson's first trip into the wilderness, in 1652 when he was sixteen, was one he did not intend to make. While out hunting ducks near the French settlements on the St. Lawrence River, he was captured by a Mohawk raiding party and taken off to their village in central New York. Though Radisson was not sure what route the Indians took, they probably followed the Richelieu River to Lake Champlain and Lake George and then went over to the Hudson or Mohawk river.

Adopted into the tribe, young Radisson lived for a time with a prominent Mohawk family. Once, after escaping, he was brought back and subjected to some of the customary torture techniques. In later life, while living in England, he wrote of his torture and about all of his wilderness adventures in an erratic but often charming English.

"They plucked four nails out of my fingers and made me sing," Radisson wrote. Then, "A woman came with her boy, enticed him to cut off one of my fingers with a flint stone. The boy was not four years old. This boy takes my finger and begins to work, but in vain because he had not strength to break my fingers. So my poor finger escaped, having no other hurt done it but the flesh cut round about it. His mother made him suck the very blood that runned from my finger."

Next day an old man "holding in his mouth a pewter pipe burning, took my thumb and put it on the burning tobacco, and so smoked three pipes one after the other, which made my thumb swell, and the nail and flesh became as coals." That night they burned the soles of his feet and ran a red-hot poker through one foot.

Eventually Radisson's Indian mother and father intervened, saving the youngster from further harm and perhaps death. They took him to their house where the mother greased and combed his hair, oiled him and tended to his wounds. "Then begins my pain anew," reported Radisson, "for she cleans my wounds and scrapes them with a knife and then thrusts a stick in them and then takes water in her mouth and spouts it to make them clean. Meanwhile my father goes to seek roots, and my sister chaws them, and my mother applies them to my sores as plaster. The next day the swelling was gone; in less than a fort-night my sores were healed, saving my feet, that kept [me] a whole month in my cabin. . . . I remained only lame of my middle finger that they have squeezed between two stones."

After his recovery young Radisson and his Indian brother joined a military expedition to the west, around Lake Ontario. Where they went is a matter of conjecture but after reaching Lake Ontario they had to wait fifteen days for the ice to thaw before embarking on that "sweet sea."

By the time the boys launched themselves on Lake Ontario, "The weather was lovely, the wind fair, and nature satisfied. Tending forward, singing and playing, not considering the contrary weather past, [we] continued six days upon the lake, and rested the nights ashore. The more we proceeded on our journey, the more pleasant the country."

After "ending the lake," the party traveled for many days, sometimes on a river, sometimes on foot. Somewhere along the way there was an unnerving encounter with a strange beast, small but frightening, which was clinging to a tree as the boys' boat passed beneath it. Radisson said it was "a snake with four feet: her head very big like a turtle, the nose very small at the end, the neck of five thumbs wide, the body about two feet, and the tail of a foot and a half [and] of a blackish color, [all] into a shell small and round, with great eyes, her teeth very white but not long."

The creature awakened with a start and fell into the boat, causing consternation aboard. "There is the question [of] who was most fearful. As for me, I was quaking," admitted Radisson. Unfortunately the boys could not kill this miniature dragon for fear of harming their boat. Instead they rowed on, hoping to find a good landing spot where they could turn the boat upside down and "be rid of such a devil."

A squirrel clambered aboard, offering some comic relief. The bushy tailed one, scared to death, ran up and down the boat as if rabid. Every time the squirrel came near it the creature rose up and "made a kind of a noise." Finally the animal put its forefeet on a side of the boat and the boys saw their chance. Leaning on that side of the boat, they tipped it and at the same time they gave the little beast a helping hand into the river with their oars. They then beat it to death in the water.

In another place in his writings Radisson calls this little reptile a sea serpent. What was it? Perhaps it was a harmless iguana—some species of the big lizards lived in those latitudes.

Eventually the raiding party made its way around to what must have been Lake Champlain, "a delightful place with a great many islands." There they killed many bears, deer, and "castors," as the French called beavers. "We took above three hundred castors there and fleeced off the best skins," reported Radisson. These skins would hold bear oil as well as a bottle.

When the party returned home with prisoners and several heads (scalps), their Mohawk kinsmen held a great feast in their honor. The heroes were favored with the choicest meats as well as "a most dainty and cordial bit" called "salmagundy," which was the best dish these Indians had to offer. Radisson describes it thusly:

First, when the corn is green, they gather so much as need requireth, of which leaves they preserve the biggest leaves for the subject that follows. A dozen more-or-less old women meets together alike, of whom the greatest part wants teeth, and see-eth not a jot, and their cheeks hang down like an old hunting dog, their eyes full of water and blood shot. Each takes an ear of corn, and puts it in their mouths, which is properly as milk, chaws it, and when their mouths are full spits it out in their hands, which possibly they wash once [in] one year. Their hands are white inside by reason of the grease that they put to their hair, and rubbing of it with the inside of their hands, which keeps them pretty clean but the outside in the rinkness of their wrinkled hands there is a quarter of an ounce of filth and stinking grease. So, their hands being full of that mince meat minced with their gums, [they] fill a dish. So, they chaw chestnuts; then they mingle this with bear's grease or oil of [sun] flower. . . . So, having made a mixture, they tie the leaves at one end, and make a hodgepot and cover it with the same leaves, and tie the upper end so that what is within those leaves becomes a round ball, which they boil in a kettle full of water or broth made of meat or fish. So there is the description of the most delicious bit of the world.

Later on Radisson escaped again and fled to the Dutch outpost of Fort Orange (later Albany) on the Hudson. Eventually the Hollanders helped him make his way to France.

Before long Radisson was back in Canada and, before he had been there any time at all, wanted to be on the trail again. The troublesome Iroquois were showing signs of friendship and had asked for Jesuit missionaries to visit. Despite his earlier experiences in Iroquois lands, Radisson volunteered to accompany the priests. He was, it seems, a born explorer.

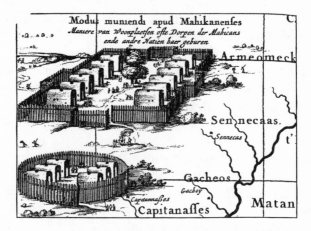

As Radisson's party traveled along the St. Lawrence and into New York, the Frenchman was enchanted with the game he saw. The deer were so plentiful the men hunted them as much for sport as for food. Once they hung a bell around a deer's neck and laughed at the consternation it caused when the deer was let loose among its fellows: "What a sport to see the rest fly from that that had the bell."

On another occasion a "very remarquable" thing happened. "There comes out of a vast forest a multitude of bears, three hundred at least together, making a horrid noise, breaking small trees, throwing the rocks down by the waterside. We shot at them, but [they] stirred not a step, which frightened us that they slighted our shooting. We knowed not

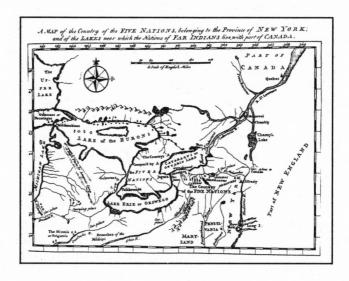

whether we killed any or no because of the dark; neither did we venture to go see. The wildmen [Indians] told me that they never heard their father speak of so many together."

Since this bear convention convened in the darkness, Radisson undoubtedly exaggerated their number. Bears were thought of as solitary animals, but there is no reason why there should not have been a goodly number of them, though not nearly as many as the Frenchman thought. It is likely that this convocation was an event of the mating season. New England settlers, later, remarked that when in rut black bears gathered in considerable numbers—twenty, thirty, perhaps forty of them, all putting up a hideous roaring.

As he came to Lake Onondaga, near where Champlain had been forty years earlier, Radisson thought it "a most pleasant country, very beautiful." On all sides were fields of Indian corn and "citruls" (pumpkins), while the woods were full of oak and chestnut and wildfowl. Ringdoves— passenger pigeons—had gathered at a salt spring near present-day Syracuse, where fifteen hundred or more could be caught with one net. Hogs, given to the Onondagas by the French, were "so fat they were not able to go."

The Jesuits, who had gone ahead, had already established themselves in a fort. One priest decided this would be "one of the most commodious and most agreeable dwelling places in the world, without excepting even the levee of the River Loire, if its inhabitants were as polished."

Many kinds of fruits grew near Lake Onondaga, "all of which excell ours in beauty, fragrance, and taste." These were plums, grapes, stoneless cherries (cranberries), and a fruit "the color and size of an apricot, whose blossom is like that of the white lily, and which smells like citron"—the May apple again. The roots of "a wonderful tree" provided dyes and supposedly healed wounds—the ubiquitous sassafras.

Unfortunately the area did not turn out to be truly commodious. The Onondaga Indians grew increasingly hostile and the French quickly decided to retreat to their Canadian settlements. One night, while the natives slept, the Frenchmen tied a bell to a hog to lead their drowsing hosts into believing they were still there. After returning to his base camp Radisson, not one to stay put, was off again. He and his brother-in-law Médard Chourat, Sieur des Groseilliers, set out to "discover the great lakes the wildmen speak of." Some of that area, perhaps most of it, had already been discovered, but not much of those journies has been chronicled.

Champlain had flirted with the eastern borders of the Great Lakes in

1615. Even earlier, in 1610, he had sent Étienne Brulé deep into the region to explore, learn the languages and disposition of the natives, and lay the groundwork for French-Indian fur trading. Brulé lived among the Hurons and journeyed on Lakes Huron, Ontario, and Superior.

Another daring Frenchman, Jean Nicolet, had spent eight years with the Nipissings on the upper Ottawa River, joining in their fishing and hunting, learning their language and mores. Later Champlain sent him on a mission to the Puans on the Lake of the Stinkings—the Winnebagos of Green Bay. This was in 1634, when Europeans were still expecting at any moment to run into China. The *Jesuit Relations* tell us that Nicolet appeared before the astonished Winnebagos in a damask robe embroidered with flowers and birds, prepared to greet any mandarins who might be about.

The *Jesuit Relations* mention two young Frenchmen who suddenly emerged from the tangled wilderness of the Great Lakes country in 1656. They had traveled as far as Wisconsin in "little gondolas of bark," or birchbark canoes. They had been on at least some of the Great Lakes and had met many of the tribes living on those shores. They certainly had been to Green Bay, already an important station in a vigorous fur trade.

There is little doubt these two anonymous Frenchmen were Radisson and Groseilliers, yet there is no record of where they went and what they saw. What Radisson wrote years later may have been a composite of this earlier trip and later ones, those we will consider now.

The small party of Radisson, Groseilliers and natives set off up the fiercely rushing Ottawa River and soon found themselves in the harsh country that had so tortured Champlain's men. "The most parts there abouts is so sterile that there is nothing to be seen but rocks and sand and . . . trees that grow miraculously, for the earth is not to be seen that can nourish the root."

Except for an occasional bear and a few very small fish, there was no food. Eventually the men were reduced to eating *tripe de roches,* a lichen growing on the rocks of northern lakes that somewhat resembles bits of tripe. The Indians, eating it when they had to, called it *windigo wakon.* A *windigo* was a wood sprite so hungry that it ate off its own lips. Scraped off the rocks and boiled, the substance "became like starch, black and clammy. . . . I think if any bird lighted upon the excrements of said stuff they had stuck to it as if it were glue."

At least the stuff kept the men alive.

At one time Radisson and Groseilliers gathered half-ripe gooseberries

and blackberries, stuffing themselves so that their bloated bellies pre-
vented them from drawing on their shoes and stockings.

Arriving at Lake Nipissing, the expedition found it crammed with fish
in waters "clear as crystal." There was such an abundance of otters
Radisson and Groseilliers seemed to have been persuaded that the sleek
animals had "all gathered there to hinder our passage." The trip down the
French River to Georgian Bay was easy and once there the Frenchmen
found the shores of the bay, part of Lake Huron, "most delightful to the
mind, the land smooth, and woods of all sorts." On the offshore sandbanks
there was "such an infinite deal of fish that scarcely we are able to draw
our nets. There are fishes as big as children of two years old; there is
sturgeon enough and other sorts that is not known to us."

Where Radisson and Groseilliers went from Lake Huron is not clear.
Radisson's writings are confusing—he had no maps, kept no journals—
and he goes over the same material more than once. Different tribes
confused matters further by calling rivers, lakes, and mountains by names
of their own devising. Apparently the explorers passed through the Straits
of Mackinac into Lake Michigan and Green Bay, sailed Lake Superior,
and went as far as the Mississippi River, probably somewhere in Minnesota.

Radisson called Lake Michigan the "Lake of the Staring Hairs" because
"those that live about it have their hair like a brush turned up." The
Staring Hairs, probably Winnebagos, hung copper ornaments from holes
in their noses and ears, and stuffed the ornaments with swans' down when
the bitter winter wind swept in from the lake. This was not so much
because of the cold, Radisson thought, as "to make them gallant."

The two Frenchmen believed Lake Michigan "the delightsomest lake
of the world," and were impressed with its tall trees, sandy shores, and
many fruits. There were "she goats, very big," perhaps pronghorn antelope; plenty of deer and buffalo; and "so many tourkeys the boys threw
stones at them for recreation."

Around the lakes they made the acquaintance of Ottawas, Ojibways,
the Fire Nation (Mascoutens), and People of the Wild Oats (Menominees). Farther west, on the edge of the Great Plains, they came upon
the Nation of the Beef (boeuf or buff, the Buffalo People). These were
the Nadowessiek, called in other places the Tatarga. Obviously they were
Sioux, for their word for buffalo was tatanka, and a division of the Sioux
nation was known by that name.

The Frenchmen's meeting with the Sioux was on "the forked river, so called because it has two branches, the one towards the west, the other towards the south which we believe runs towards Mexico, by the tokens they gave us." Indians to the south, Radisson and Groseilliers heard, warred with men "that build great cabins and have great beards." The forked river could only be the Mississippi, with the Missouri its northern arm. Below the junction of the two rivers the Indians made war against the Spaniards farther south.

The explorers spent the winter living well. "The snow proved favorable that year [not much of it, that is], which caused much plenty of everything." The snow that did fall did not stop animals like the moose from migrating: "a mighty strong beast, much like a mule, having a tail cut off two or three or four thumbs long, the foot cloven like a stag. He has a muzzle mighty big. I have seen some that have the nostrils so big that I put into it my two fists at once with ease."

Deer and beaver were joined by buffalo up from the plains. In his turn Radisson was intrigued by the great woolly beast:

> The buff is a furious animal. . . . The horns of buffs are as those of an ox, but not so long, but bigger and of a blackish color. . . . He is reddish, his hair frizzled and very fine, all parts of his body much unto an ox. The biggest are bigger than any ox whatsoever. . . . It's a pleasure to find the place of their abode, for they turn round about, compassing two or three acres of land, beating the snow with their feet and, coming to the center, they lie down and rise again to eat the boughs of trees that they can reach. They go not out of their circle that they have made until hunger compells them.

On a later trip to the lake country, Radisson and his brother-in-law headed straight for Lake Superior. They portaged around Sault St. Marie, entered the lake, and followed its southern shoreline. The shores, Radisson thought, "are most delightful and wonderous, for it's Nature that made it so pleasant to the eye, the spirit and the belly." Of course the belly was satisfied by the plentiful deer, moose, beavers, bears, and even "cats of the mountains"—panthers or wildcats.

Bustards, as the French called wild geese, had been so long undisturbed they were fearless of humans. After creeping up on some of them, Radisson related how the birds, "seeing me flat upon the ground, thought I was a beast as well as they, so they come near me, whistling like goslings, thinking to frighten me. The whistling that I made them hear was another music than theirs. There I killed three and the rest scared, which nevertheless came to that place again to see what sudden sickness befelled their comrades. I shot again; two paid for their curiosity." In a few minutes Radisson had five days' food supply.

At Whitefish Bay Radisson and Groseilliers discovered legions of "a fish they call *assickmack*"—the famous Lake Superior whitefish, the best eating in these waters. In other places were sturgeon "of a vast bigness" and pike seven feet long.

Near Munising, Michigan, at what is now Pictured Rocks National Lakeshore, the waves had carved the sandstone cliffs into shapes like those in the great deserts of the West: steeples, pulpits, arches, ship prows. Waves crashing into nearby caverns caused the Indians to think the gods of thunder dwelled here.

On the rocks was a drawing of what the Frenchmen took to be the devil. Indians venerated the figure, flinging it tobacco and other sacrifices. This was one of many representations not of the devil but of the *manitou*, the deity, that could be found in the American wilderness. This one may have been the same figure later travelers called the Ghost.

Near here was the Grand Portal, a natural rock bridge spanning nearly six acres of water. "The lower part of that opening is as big as a tower, and grows bigger in the going up. A ship of five hundred tons could pass by, so big is the arch." The lake was rough here and the beating of wind and wave against the rocks over the centuries had created this natural masterpiece. The waves still went in and out of nearby caves "like the shooting of great guns." The portal collapsed about 1900.

At some spots along the shore were meadows "as smooth as a board," and behind some of them muskeg swamps—abandoned beaver pools that had silted up and become dangerous sinkholes. "Trembling ground," Radisson called them and warned that in such bogs as these "if you take not great care you sink down to your head or the middle of your body. When you are out of one hole you find yourself in another." Once the natives may have saved Radisson's life by advising him that when the trembling ground began to give way he should "cast my whole body into the water on sudden. I must with my hands hold the moss, and go like a frog, then to draw my boat after me."

Portaging at the base of the Keweenaw Peninsula, the Frenchmen found chunks of copper everywhere, some very large. Indians told them the mountains they could see were "of nothing else." Here was the source of the seemingly endless supply of primitive North America's most precious metal, that through vigorous trading had filtered into the far corners of the continent.

Radisson and Groseilliers wintered at a Menominee village somewhere south of the western end of Lake Superior. It was an unusually hard winter with snows so heavy "it is to be believed the sun was eclipsed for two months." The snow was "as if it had been sifted," making it difficult to get about even on snowshoes six feet long and a foot and a half wide. "We felled over and over again in the snow," wrote Radisson, "and if we were alone we should have difficulty enough to rise again."

Hunting in this sort of weather was impossible, so hosts and guests alike faced starvation. Apparently some went out to search for roots, but the snow was five or six feet deep and the men could find none. To survive first they ate the inner bark of trees, dried and boiled to make a broth. Next came the local dogs, and after they were devoured, their bones were boiled two or three times to make a broth.

In the middle of the famine two Sioux visitors arrived. The pair looked well fed themselves, yet the dog accompanying them was emaciated. Nevertheless, Radisson stole the animal away in the night and killed it. It was quickly broiled, "guts and all," and cut into small pieces. The bloody snow where the dog had been killed was put in the kettle for seasoning.

Finally for dinner came the skins the Indians had been saving to make clothes and shoes. After the hair was burned off the skins they were chewed up "so eagerly . . . that our gums did bleed like one newly

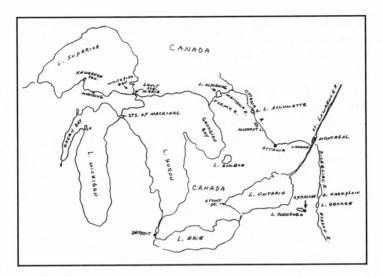

wounded." Before the winter was over, Radisson wrote that over five hundred Indians had died.

When winter ended and food became available the Menominees held a great feast for the dead, gorging themselves for days. Neighboring tribes attended, including a delegation of eastern Sioux from central Minnesota. The Sioux wives contributed wild rice and corn to the celebration. The Sioux men, "arriving with incredible pomp," contributed only their splendid presence. They dressed in deer or moose hides, buffalo coats, and beaver robes died white; their stockings were embroidered with pearls and painted porcupine quills. The men's hair "was turned up like a crown and cut very even, but rather so burned, for the fire is their scissors. They leave a tuft of hair upon the crown of their heads, tie it, and put at the end of it some small pearls or some turquoise stones." A mixture of thick grease and clay kept these topknots in place.

From the *Jesuit Relations* it appears that Groseilliers was the leader of these expeditions, and it is unfortunate that we have only Radisson's confused narratives to study. At any rate, Radisson was captivated by this magnificent unspoiled wilderness and stated:

The further we sojourned the delightfuller the land was to us. I can say that in my lifetime I never saw a more incomparable country. . . . The country was so pleasant, so beautiful and fruitful that it grieved me to see the world could not discover such enticing countries to live in. This I say because the Europeans fight for a rock in the sea against each other, or for a sterile and horrid country. Contrariwise, these kingdoms are so delicious and under so temperate a climate, plentiful of all things, the earth bringing forth its fruit twice a year, the people live long and lusty and wise in their way.

Despite Radisson's problems with the English language, perhaps no one ever said it better.

The French had now sprinkled Canada with colonists and were casting an inquiring eye on the dimly perceived great river of the interior. The questions were: Did the Mississippi River flow west or south? Did it empty into the Pacific Ocean, the "Gulf of the Mexicans," or the Vermillion Sea as the Gulf of California was called?

French authorities decided to find out.

INTO THE INTERIOR
Joliet, Marquette, and La Salle

For their Mississippi adventure the French government in Canada picked Louis Joliet, a fur trader, and Father Jacques Marquette, a Jesuit priest. Joliet was familiar with some of the Great Lakes country and Marquette, having worked in missions there, spoke six Indian tongues.

Joliet remains a shadowy character in the annals of exploration. It is known that he went to Jesuit schools and once intended to be a priest himself. His brother Lucien had gone into the Great Lakes country and was never seen again.

As for Marquette, he was a gentle and unassuming cleric, an old-style missionary who was not afraid of death. He was particularly devout—even for a priest—and apparently was absolutely selfless. He had utterly dedicated himself to spreading Christianity among the heathen aborigines of North America.

Down the Mississippi with this unlikely pair went five companions, all seven traveling in two birchbark canoes. Near the end of their journey one of the canoes overturned, leaving Joliet's journals at the bottom of the river. What we know of the trek comes from the much briefer notes of

Marquette, giving history the impression that he was the leader rather than Joliet.

Marquette and Joliet were a good team. Both men were in awe of the wonders they saw and like that other Frenchman, Radisson, appreciated the New World wilderness for its beauty and abundance of life. Perhaps more than any other explorers, they realized the importance of their discoveries, allowing them to be more responsible.

Joliet and Marquette's journey began in the spring of 1673 as the men followed the usual Indian route from Green Bay on Lake Michigan up the Fox River and down the Wisconsin River to the Mississippi. On the Fox they stopped for a while to visit with the friendly Menominees. This far north the staple of the American Indian, maize, grew reluctantly; the chief crop was rice—"wild oats" the early comers called it. It grew in the region's numerous shallow lakes and streams, so thick travelers sometimes had to hack a path through them for their canoes.

Harvesting rice was a simple matter, Marquette explained: "The Indians go in canoes across the fields of wild oats and shake the ears on the right and left into their canoes. The grain falls easily if it is ripe, and in a little while their provision is made." Then the rice was dropped into a deerskin-lined hole and flailed with sticks to loosen the husks; winnowing was done by tossing it into the breeze. It then was ready to be fried and pounded into meal: "The grain is not thicker than our oats, but as long again, so that the meal is much more abundant."

The Menominees were taken aback to learn that this tiny group of Frenchmen planned to go down the great river. They warned of hostile tribes along the way and of fearsome monsters living in the river's depths. If the travelers survived the voyage they would be burned to death by the fierce sun at the mouth of the river, the Indians believed.

While visiting with the Fox Indians a little farther on, Joliet and Marquette paused to investigate the wonderful properties the Indians claimed for a certain unidentified herb, said to be a specific against snakebite. Snakes also fled from anyone rubbing himself with this marvelous root and two or three drops of the plant's liquid put on a serpent's tongue assured its immediate demise. The drug must have worked the same way one catches a bird by putting salt on its tail.

Before leaving the Fox River the *voyageurs* stopped off at a village of the Mascoutens or Fire Indians, a beautiful spot on a high eminence. From here: "The eye discovers on every side prairies spreading away beyond its reach, interspersed with thickets or groves of lofty trees." Before they could reach these attractive lands the Frenchmen had to cross the flat, swampy watershed between the Fox and Wisconsin Rivers, not easy at this time of year. If they had come sooner they could have floated their canoes across the drowned prairie, but it was now too late and Joliet and Marquette were forced to portage over ground still so wet from the recent spring floods that it was "cut up by marshes and little lakes."

Fortunately this portage—at present-day Portage, Wisconsin—was only a mile and a half. They then entered the Wisconsin River, "very broad, with a sandy bottom, forming many shallows." The Frenchmen found the Wisconsin a tranquil stream full of islands choked with vines and surrounded by open prairies and woodlands. There was little small game, yet deer and moose were there "in considerable numbers."

When the party reached the Mississippi River, near Prairie du Chien, the scenery changed. There were fewer swamps and marshes and instead "very high mountains" on the west bank and "fine lands" on the east bank. Lining the river were black oaks and white oaks, black walnuts, ashes, elms, and dogwoods.

"From time to time," wrote Marquette, "we came upon monstrous fish, one of which struck our canoe with such violence that I thought it was a great tree about to break the canoe into pieces." This may have been one of the huge Mississippi River catfish like those seen by De Soto in Arkansas. More likely, perhaps, it was one of the giant sturgeon that dwelled in the upper Mississippi's depths.

The Mississippi was an ancient body of water and it stood to reason that it held some old forms of life. The great sturgeon was one of them. Even older was the "very extraordinary kind of fish" that the Frenchmen found in their net one day, one of the truly curious specimens of the ichthyological world: "It resembles a trout with this difference: It has a larger mouth, but smaller eyes. . . . Near the snout is a large bone like a woman's busk, three fingers wide and a cubit long, and at the end it is circular and wide as the hand. In leaping out of the water the weight of this often throws it back."

A cubit is about the length of a man's forearm. A "busk" referred to

Spatule.

the flat bone stays women of the age used to hold out their voluminous hoopskirts.

What the astonished travelers gaped at was a paddlefish or spadefish, sometimes called spoonbill catfish though it is a member of the sturgeon clan. A grotesque holdover from one of the earth's oldest periods, the paddlefish is a living fossil. Its only kin lives in China, in the Yangtze River and its tributaries. Superficially it resembles a shark more than a trout, except for its long spatula-shaped snout (ichthyologists call it *polyodon spatula*). Scientists aren't sure what the paddle is used for, but it seems to be an aid in finding food. The fish feeds on microscopic plant and animal life and apparently finds its meals by stirring up silt in the river bottom with this appendage.

Occasionally some surprised angler can find, even today, one of these odd fish struggling on the end of his line. It is known that the paddlefish can now reach 160 pounds, and those of a hundred pounds not uncommon. Long ago, before European civilization took hold, paddlefish grew to enormous size.

One day, swimming right in front of the canoes, they saw "a monster with the head of a tiger, a sharp nose like that of a wildcat, with whiskers and straight erect ears." Apparently this was a cougar, bobcat, or lynx, but Marquette noted in his journal that they had discovered some new kind of aquatic mammal. Farther on they saw a similar creature, one the priest called a "spotted tiger."

Instead of the moose and deer the Frenchmen were used to seeing, they now found more wild turkeys and *pisikous*, or buffalo. Buffalo were new to these Europeans and they were very wary of the shaggy beasts: "They take a man with their horns, if they can, lift him up, and then dash him to the ground, trample on him, and kill him. When you fire at them from a distance with gun or bow, you must throw yourself on the ground as soon as you fire, and hide in the grass." Herds were much smaller than those on the Great Plains, but these Frenchmen had never been there and were amazed at the sight of four hundred or so of the animals together.

The flesh of the buffalo, Marquette noted, made excellent eating. A friendly Illinois tribe the explorers encountered served *pisikous* hump as the entrée at a formal sit-down dinner in honor of the Frenchmen. There were three other courses, the first being *sagamité*, soggy cornmeal mixed with fat and cooked with grease. This, or some variation of it, was the most common dish on this tribe's table. Beans, peas, and pumpkins were added in season and either fish or game when they were caught. Maggots in the meat or waterflies in the fish didn't matter—they were just more to eat.

A prominent member of the Illinois tribe, as tradition dictated, fed the guests personally, putting food into their mouths with a wooden spoon.

Another course was boiled fish. The chief broke the fish, blew on the hot pieces, and placed them in the mouths of the Frenchmen. Though it was an insult to refuse a host's food, the Illinois made an exception and allowed their guests to pass up a course of boiled dog.

Between courses dogs licked the wooden plates or they were cleaned with a bit of skin. The natives wiped their hands on a dog's hair or on their own.

Farther down the Mississippi the *voyageurs* encountered the hideous monsters the Menominees told of; they were nothing more than two figures painted in long-living color on the sheer wall of a cliff near present-day Alton, Illinois. Nevertheless all the Frenchmen were startled by the sudden appearance of the vividly depicted creatures: "They are as large as a calf, with horns on the head like a deer, a fearful look, red eyes, bearded like a tiger, the face somewhat like a man's, the body covered with scales, and the tail so long it twice makes the turn of the body, passing over the head and down between the legs, and ending at last in a fish's tail. Green, red, and black are the colors employed." They were so well painted no French artist could have done better, Marquette believed.

Only one figure was complete—much of the other one had been effaced. The complete figure became known as the Piasaw Bird and the Indians thought it had spiritual connotations. There is evidence that the drawing depicted some mythological beast half man, half bird.

The legends claimed the creature lived on human flesh, and indeed there was found in the 1880s a cave filled with human bones higher up on the cliff. The bones of course could have been the source of the legends rather than proof of them. Many Indians thereabouts were afraid to go past this point.

Just below the Piasaw Bird Joliet and Marquette witnessed the violent entry of the Missouri River into the Mississippi. Natives living on their banks thought of the two rivers as a single system, with today's upper Mississippi a tributary. Observed from their perspective it seems logical. If the first Europeans—Marquette and Joliet and then La Salle—had gone *up* the river instead of down it, they might have interpreted it the same way, and we still might today. And the river might have retained its original name, *Pekitanou*, instead of the borrowed Algonquin words *messi*, great, and *sipi*, river.

Certainly the French party was startled by the sudden rush of the Missouri into the Mississippi. "I have seen nothing more dreadful," wrote

Marquette, "an accumulation of large and entire trees, branches, and floating islands was issuing from the mouth of the river . . . with such impetuosity that we could not without great danger pass through it. So great was the agitation that the water was very muddy and could not become clear."

They had arrived at the time of the spring floods, an event that gave the Missouri its impetuosity as well as a lasting nickname—Big Muddy. Above this point the Mississippi was exceptionally clear and swift, yet from there on it was turbid. This transformation did not take place immediately; it was some sixty miles before the Mississippi managed to completely assimilate its wild neighbor. For that distance their waters flowed side by side as if neither wanted to fraternize with the other, the Missouri's dull and opaque, the Mississippi's clean and sparkling.

It was the same where the Ohio River emptied its torrents into the Mississippi. A later traveler said it was "like putting dirty soapsuds and pure water together." Below the mouth of the Ohio, the Mississippi's bottomlands began and the black earth produced plant life in profusion.

Lining the banks were the usual river trees: willows, cottonwoods, cypresses, sycamores. Some were destined to be swept away by the force of the river and create the snags and sawyers that were the eternal bane of later rivermen.

Many cottonwoods were large enough to make a pirogue sixteen or seventeen feet long. The large-trunked cypresses spread out a few feet apart to accommodate their characteristic knees, the large knobby roots that protruded from the water around them. Their dark branches fanned out far overhead, creating deep silent groves that must have been impressive in their stillness.

The patriarchs of river trees—the giant sycamores—had thrived in the Mississippi valley since, perhaps, as long as 130,000,000 years ago. They were a mottled green-brown when these wayfarers came, and by the end of summer would shed their bark like a snake shuffles off its old skin. Then they stood glistening white, even at night, and would serve as beacons for later river pilots.

Then the river swarmed with ducks and geese. Hardly molested for centuries, the birds had grown so fearless they took to the air only when forced. Someone killed "a little parroquet, one half of whose head was red, the other half and the neck yellow, and the whole body green." It was one of the little Carolina parakeets that flocked among the sycamores to feed on the trees' buttonballs, its food of choice. Though the balls are tough and prickly on the outside, nature seemed to have perfectly designed the parakeet's hooked beak for cracking them.

Of course these Frenchmen could not have foreseen it, but the Carolina parakeet was doomed to extinction. As more people came to America and more orchards were planted, it became a very unpopular bird; it had an exasperating penchant for twisting off fruits before they were ripe and dropping them on the ground. To them it seemed to be a game, for the bird didn't often pick up its plunder. To save their fruit farmers killed the parakeets, but sportsmen killed them just for fun. Others captured them, because they brought high prices in the city—they looked so pretty sitting in a cage. The last Carolina parakeet was seen in the wild in 1901.

Joliet and Marquette's route south now swarmed with passenger pigeons. They were beautiful birds with head, wings, and back of pearly gray and underparts of blushing brown. Though passenger pigeons have been extinct for the better part of a century, they were once seen along the Mississippi flyway, a great migratory route for countless ages, in incredible numbers. If they could have been counted they would have numbered in the billions. Roaring overhead like a tornado, the passenger pigeons

streamed out for as much as two hundred miles, blocking out the sun for hours at a time. This great cloud was like a single organism as individual birds flew uncannily in perfect formation, wing to wing.

The great swarms stopped overnight to feed and rest. At sunset they descended en masse, blanketing the dense hardwood forests for miles around. So many perched in a single tree, body to body and several atop one another, their weight broke off even large branches and sometimes felled an entire tree. Their favorite provender were the sweet nuts of the beech trees whose smooth lavender-gray boles once dominated many a forest in the Mississippi valley.

The passenger pigeons' flocking habits, especially their preference for huddling so close together, made them easy targets for hunters. Not only were they gunned down, they were simply knocked off their perches with

poles and clubs. Smoldering sulfur fires under their roosts stunned them and allowed them to be easily caught in nets.

Also helping in their destruction were their flight patterns. The birds did not fly as high as ducks or geese, but barely skimmed the treetops. Flocks were so low and dense almost anything hurled in their direction was likely to bring down one or two. There is a recorded instance of a bird dog springing from the top of a hill and snatching one with its jaws. Another tells of a boy spearing one with a pair of sheep shears.

The last of the great flights took place in the 1870s with the last recorded shooting in 1899. By the turn of the century the passenger pigeon was a vanished species. The sole survivor of this senseless carnage, an old female named Martha, died in the Cincinnati Zoo in 1914.

When they reached the lower Mississippi Joliet and Marquette encountered much misery by another creature of the air—the mosquito. Until then the voyagers had not been greatly troubled by these pests, but now the expedition was "entering their home, as it were." Father Marquette explained what the Indians did to escape the worst of the mosquitoes' attention: "They erected a scaffolding, the floor of which consists only of poles, so that it is open to the air in order that the smoke of the fire underneath can pass through, and drive away these little creatures, which cannot endure it. The savages lie down on the poles, over which the bark is spread to keep off rain."

It was miserably hot in this country. Natives tried to escape the torrid rays of the sun by lying under the scaffolding. For the same purpose the Frenchmen erected "a sort of cabin on the water, with our sails as a protection against the mosquitoes and the rays of the sun."

Traveling down the river between present-day Arkansas and Mississippi, the explorers began hearing of a large village at the mouth of a great river. The inhabitants of the town turned out to be the Quapaws, the river the Arkansas. Once the Europeans arrived it appeared there would be serious trouble between the French and the Quapaws until Marquette held aloft the calumet, the peace pipe. After that the Indians became friendly, treating the strangers respectfully.

The Quapaws were wretchedly poor, yet were "very obliging and liberal with what they have." They treated the explorers to dog flesh, cornbread, and the usual *sagamité*. They cooked in well-made jars of baked clay, served in dishes of the same sort of earthenware, and stored food in cane baskets or in gourds "as large as half-barrels." Dining was accomplished without ceremony: a common platter went around, everyone taking what he wanted.

Like other North American Indians, the Quapaws saved grease from cooking and either drank it with the meal or waited until it hardened and ate it. The only fruit in the village was watermelon because, according to Marquette, the tribe did not know how to properly till the soil.

The Quapaws had firearms, hoes, glass bottles, and other trade goods that could only have come from Europeans. Tribesmen said they had not traded directly with any Europeans, but had bought the items from natives downriver. Were the European traders the Spanish in Mexico or the English in Virginia? The Frenchmen didn't know and the Indians couldn't tell them. Joliet believed the goods were Spanish barter commodities and also that the Spanish domains were closer.

So, having satisfied themselves that the Mississippi dumped into the Gulf of the Mexicans, Marquette and Joliet began the long journey back to Canada. Exploration of the Mississippi River's full length had to wait for another Frenchman, the visionary Sieur de la Salle.

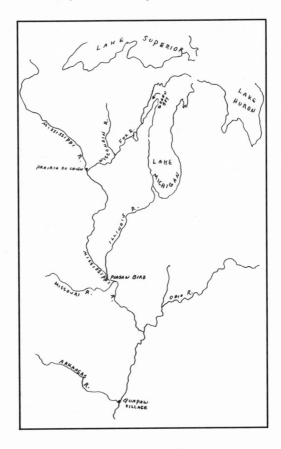

René-Robert Cavelier, known to history as La Salle, was the most tragic figure in all of French exploration in North America; his vision was the grandest, his luck the worst. If his dream had come true his beloved France would have straddled the North American continent with one foot in Quebec and the other at the mouth of the Mississippi. Instead La Salle died in an obscure Texas thicket, shot in the head by one of his own men.

La Salle was only twenty-nine when he came to Canada. He was bright, well-educated by the Jesuits, and ambitious; he was also a loner, preferring to try to do everything himself. He would have made a good *coureur de bois,* wandering among the Indians trading, trapping, and hunting. But La Salle was too clever and too ambitious for this sort of life. In the end he would leave no trace of himself.

Though his career was bound up with the Mississippi, La Salle began by exploring the Ohio River. This was in 1669, before the mission of Joliet and Marquette. The French knew there was a river called the *Ohio,* but they did not know exactly where it was or what body of water it emptied into. Perhaps—and so they hoped—it flowed into the Pacific Ocean or at least the Vermillion Sea. The stream came to be called *La Belle Rivière,* the Beautiful River. Apparently that is what the Indian word meant, though some doubt any American natives had a word so short.

Indeed the Ohio was a lovely river, its scenery seeming to change after every bend. A meandering course took it through immense forests where giant sycamores lined the banks and the short-trunked redbuds blazed with masses of pink flowers. The bottomlands were filled with cane, and every settler knew a thick stand of cane meant rich soil. The river boasted many islands large and small, all gaily festooned with vines.

Kentucky cardinals, brilliantly red, flitted among the trees, adding their color to the green, red, and yellow of the Carolina parakeets. Swarming

everywhere were flocks of wild geese, ducks, partridges, and quail. Herds of deer stalked the woods, as did black bears, while thousands of squirrels, black and gray, swam from one side of the river to the other. Eventually many of these creatures would drown and because of it the river smelled in some places.

Early comers loved to kill squirrels, it seems. After the first frontiersmen came to present-day Kentucky, on the south side of the Ohio, squirrel hunting became a practiced art. Hunters boasted of their skill with the long Kentucky rifle, and some claimed a squirrel was not good eating unless shot squarely in the left eye. Distinguished woodsmen, such as Daniel Boone, did not really shoot squirrels; they simply made their shot splinter the tree bark where the animal stood, causing the squirrel to have a concussion. "Barking off," it was called.

Practically nothing is known about La Salle's trip down the Ohio River. Apparently he kept an account of it, but later generations lost it. La Salle traveled at least as far as the great falls below present-day Louisville, where his few companions deserted him. Continuing to wander the Ohio country alone, La Salle lived on the game he killed and gifts of food from natives. He picked up all the information he could, made maps, and eventually learned and spoke eight Indian dialects.

Some historians believe the Frenchman went as far as the confluence of the Ohio and Mississippi. Whether or not La Salle went this far, he must have seen some of the mysterious mounds left in the Ohio valley by Indian societies already vanished. For about two thousand years mound building flourished in the Ohio and Mississippi valleys. Earlier natives had built small hump-shaped mounds as burial places; later Indians supplanted these with large pyramid-shaped mounds and built temples on them.

Most likely La Salle saw the burial mounds of the Adena culture, named after a place in Ohio where the first one was found. The state is filled with such mounds—almost ten thousand of them—with the most notable one being the Great Serpent Mound at Peebles, Ohio, near the Ohio River. It curls along for 1,330 feet in the form of a snake that seems to be swallowing an egg. Many primitive cultures thought of the serpent as the giver of life and the egg as a symbol of birth. Surely the proud natives would have shown La Salle this special treasure, at least.

When La Salle, not yet thirty years old, emerged from the wilderness he already had his scheme of empire firmly in mind. He started putting his plan into action by building a blockhouse on the Niagara River to control the Great Lakes trade. The Niagara River connects Lake Ontario and Lake Erie, making it the northern door to travel on the lakes.

The blockhouse was near Niagara Falls, one of the great spectacles of the North American wilderness. Here the Niagara River drops from Lake Erie, higher above sea level, to the level of Lake Ontario. The falls "forms vapors one can see from a distance of sixteen leagues and it can be heard from afar when the air is calm," wrote La Salle's chief lieutenant, Henri de Tonti. "Once swans and bustards [geese] are in its current, they are unable to rise and are dead before they are at the foot of the falls."

Living in the blockhouse was Father Louis Hennepin, a garrulous Recollect priest who also described the falls. To him they were "the most beautiful and at the same time the most frightening cascade in the world." As in everything else, he exaggerated their size. They were "six hundred feet and more," he exclaimed. Their actual height was 167 feet.

The Niagara Falls have been slowly retreating for centuries. When La Salle and his party saw them they were farther downstream than they are now. Goat Island separates them into the American Falls and the Canadian—or Horseshoe—Falls. At one time, legend has it, there was a third falls at right angles to Horseshoe Falls. Still earlier—much earlier—all three could have been one violent tumble of water.

After securing this vantage point on the river, La Salle spent six months building a forty-ton bark he named the *Griffon*. He sailed—and sometimes towed—the ship across the lakes to the French trading post at Green Bay. Here he loaded the *Griffon* with furs and sent it back; it was never seen again.

Soon La Salle and a small party set out in canoes to follow the coast of Lake Michigan south; it turned out to be a desperate journey. It was September, late in the year to be starting a voyage in these climes, and the weather turned nasty. Several men barely escaped death when their canoe overturned in the icy waters. Later there came a time when the food ran out except for a little parched corn; hunger drove some of the men to try fruits they did not recognize, causing them to fall violently ill. Once the Frenchmen stayed alive by eating what remained of a deer after they had chased off the buzzards and eagles.

La Salle ordered a halt to his journey at the mouth of the St. Joseph River while waiting for his lieutenant, Tonti, to catch up with him. La Salle kept his men busy building Fort Miami, the first of a long chain of French forts to arise in the interior. While working the men sustained themselves entirely on bear meat. The woods were full of fat deer and *cocs d'Inde,* as the French called wild turkeys, yet La Salle would not give the explorers time off to hunt them. The Frenchman seemed driven to create his wilderness empire as quickly as possible.

The bears were another matter—they did not have to be hunted. Many came to the water's edge in search of the grapes they loved, grapes as big as plums and hanging in clusters a foot and a half long. Though the Frenchmen tired of it as a steady diet, bear meat tasted best in the fall of the year because the animals had fattened themselves up for hibernation. The men made wine from the grapes and thought it "more relishing to us than any flesh."

After Tonti arrived La Salle's expedition set off on the chill waters of the St. Joseph River; they were looking for the portage that would take them to the Kankakee River. From the Kankakee they planned to go to the Illinois River and follow it to the Mississippi.

It was now December. The men's hands froze to the paddles, frost powdered their beards, and they slept with their moccasins tucked under their bodies to keep the leather from freezing. Unfortunately paths indicating a portage are not easily spotted in the wilderness and the travelers overshot the one they were looking for. While searching for this opening La Salle was lost in a snowbound forest. An experienced woodsman by this time, he found his way back to camp carrying two opossums he had clubbed in the head while they swung by their tails from a limb.

Shortly afterward La Salle found the portage near present-day South Bend, Indiana, and his men carried the canoes some five miles to the Kankakee River. What they passed through was drowned country, clogged in some places by fallen trees and in others by beaver dams creating "quagmires that one can scarcely walk over." The Kankakee itself twisted and turned over flat land, and the party made less than five miles a day. For long stretches they could find no land dry enough for a camp.

After the expedition entered the Illinois River the landscape began to improve. There were still marshes, but beyond them were "fine fields as far as you can see, broken here and there with groves of trees." Many groves were entirely of oaks "more prodigious" than those of Canada.

Here at the edge of prairie country, the Frenchmen expected good hunting, but they were disappointed. Much of the countryside was black where Indians had burned over the plains trying to force buffalo in the direction they wanted them to go. The fires had flushed out birds and game, but there were no buffalo. All the Frenchmen could find were scrawny geese and a few winter-lean deer.

There were rumblings of discontent among the men until they stumbled upon "a prodigious big wild bull, lying fast in the mud of the river." Here was about half a ton of good beef, enough provision to last for some time. After Tonti shot it the party had "much ado" to get the buffalo up from the mire. Finally twelve men slung it about with a cable and with great effort hauled the great beast out. For days they feasted on delicious buffalo steaks, and the rest of the meat was smoked for the downriver voyage.

Near a cliff outcropping known as Starved Rock, near present-day Ottawa, Illinois, the Frenchmen at last came upon a village of the Illinois Indians. It was a large town of some 450 lodges, rounded structures of bent poles covered with rush mats "so closely sewed together that no wind, rain, or snow can go through." These were multifamily longhouses with four or five fireplaces in each. On closer inspection the explorers were disappointed: nobody was at home. All the Indians—men, women, and children—had picked up and gone on buffalo hunts.

Out of provisions again, the Frenchmen stole thirty or forty bushels of corn from pits where the Indians stored their food. Filching food was a high crime in the wilderness, and when La Salle came upon the Illinois hunting camp a few days later he mollified the natives by paying for the corn with steel axes. The camp was just south of present-day Peoria, Illinois, and here La Salle built his next stockade, Fort Crèvecoeur.

La Salle eventually left the fort in command of Tonti and with four hardy men started back to Canada for supplies. The hardships of the trip almost ended the young leader's dreams of empire.

The journey began on the first of March, the worst time of year for a trek in that part of the country. The nights were cold and during the day the sun turned the prairie into vast tracts of mud and half-thawed snow. Meadows were standing in water, the travelers sometimes walking knee deep in it, while brambles cut their faces and ripped their clothes. Their feet bled and every so often they had to stop and make new moccasins. Sometimes the men slept curled up on stumps, the only dry places. Every morning their clothes were frozen and they had to thaw them out in front of a fire before continuing. The thick ice in streams had not melted and the Frenchmen had to chop channels through it for their canoes. Despite the arduous journey, La Salle and his men reached their destination.

On the way back to Fort Crèvecoeur La Salle's party found that the Illinois plains, now that the burned-over grass had grown out again, were swarming with buffalo. Stopping to hunt, they killed twelve buffalo and some geese, swans, and deer. Those who stayed to hold the fort would surely be glad to see them coming with so much meat. But when La Salle reached the site of the Starved Rock village he knew something terrible had occurred.

The village was no more—all about lay a scene of desolation and death. Nothing was left of the town except heaps of ashes, charred lodgepoles, and the frameworks of houses. Human skulls perched on top of the poles, picked clean by carrion birds. A nearby graveyard had been ravaged and

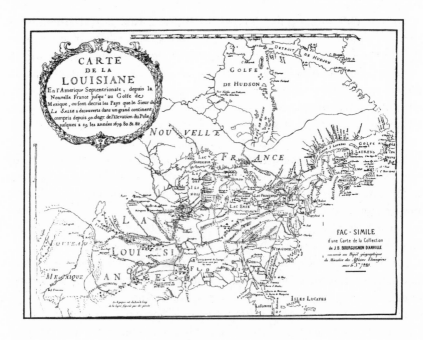

the bones of the dead lay intermingled with the corpses of recent victims. La Salle knew immediately what this gruesome tapestry meant: The Iroquois had invaded the Illinois country.

The village was some 250 miles north of Fort Crèvecoeur. As the party continued down the Illinois River they passed again and again the abandoned campsites of the Illinois as they had retreated in front of the advancing Iroquois. When they reached the fort they found what they feared: It had been demolished and there was no sign of survivors. Despondent, La Salle returned to Fort Miami on the shores of Lake Michigan.

Before he left Fort Crèvecoeur, La Salle instructed Father Hennepin and two *voyageurs* to follow the Illinois from the fort south to the Mississippi and then travel up the great river as far as they could. Clearly one of the other men was the leader of this little expedition, but Hennepin kept the records and in his accustomed way the mendacious friar put himself in the forefront. When he published these memoirs later Hennepin claimed that he also followed the Mississippi south to its mouth, a patently absurd declaration. Tonti was of the opinion La Salle sent Hennepin on this mission to get rid of the meddlesome fellow for a while. He may well have been right.

The three men headed south on an Illinois that broadened and deepened as it groped its way toward the Mississippi. It was a placid river, flowing "so softly that the current is hardly perceptible, except when it swells." Vast meadows and forests stretched endlessly and the soil was so richly black it "looked as if it had been manured." The richness was courtesy of rotting vegetation over the centuries, with countless buffalo chips and bones thrown in.

After turning north the party found the upper Mississippi, flowing fresh from its hidden springs in the north and not yet wed to the turbulent Missouri. It was spring and trees were budding as the fields turned white and bluish-purple with euphorbia and gentian. Grapevines draped limbs, sweet honeysuckle fell from cliffs.

The three Frenchmen must have been struck by the exotic beauty of the landscape. There were domed rocks, tower rocks, fortress rocks, rocks that seemed to have been sheared off by some great cosmic hand. The men also came to a cliff where, according to an Indian legend, a maiden had jumped to her death because of unrequited love.

Here game was plentiful—buffalo, deer, beaver, and wild turkey. Even though it was Lent, these faithful Catholics devoured their meat for the wilderness had a way of suppressing religious convictions in favor of practical necessity.

While sitting around their camp one afternoon, somewhere near the mouth of the Wisconsin River, Hennepin and the other two men were suddenly confronted by a war party of Sioux. Luckily they saved themselves from immediate extinction by presenting the natives with knives, hatchets, and other truck. Hennepin tried to further calm the Indians by reading from the scriptures, but their reaction wasn't positive; the warriors howled, made threatening gestures, and by other signs showed that they thought the Bible dangerous. They seemed to think this strange gray-robed man was calling down a curse on them. Fortunately the priest discovered that singing the service, loudly and cheerfully, brought a joyous response. Singing was something these Indians understood, even if their howls and laments were far from what the French considered vocalizing.

Soon the Sioux headed north up the Mississippi with the Frenchmen in tow. Apparently Hennepin bemoaned his fate so often and so loudly the other two Frenchmen refused to travel with him. The warriors relegated Hennepin to the worst of their canoes, making him share it with an old woman and a child. As he bailed water out of the leaky vessel, the priest noted with wonder how the woman was able to discipline her child by thumping it on the head, at each stroke, with the other end of the paddle.

Every night the captives expected to be hacked to death while they lay sleeping, perhaps with the very hatchets they had given the Indians. Sometimes the natives stopped their trek to hunt buffalo for replenishing their food supply. This was always accompanied by wild dancing and screeching by painted hunters.

Nineteen days after the Frenchmen's capture the party left the Mississippi near the site of present-day St. Paul, Minnesota. The Sioux destroyed the Europeans' canoe and confiscated their possessions. The chief warriors also took the priest's vestments, something they had been wanting since first seeing them.

The party then struck out overland for the Sioux villages on the shores of a large body of water known today as Mille Lacs in Minnesota. The Indians, said Hennepin, were so strong the Frenchmen could not keep up with them. To speed the Europeans along the warriors had set fire to the prairie behind them. Ice in the creeks cut their legs as the Frenchmen waded across while Hennepin swam the larger streams and nearly perished of the cold when emerging. The priest's two companions couldn't swim, so Indians carried them across.

When the party reached the villages on Mille Lacs the French saw more than one kind of dwelling. Some houses were like those the Europeans had seen in the Illinois country and others were made of skin stretched over a conical framework of branches—the famous tepee of the Plains Indians. At first it appeared the newcomers were in for a rough time and might even be burned at the stake, but they were not harmed.

One of the leading Sioux men adopted Hennepin into his family, introducing the priest to his several wives and large assortment of children. The priest was exhausted after the arduous journey and the Indian family helped him regain his strength. They fed him large bowls of wild rice mixed with dried berries and a small boy rubbed his feet with wildcat oil—natives believed the animal's fierce strength could be given to a man in such a manner. Three times a week the Sioux also gave the Frenchman a type of sauna in a little hut closely covered with buffalo hides. In a short time Hennepin was feeling fit.

The priest made himself useful around the villages by shaving the heads of children, a tribal custom, and dosing the sick with European remedies. The Sioux were particularly smitten by Hennepin's compass with the little flickering needle. They also stood in awe of the priest's metal pot with legs shaped like the legs of a lion—they wouldn't touch it without first wrapping it with a beaver skin so its magic would not rub off on them. In such ways, Hennepin said, did the priest gain the respect of these Sioux, who decided he must have occult powers. From then on this tribe called all Europeans "spirits."

There came a time when there was nothing to eat except wild berries. The Sioux then headed south for the buffalo grounds, taking the Frenchmen with them. Traveling down the Rum River they eventually came to the Mississippi. Once at their destination Hennepin and one of the other Frenchmen were allowed to go off buffalo scouting on their own. While searching for the animals they lived on an occasional deer and especially on turtles. Most of their deer meat spoiled because they did not know how to smoke it.

Later on the men set out trotlines in the Mississippi. Suddenly there was turmoil around one of the lines and the Frenchmen hauled in two large catfish. They were amazed at the size of the fish, together weighing over thirty pounds. Little did they dream that there were catfish in the lower Mississippi making these specimens look like minnows. Another time they scared an otter away from its prey and then gaped at the odd creature they had rescued—a paddlefish. Despite its eccentric appearance, they ate the fish and were pleased with its taste.

Finally buffalo appeared, coming down to the water's edge to drink. After shooting a cow in shallow water the men were unable to get her out. So they butchered the animal where it lay, feasting on their first food in two days. The Frenchmen ate themselves sick, in fact, and remained on the site for two days to recover.

After Hennepin and his companion joined up again with the main party they met a five-man exploring expedition headed by Daniel Graysolon Du Luth, after whom Duluth, Minnesota, was named. The Sioux took all the "spirits" to their Mille Lacs villages and threw a banquet in honor of Du Luth. Then the eight Europeans headed for Green Bay, eventually making their way to Canada.

While spending the winter at Fort Miami, La Salle heard joyous news: Not all of those left behind at Fort Crèvecoeur had been destroyed by the barbarous Iroquois. Tonti and some of the others had turned up—a little banged up but all right—at the French post of Michilimackinac on the northern extremity of Lake Michigan. After joining Tonti, La Salle and his lieutenant and a large group of Frenchmen and Indians at long last began their descent of the Mississippi.

In the waning days of 1681 the party traveled to the Illinois River then started downriver. At this time of year everything was frozen: "We continued our route over the ice, pulling our canoes and equipment not only to the village of the Illinois, where we found no one, all having gone to winter somewhere else, but for thirty leagues farther down, to the end of Lake Pimetoui [Lake Peoria]." Lake Peoria was really three connecting bodies of water. In the summer, when the water was low, Indians ditched the lowest lake, providing themselves with fish in great quantity. While the La Salle party was there they caught a *barbue*—a catfish—of such extraordinary size it provided supper for all.

Soon the ice broke and La Salle's party descended to the Mississippi. Traveling was easy now, the hunting and fishing fine. In their turn these Frenchmen were surprised, and some a little frightened, by the sudden roiling of the Mississippi where the Missouri River poured in its turbulent waters. At an early rest stop the party's hunters killed seven buffalo, four deer, turkeys, swans, and "bustards."

The countryside here was beautiful, with "nut trees, plum trees, oaks and maples on low ridges here and there, also tall grass as fine as in our

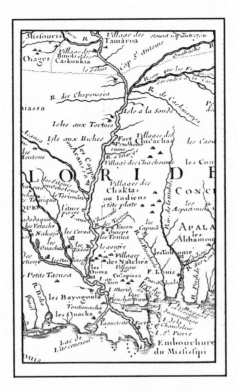

meadows." This was our earliest description of St. Louis, later the gateway to the West.

Just south of here La Salle paused at a large Indian village, but everyone was away on a hunt. This was probably Cahokia, an ancient town that once was a center of the mound-building culture where some eighty-five mounds have been found. Archaeologists believe that about nine hundred years ago Cahokia was the largest town in North America with perhaps seventy-five thousand inhabitants.

Spring was coming and the landscape was changing. Early morning mists rose from the river and birds and beasts strange to these northern eyes appeared. Though it was early March, flowers were also beginning to open. The party had traveled to the great alluvial plain of the lower Mississippi valley, and shortly they saw on the left "ridges arising at a distance from the river. The land is red, as shown by the ravines in the ridges." These were the Chickasaw Bluffs near the site of present-day Memphis, Tennessee.

Here La Salle encountered the fierce Chickasaw Indians who, after a few tense moments, treated the exploring party with respect and considerable awe. Some touched the Frenchmen's weapons or personal belongings and then touched the men themselves, believing that some of the mystic power of these bearded visions would be imparted to them. A few rubbed a priest's cross.

Many of these natives had "flat heads," a bizarre affectation common to several tribes of North American Indians. To produce this effect natives' heads had been bound between two boards in infancy. The term flat head is misleading since the practice left the Indian with more of a pointed head than a flat one.

Nevertheless the Chickasaws were robust and altogether rather attractive, especially the women. Even more attractive were the Quapaws who lived near the mouth of the Arkansas River. These same Indians had cordially received Joliet and Marquette only a short time before. According to La Salle, "The whole village came down to the shore to meet us. . . . I cannot tell you the civility and kindness we received from these barbarians. . . . The young men, though the most alert and spirited we had seen, are nevertheless so modest that not one of them would take the liberty to enter our hut, but all stood quietly at the door. They are so well formed that we are in admiration of their beauty."

Later comers would also admire the physique and comeliness of the Quapaws. Early French settlers of the region called them *Les Beau Hommes*, the Good-Looking Men.

La Salle found the landscape of Arkansas good-looking as well. Quapaw villages were on high natural levees that protected them from floods, provided good drainage, and had rich soil. Covering the houses was "the bark of trees that resemble cedars with trunks more than a hundred feet tall without a branch and of which they make their pirogues that go as well as bark canoes do."

These were the great bald cypresses found in plentiful splendor along the lower Mississippi. There were also many fruit trees—peaches, plums, mulberries, "and others of unknown names." Undoubtedly some of the "plums" were persimmons, and some of the real plums were served up as prunes. A mention of "cocks and hens" must have meant the Quapaws kept chickens as well as turkeys. The chickens would have been brought up from Spanish domains in Mexico.

The Quapaws entertained the explorers with dancing and ceremonies. To return the favor La Salle marched his men to the public place in the middle of the village and had them sing songs from home and erect a cross. He then issued a proclamation formally taking possession of the land for his sovereign, Louis XIV. The Quapaws joined in the merriment, blissfully unaware they had just been made subjects of a far-away white sachem wearing makeup and reeking of perfume.

A French priest next preached to them a sermon on the Christian doctrine of salvation. Even though they couldn't understand it, the natives loved the sermon and shouted their approval every time the priest paused for breath.

Traveling a little farther down the Arkansas La Salle next stopped to visit the Taensa Indians. He sent a delegation under Tonti to pay a respectful call at their main village, reached by going up a channel leading to the oxbow lakes around present-day St. Joseph, Louisiana. The Taensa, like other Indians from here to the Mississippi's mouth, had an elaborately formal culture and their chiefs enjoyed absolute authority. "I was never more surprised as on entering the cabin of the chief," wrote Tonti. "One recognizes in this nation some of the qualities of a civilized people. We entered a cabin of forty foot frontage. Its walls were of mud, two feet thick and twelve high. The cover is in the form of a dome, of mats of cane, so well made that no rain passes through."

The chief reclined on a couch, attended by almost sixty elders who raised their arms crying "Ho! Ho! Ho!" The emmisaries were well received, the Taensa showing a desire for friendship by joining their own hands. Tonti was embarrassed because he could not do the same—he had lost a hand in a European war—but directed his men to do so.

On their journey the Frenchmen next stopped to visit a town of the Natchez Indians. The village had a public square surrounded by private dwellings with important men having two-story houses, the upper floor supported by posts and reached by a portable ladder. There was a temple in the middle of the square, a large oven-shaped building with wooden pillars carved in the likeness of a serpent, and situated on a mound. Though the Natchez worshipped the sun, the temple was lined with idols of different animals carved in wood, bone, or baked clay.

Their chief, known as the Great Sun, lived on a nearby mound in a large cabin similar to the temple. Anyone entering the chief's quarters had to pass around a stone in the middle of the room and salute the chief with a howl. Conversation was punctuated with the same howling, followed by a parting screech when the visitor left.

When a Great Sun died his bones were stripped of flesh and laid in the temple to be tended by two aged priests. To serve the chief in the afterlife, his servants would be strangled with a cord of twisted buffalo hair. Wives would be sacrificed unless they were nursing an infant. But if wives wished not to be denied the honor of being laid to rest with their husbands, they could choose death. The women would give away—or have strangled—any suckling children.

The Natchez's concept of an afterlife was not unlike the Christian's. Heaven was supposed to be a place of perpetual feasting and festival. Hell was a place covered with water where natives went to be eternally ravaged by monstrous mosquitoes and there was nothing to eat except rotten fish.

The woods along the lower Mississippi were full of bears, especially black ones. Many came south in the fall when the weather turned cold farther north. Here bears found the grapes, honey, roots, and acorns they loved, especially along the river's banks. Their paths to the water were so beaten it appeared as if a thousand men had passed that way.

Natives killed bears as much for their oil as for their flesh. They went through the woods tapping hollow trees until they located one of their prey and then smoked it out by building a cane fire at the tree's base. Other hunters brought in a deer and made a cask of its skin by stripping it off whole, cutting off the legs, and stopping up the holes. After boiling the bear's flesh and fat together, they poured the substance into the cask. In a few days oil formed on top and a thick layer of lard at the bottom, both important in cooking. Lard, the Indians thought, was good for certain ailments, such as the one Europeans called rheumatism.

Finally La Salle saw the Mississippi River divide into three channels, and soon the party found themselves coasting on the broad waters of the Gulf of Mexico. The Frenchmen had proved beyond a doubt that a waterway existed through the interior of the continent. La Salle erected a large column, assembled his men, and took formal possession of all lands drained by the river; he named the region Louisiana after his king. All that remained now, La Salle thought, was to secure the river's mouth by building a fort and establishing a colony there.

This seemed simple enough, but the attempt was destined to end in tragedy.

La Salle returned to Canada and then went home to France. But in 1684 he was back in the Gulf of Mexico with three boatloads of prospective settlers, many of them former residents of French jails and waterfronts. The venture was ill-fated from the start.

Overshooting the mouth of the Mississippi, La Salle's ships landed at Matagorda Bay in Texas. The Frenchman decided to settle his people there for the time being and search for the Mississippi River later. After moving farther inland, La Salle built a stockade, Fort St. Louis, and other structures at the end of what is now Lavaca Bay.

It was a promising site. The fort was on a hill and from there the French could see "vast and beautiful prairies, extending very far to the westward, all level and full of greens, which afford pasture to an infinite number of beeves [buffalo] and other creatures." In other directions were more plains, broken here and there by "tufts of woods." The trees were oaks— red, white, and live—mulberries, hackberries, persimmons, and cotton-woods.

On the trees grew lots of grapes, good food if the men could get to them before the animals did. The fruit proved fleshy and tart, not good for wine and instead were used in soups and sauces.

There also was the old reliable prickly pear that to these Europeans had "leaves like rackets . . . The blossoms grow out about the leaves and of them comes a fruit resembling figs. But the leaves are full of prickles, which must be carefully rubbed and taken off before it is eaten." One famished soldier did not trouble himself to remove the spines and after eating the fruit died.

La Salle's first meeting with the local Indians was pleasant enough. A group of them laid down their arms and advanced to meet the French, "caressing us after their manner, and stroking first their own breasts and then ours, then their own arms and afterwards ours. By these signs they gave us to understand that they had a friendship for us, which they expressed by laying their hands on their hearts, and we did the same on our part."

After a little trading, always a prerequisite, the natives took the new-comers to their village. There were about fifty cottages made of bent poles covered with rush mats and "looking like great ovens." The Indians fed their guests buffalo and porpoise meat.

These natives turned out to be the Karankawas living between Mata-
gordo and Galveston bays, just as they had when Cabeza de Vaca and
other survivors of the Narváez expedition were on these shores 150 years
earlier. The Karankawas were sometimes friendly and sometimes not,
taking every opportunity to slip up on La Salle's fort "howling like wolves
and dogs." Two or three musket shots usually put them to flight.

The Karankawas seemed to be living in relative ease, the buffalo providing them with most of their food. This was in stark contrast to the
desperate conditions Cabeza de Vaca and travelers found here, but in his
time apparently not many buffalo wandered this far south. The Karankawas used heavy dugout canoes like natives along the Mississippi, convincing La Salle that he was not far from the great river.

One of La Salle's ships had capsized when it came into Matagorda Bay
and most of the expedition's food stores were lost. For a time there was
little to eat except flour mixed with the brackish water of the bay, then
someone noticed how the waters "worked and bubbled up . . . occasioned
by the fish skipping from place to place." It proved easy for the French
to catch all the fish they wanted in nets, including catfish, mullet, trout,
eels, "and others whose names we know not." Sometimes a great sea turtle
wandered ashore, and there were many of the small variety living in
shallow pools. Oysters, good-size ones, were plentiful and when the men
pushed their log dugouts into the water they slashed their feet on the
shells.

The marshes here were havens for ducks, plover, swans, teal, snipe, and
"partridges." The so-called partridges were of two kinds, "one large, the
other small, these being the better. The large ones are like pheasant and
spread a fan as turkeys do and have a cloche at the side of the throat."
The description identifies the first as prairie chickens. The smaller and
"better" birds probably were quail.

In large part it was the *boeuf* that sustained the little colony during its
brief existence. Henri Joutel, La Salle's chief aide on this expedition,
wrote that the shaggy ones were "our daily bread" and describes what the
buffalo chase was like for himself and other novice buffalo hunters.

On his second hunt Joutel found himself crawling around on his knees
in a herd of several thousand buffalo. He fired right and left, but to his
"great vexation" could not bring one of them down. "Though I was tired,
I tried again, approaching another band, and I fired a number of shots,
but not a buffalo would fall. At last, as I was going back to rejoin my men,
I saw a buffalo lying on the ground. I examined it and found that the bullet
had gone in near the shoulder. Then I found others dead like the first."

Joutel had learned the first lesson of the buffalo hunter: these animals rarely fell at once unless hit directly in the spine.

Two of the three priests at the fort also learned that lesson. One put a shot into the shoulder of a big bull and waited for it to collapse. Instead the enraged animal turned and butted the shocked priest to the ground—he was lucky to escape alive.

The other father approached a prostrate buffalo he assumed was dead and punched it with the butt of his gun. In a final burst of fury the beast jumped up and trampled the priest, almost killing him.

Two birds there especially intrigued the Frenchmen. One filled its enormous pouched bill with fish, the other had a long flat bill and beautiful rose-red plumage. These birds, of course, were the pelican and roseate spoonbill. A *mouche* (fly) with iridescent wings, probably a dragonfly but perhaps a hummingbird, also fascinated the settlers.

One day, while reaching into a hole after a turtle, the colony's surgeon was "bit by some venomous creature, which we supposed to be a sort of toad, having four feet, the top of his back sharp and very hard, with a little tail." This was the Frenchman's first meeting with the Texas horned frog, and though this exotic creature is not venomous the surgeon's arm swelled and he eventually lost a finger.

Another settler reported the attack of a denizen that was certainly venomous—the rattlesnake. Although his leg was amputated, this Frenchman died. Several of the camp's animals were rattler victims too. Once a dog was bitten and its head became swollen. But the dog survived and became a fine lookout, circling a rattler and barking until someone came to kill the miscreant. When some settlers finally tried eating rattlesnake meat they found it "not amiss."

Alligators were thick in the lagoons, some of them "of a frightful magnitude and bulk." Joutel killed many of them, including one he says was "between four and five feet around and twenty feet long." Like other early comers they called these reptiles crocodiles and were astonished to learn that a creature so large was the product of an egg and normally only thirteen inches long at birth.

Some of the Frenchmen shot alligators for amusement and once a hunting party watched Indians torture one. After putting out its eyes, the Indians tied it to a stake and ran firebrands over it.

After staying at the fort awhile La Salle set out in search of his lost love, the elusive Mississippi River. His small party traveled east along the coast for some distance and then turned north. They didn't go far this first time, some of his men becoming lost and the rest returning in rags.

On a second expedition La Salle's party headed straight into the interior of Texas, angling slightly northeast. They found the land fine and green, the buffalo and turkeys plentiful. While crossing a stream—it must have been the Colorado River of Texas—one of La Salle's servants was "dragged down to the bottom of the water and devoured by an alligator." Another man mired down in the river mud and almost suffocated before they could get him out.

Several members of the party deserted to take their chances in the wilderness while others became lost and presumed dead. Just beyond what probably was the Trinity River fever struck down La Salle and his nephew and they were incapacitated for two months. By then the party's ammunition was exhausted and La Salle ordered a return to Fort St. Louis.

Although suffering from a hernia, La Salle went out on a third and fatal trip in 1687, accompanied this time by Joutel. Not far north of Matagorda Bay friendly Indians called the Ebahamo, thought to have been Tonkawas, told the Frenchmen that a journey of a few days would bring them to men like themselves, other "hairy mouths." La Salle did not know whether this meant French or Spaniards, but the party pushed on.

It rained for weeks at a time and La Salle's men had to remain in a water-soaked camp. Because the rains had swollen them to twice their normal size, streams had to be detoured or crossed by felling trees and constructing boats covered with buffalo hides. Dissension soon plagued the group and mutiny was at hand. Shortly after crossing the Brazos River, somewhere near the present-day town of Navasota, Texas, Frenchmen shot and killed La Salle and four others.

So ended the grand aspirations of the Sieur de la Salle. One could say the wilderness claimed him and his dream of a mighty French empire in the New World.

The conspirators, knowing it would not be in their best interests to return to Fort St. Louis, took control of the expedition and forced the others to continue on with them. Shortly they came to the land of the Ceni Indians, visited by La Salle on his second trip. They found the Cenis, a Caddoan people, in their villages of dome-shaped wooden huts covered with mats of woven grass or hides. These natives tilled the earth with wooden mattocks or the shoulder blades of buffalo, growing corn, beans, squash, and watermelons.

Sharing their food, the Ceni served a lot of corn prepared as bread, pone, or mush. It was also roasted and drunk with water or boiled in the husk like tamales. The Frenchmen welcomed the change from buffalo, turkey, and deer meat.

Joutel, who was not killed, said the Cenis were "generally handsome, but disfigure themselves by making scores, or streaks, on their faces, from the top of the forehead down to the nose to the tip of the chin." The streaks were apparently tattoo marks made by pricking the skin and mixing the blood with powdered charcoal.

The party plunged onward, hoping soon to come upon the Mississippi and then find their way to Canada. In time they came to other Caddoan tribes living in northeast Texas and southwest Arkansas, all of them residing in villages much like those of the Cenis. It was the custom of these people to carry visitors into town on their backs and give them a ceremonial bath. Since the French were fully clothed, the Indians contented themselves with washing the visitors' faces.

The Caddoes were a closely organized confederacy and lived in some affluence on the wide, fertile plain of the Red River. Tribes from far away came in search of the Osage orange trees growing only in northeast Texas, southwest Arkansas, and a bit of Oklahoma. The Osage orange, a member of the mulberry family, was the wood of choice for making fine bows. The French called the trees *bois d'arc,* bow wood, and their mention in Joutel's *Journal* seems to be the first report of them in early accounts of travel in the North American wilderness.

After resting briefly near present-day Camden, Arkansas, where de Soto had wintered long before, the party found themselves following the course of what once had been a large river, known today as Bayou Bartholomew. Here the Frenchmen, none of whom had come down the Mississippi with

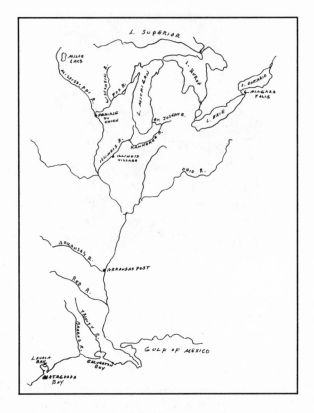

La Salle, saw their first stands of bald cypress, always an impressive sight. The bayou took them to the Arkansas River and soon the men were enjoying the company of other Frenchmen at Arkansas Post, built by Tonti near where the Arkansas flowed into the Mississippi. Eventually the Frenchmen made it to Canada.

What became of those left at Fort St. Louis? Smallpox ravaged the little settlement and the survivors were taken into slavery by the Indians or the Spanish.

Frenchmen continued to filter into the Mississippi valley, building forts and trading posts and giving a Gallic flavor to settled parts of the Louisiana Territory. But France had a tenuous hold on this vast wilderness and in time would sell it to the fledgling United States of America at a bargain price.

France was not sure exactly what it had sold and the United States had only a hazy idea of what it had bought. Someone had to find out and that expedition, the last great charge into the American wilderness, would in many ways be the most remarkable of all.

THE FINAL CHARGE INTO THE WILDERNESS
The Lewis and Clark Expedition

I t would be more than a hundred years after La Salle's death before anyone would explore the last great region of what is now the United States. Maps of the time showed a wide white slice through most of the country west of the Mississippi River, representing territory almost totally unknown.

In 1803 President Thomas Jefferson made a surprise move when he bought this vast mystery from France at the inexpensive price of about three cents an acre. This great domain was known as the Louisiana Territory, and the question on every American's lips was: What the devil is out there?

To head an exploring expedition Jefferson picked his protege Meriwether Lewis, the young army officer he had recently made his private secretary. To share the burden of command Lewis chose his good friend William Clark, younger brother of the revolutionary war hero George Rogers Clark.

Lewis and Clark, although friends of long standing, were opposites when it came to personality. Only twenty-nine years old when the westward trek began, Lewis was the scion of landed gentry in Virginia and fairly well educated by the standards of his day. He was also something

of a hypochondriac, taking on the trip a satchel full of medicines. But the trip changed him—he discovered that he didn't need these medicines. The wilderness filled him with an indescribable joy, and he took great delight in finding out what was around the next bend in the river. Still at times he showed his old moodiness, an emotional bent that would have tragic consequences when the trip was over.

The enlisted men of the expedition respected Lewis, but they adored Clark. Although invariably laconic in his journals, Clark was outgoing and cheerful in person. The thirty-three-year-old redhead was a sharp observer of nature and well versed in the lore of the woods. He was an expert boatman as well and on several occasions saved the company from disaster. The drawings in his journals were almost professional looking.

Between forty and fifty men—there is no definite figure—went on the journey. Most of them were soldiers, some scheduled to turn back after the first leg of the trip. There was also a handful of *engagés,* French frontiersmen hired mainly for hunting. Clark's black bond servant York went along too and Lewis brought his 150-pound Newfoundland dog Scammon (also known as Scannon or Seaman).

The expedition called itself the Corps of Volunteers for North Western Discovery, or Corps of Discovery for short. It set out hopefully in the spring of 1804 from the little trading town of St. Louis near the confluence of the Mississippi and Missouri rivers. The men planned to follow the Missouri to its headwaters, wherever they were, and then go on to the Pacific Ocean by whatever route they could find.

Their transportation was a fifty-five-foot keelboat—the men called it a barge, an apter description—and two pirogues. They were traveling up river against a strong current, making the keelboat's sails virtually useless and requiring the men to labor hard at the oars. Much of the time they poled the keelboat along or their four horses pulled it from shore.

Problems cropped up immediately. Sometimes the current was so swift the corps could make little progress by any means, and the Missouri was infamous for its sharp snags and collapsing banks. The snags could rise up suddenly like a river monster and punch holes in the bottom of the boat. The party had scarcely begun its journey on the Missouri when they had to stop and reload, shifting the heavy baggage to the stern so their craft would ride up more gently on snags and suffer less damage.

Along the lower river some of the trees—cottonwoods especially—were huge. When one of these Goliaths washed away into the river it became a dam catching everything that passed its way—trash, branches, entire trees, dead animals. The French called such an impromptu obstruction

an *embarras*. Men of the corps sometimes had to crawl carefully over this river block and cut their way through it with axes.

Clay and sand banks on the river were deceiving and dangerous. The Missouri could cut sharply into them and cause a collapse without warning. Once the men barely escaped a cave-in as they rounded a bend; another time a bank collapsed in the middle of the night while the expedition was camped on it. A guard noticed the crumbling and aroused the others in time to escape before their lodgings slid away.

Fearsome Missouri River mosquitoes tormented the men until they were "covered with blood and swelling." The great flies known as greenheads bothered both men and horses. Sometimes the horses, dripping blood, bolted from camp in a frenzy of pain. Ticks were an aggravation too as were the large black gnats "which do not sting but attack the eyes in swarms and compel us to brush them off or have our eyes filled with them." The men had to set fires at night to ward off these troublesome pests.

Though the lower Missouri flowed through prairie country there were a good many trees lining its banks—cottonwood, cedar, ash, hickory, oak, walnut, and willow. Farther upriver most trees disappeared except willows and dwarf cottonwoods. There the prairies came right down to the river's edge, spreading over the land like a rich green carpet.

The pasture land was lush, grass growing "so thick and tall that it was both painful and difficult to walk along, even at a very slow pace." This grass, when dry, was tinder for savage prairie fires. One day the camp barely escaped going up in smoke during one such harrowing disaster, a roaring fire that swept past "with great rapidity and looked tremendous." Two natives did burn to death and several others were injured. An Indian mother saved her little boy by throwing a green buffalo hide over him, skin outside. Sometimes animals got trapped in one of these fast-moving conflagrations and were roasted to a horrible death. Buffalo in particular perished because their propensity for gathering in large herds made it difficult for them to avoid fire.

Animals the West is famous for were not prevalent along the lower Missouri, yet there was wildlife aplenty. The distinctive cries of sandhill cranes were heard over the sounds of the river, though often the birds flew too high to be seen. Pelicans flocked to the river islands and their eggs, with those of ducks and geese, "were found every moment on sandbars." Wild turkeys too roosted in the trees stretching their necks to watch the strange procession of humans go by. The green, yellow, and red of the Carolina parakeet was everywhere.

Though normally traveling in small detachments, parakeets on the Missouri grouped themselves into large flight squadrons. Once on the ground, the fearless little birds would stand at someone's feet. If fired into they did not take flight, but only looked around dispassionately at their wounded comrades as they lay dying.

With game animals scarce along this stretch of the river, Lewis and Clark's men ate mostly from their own larder: salt port, parched corn or hominy, flour, cornmeal, and that old Indian favorite, grease. When the engagés bagged two or three animals the men enjoyed fresh meat, perhaps topped off with suet dumplings made of flour mixed with fat and boiled in water.

Hunters went ahead of the boats and hung what they killed from tree branches overhanging the river, out of the reach of predators. One night Clark awoke to see a huge snake rising from the water toward a hanging deer. He killed it, but he didn't say how.

The expedition was now beyond the mouth of the Platte River, and animals began to appear that few corps members had ever seen before. One was something like a beaver in size and shape, with mouth and ears like a dog's and legs "just sufficient to raise his body off the ground." This little animal French-Canadians had named brarow for the way it burrowed into the ground. Americans corrupted the name into badger.

Another burrowing creature was one the engagés, who had seen it before, called le petit chien—little dog of the prairie. The Americans called it a ground rat or barking squirrel, but in later times became known by the French name. It is not a dog of course, but a member of the squirrel clan.

Lewis halted the expedition here to inspect a prairie dog town that "covered four acres of ground on a gradual descent of a hill, and contains great numbers of holes on the top of which those little animals sit erect and make a whistling noise, and when alarmed step into their hole." The men didn't realize that this was a village of little consequence, that some prairie dog settlements spread out over a hundred acres or more.

The prairie dog's whistling noise was a series of sharp yelps, a warning cry. As the strangers approached, the animals disappeared into their burrows. Determined to send one of them home to Jefferson, Lewis had some men dig into a burrow and six feet down they realized, by running a pole in, they were not half way down. Now and then one of the prairie dogs would poke his head out of his hole and taunt the men with whistling. An exasperated Lewis called in his entire force. After flushing out the hole with four barrels of water their catch was one live and one dead prairie dog plus two frogs and a rattlesnake.

Later Lewis and Clark had each man kill a prairie dog "to make sure of our supper." This proved unnecessary after the men killed several elk. Lewis had a couple of the prairie dogs roasted anyway just to satisfy his curiosity about their taste; he pronounced the meat good.

Just getting a good look at another animal native to this area, the pronghorn antelope, proved difficult. For they "generally select the most elevated point in the neighborhood, and as they are watchful and extremely quick of sight, and their sense of smelling very acute, it is almost impossible to approach them within gunshot. Often they would flee at a distance of three miles, though Lewis once managed to get close to a small herd:

> They did not discover me distinctly and therefore did not run at full speed, though they took care before they rested to gain an elevated point where it was impossible to approach them under cover, except from one direction in which the wind blew toward them. Bad as the chance to approach them was, I made the best of my way toward them, frequently peeping over the ridge with which I took care to conceal myself from their view. The male, of which there was but one, frequently encircled the summit of the hill on which the females stood in a group as if to look out for the approach of danger. I got within two hundred paces of them when they smelled me and fled.

The pronghorn antelopes disappeared so quickly that the captain was astonished: "It appeared rather the rapid flight of birds than the motion of quadrupeds. I think I can safely venture the assertion that the speed of this animal is equal, if not superior, to that of the finest blooded courser."

It was true; the pronghorn of the western shortgrass plains was the swiftest creature on the continent, able to travel at about sixty miles an hour. Actually antelope is a misnomer—Clark gave it the name after finally managing to shoot one. The French called it cabril, or goat, but to Clark it was "more like the Antilope or gazelle of Africa than any other species of Goat." The species was found nowhere except western North America.

The pronghorn's remarkable powers of sight and smell allowed it to spot danger at a great distance. Lewis and Clark could not have known it, but the animal had a peculiar warning system that would have greatly intrigued them. There was a white spot on the pronghorn's rump and when frightened the muscles contracted so that the white hairs rose and the patch flashed in the sunlight like a tin pan. At the same time a gland in the animal gave off a musky odor, also warning others of its kind.

But eventually the men found the animals not so difficult to kill for they were "very inquisitive usually to learn what we are as we pass, and frequently accompanying us at no great distance for miles, frequently halting and giving a loud whistle through their nostrils."

On the day Clark killed the first pronghorn one of his men brought in a hare with ears like a jackass's: "The ears are placed at the upper part of the head and very near to each other. . . . The animal moves them with great ease and quickness and can contract and fold them on his back or dilate them at pleasure." The little animal, soon to be renowned for these great long ears and its jumping ability, was from then on known as the jackrabbit. After he measured its leap at twenty-one feet, Lewis began to have doubts that the pronghorn was the fastest animal on the plains.

Pronghorn and jackrabbit skins were soon made ready for shipping home, and shortly Lewis's traveling museum of natural history boasted other specimens. One was a magpie, a brilliant black and white bird with a glossy tail. Although there were magpies in Europe, no one knew they existed in America. Eventually Lewis caught four of the birds and nursed them through the winter. He planned to send them home to Jefferson, an amateur ornithologist who already had a tame mockingbird hopping around the presidential mansion.

The party also saw "a curious kind of deer," dark gray, with long hair and ears and "a tuft of black hair about the end." It jumped more like a sheep or goat than a deer. The engagés called it the black-tailed deer, but Americans named it the mule deer, a name the animal retained.

Another animal that bothered the expedition for weeks before Clark killed it was a wolflike creature that "barked like a dog." Clark called it a prairie wolf, but it is known to us now by the Spanish name, coyote.

Soon buffalo, in small herds, began to appear. When the first buffalo was shot Lewis sent eleven men to haul it in. The engagés, hired mostly for this sort of work, skinned the animal and cut off the choice parts, mostly hump and tongue. The Frenchmen, like the Indians, were also fond of the fat.

Shortly the men were killing buffalo everywhere—on the plains, on river terraces, on islands. Even York, who couldn't legally carry a gun, took his turn.

Coming into the point where the Big Sioux River enters the Missouri near present-day Sioux City, Iowa, the expedition noticed a conical hill in the middle of a great plain. Perhaps an ancient mound, the hill was said

by natives "to be the residence of devils." These alleged devils were in human form, but said to be only eighteen inches high. The Indians claimed these creatures would kill anyone approaching the hill, which sounded too much like a challenge for Lewis to ignore. He inspected the place and found only a great swarm of insect life being fed on by bats and swallows. This swirling mass must have been the origin of the fantastic stories, Lewis concluded.

Just beyond the Niobrara River, gateway to the high plains, Lewis made a startling discovery: a huge skeleton "in a perfect state of petrification." It was forty-five feet long and he assumed it was the fossil of a great ancient fish, though it was more likely the remains of a dinosaur. This could be his most impressive specimen, Lewis thought, but there was no way to get it home. He contented himself with breaking off a few bones to send back East.

While ascending the lower Missouri Lewis and Clark counciled with the region's Otos, Omahas, Mahas, and Missouris, all of them friendly but living in fear of the Teton Sioux. The Sioux were the most bellicose tribe of the northern plains, according to Lewis "the vilest miscreants of the savage race." Their name meant "enemy" and their universal signal was a hand swiped across the neck—cutthroat. Their first village was at the mouth of the Bad River where Pierre, South Dakota, stands today. Their lodges were like nothing the Americans had seen before—"of a conic form, covered with buffalo robes and painted different colors, and all compact and handsomely arranged."

The Tetons themselves were far from handsome, the Americans thought. In his characteristically cryptic remarks Clark called them "generally ill-looking and not well made; their legs and arms small generally;

high cheekbones, prominent eyes. They grease and black themselves with coal when they dress." Their warriors shaved their heads except for a plaited roll and wore polecat skins or buffalo robes decorated with porcupine quills.

At a banquet the Tetons honored the distinguished representatives of the Seventeen Great Nations of America—that is, the United States. The meal featured pemmican, groundnuts, and boiled dog. On this journey the Americans, except for Clark, learned to relish dog almost as much as any other meat. Clark refused to eat dog except on important ceremonial occasions such as this. Despite the subdued gaiety of the banquet, there were some tense moments before the expedition moved on up the Missouri.

The Corps of Discovery spent their first winter among the Mandan Indians in central South Dakota. The men built a stockade, Fort Mandan, and moved into it in November. Already the cold was teeth-gritting—and that was only a foretaste of real winter weather. Eight days before Christmas the thermometer stood at forty-five degrees below zero.

Lewis and Clark's party stayed inside as much as possible, but the Mandans were not intimidated by frosty mornings; they went about their business as usual. If it wasn't too cold—say no more than twenty degrees below—some of these Indians played lacrosse on the ice. An awed Lewis wrote, "The customs and habits of these people have inured them to bear more than I thought possible for man to endure." The captain, considered something of a magician by these Mandans, also spent much time treating his men and the natives for frostbite and occasionally amputating "frosed" toes.

To check on weather conditions, Lewis set a bottle of whiskey out in the snow to see how long it took the liquor to freeze. If it took longer than fifteen minutes the weather was good enough to hunt buffalo. Not much meat could be brought back though; most of it was picked up later by sled. Two American hunters, lost in the snow, survived by eating a wolf.

The Mandans were an amiable sort and the corps would consider them the most attractive of all the Indians they met on the expedition. Clark, rarely one to pass out compliments, thought Mandan women "the handsomest in the world."

Mandan wives took part in rituals designed to assure success in upcoming buffalo hunts. This "curious custom" Clark described thusly:

> The old men arrange themselves in a circle, and after smoking a pipe which is handed them by a young man dressed up for the purpose, the young men

who have their wives back of the circle go each to one of the old men and with a whining tone request the old man to take his wife, who presents herself naked except for a robe, and sleep with her. The girl then takes the old man (who very often can scarcely walk) and leads him to a convenient place for the business, after which they return to the lodge. If the old man (or a white man) returns to the lodge without gratifying the man and his wife, he offers her again and again. Some of the soldiers joined in these sacred doings and were "untiringly zealous in attracting the buffalo."

At this point Lewis and Clark sent the keelboat back to civilization bearing reports, letters, pressed plants, pottery, buffalo robes, bows and arrows, Indian costumes, tobacco seeds, and a box of "earths, salts, and minerals." Also going were the skins or skeletons of a weasel, gopher, pronghorn, jackrabbit, coyote, and red fox. In cages was Lewis's traveling plains menagerie: a prairie dog, a sharp-tailed grouse, and four magpies. Men who had never intended to go farther returned with the boat, leaving about twenty-eight soldiers, hunters, interpreters, and York.

Clark's servant intrigued the Mandans, as he did all Indians the expedition encountered. York was a large, muscular man and when he danced— as he was fond of doing—the natives were absolutely delighted. They found it hard to believe that one so big could be so agile. Also it was hard for them to believe a man could be black, and some tried to rub off the "paint" with moistened fingers. For his part, York seemed to enjoy his status as a curiosity.

At Fort Mandan the corps picked up two new members: Toussaint Charbonneau and his wife Sacagawea, who was about fifteen years old. Charbonneau, a French-Canadian, had lived with the Mandans for some time and it was said he had won his young Indian wife gambling. Lewis and Clark thought the Frenchman would be valuable as an interpreter and that Sacagawea, a captured Shoshone, would know the Rocky Mountain country.

Near winter's end the squaw gave birth to a baby boy. This was her first child and "her labor was tedious and the pain violent"; none of the thirty-one medicines Lewis carried helped her labor. Another French-Canadian now traveling with the party suggested giving Sacagawea a small portion of the rattle of a rattlesnake crushed in water. He said he had administered this remedy many times and it always worked. Lewis, though with serious doubts, allowed him to try it: "Whether this medicine was truly the cause or not I shall not undertake to determine. But I was informed that she had not taken it for more than ten minutes before she

brought forth. Perhaps this remedy may be worthy of future experiments, but I must confess that I want faith as to its efficacy."

The captains soon learned they had made a mistake by leaving their two pirogues in the water all winter—they were frozen solid. In late winter, when they were ready to start repairs on them, it was no easy task getting the boats out of the ice. Knowing Indians boiled water by dropping in hot stones, Lewis and Clark decided to try to break up the ice with the same technique. But when they were dropped in a fire to heat them, the ice-cold stones exploded. But after a great deal of tiresome work the party at last chopped the boats out with iron spikes tied to poles. After cutting trees and building four more dugouts, Lewis and Clark declared themselves ready to push on as soon as the ice melted in the Missouri.

Spring came and geese, ducks, and swans flew noisily overhead. Melting snow and ice turned the Missouri into a mighty swirling torrent, carrying with it large chunks of ice and a good many buffalo dead and alive. The members of the expedition were impressed with the adroitness of the Mandans in leaping from one ice cake to another trying to retrieve the buffalo. The natives tried hardest to snatch up the dead ones, for many Indians were fond of putrid meat.

The Corps of Discovery pushed off again in April 1805. The little fleet of six boats,

> although not quite so respectable as that of Christopher Columbus or Captain Cook, was still viewed by us with as much pleasure as those deservedly famed adventurers ever beheld theirs, and I dare say with quite as much anxiety for their safety and preservation. We were now about to

penetrate a country at least two thousand miles in width, on which the foot of civilized man had never trod.

Ascending the Missouri, the expedition soon discovered, was harder work than before; the treeless plains and spring rains added new difficulties. Gale force winds sweeping off the denuded plains made poling and towing excruciating and whipped up dust storms that all but blinded the men: "So penetrating is this sand that we cannot keep any article free from it. In short we are compelled to eat, drink, and breathe it."

Because of the rains men had to pull towropes in water up to their armpits and struggle with banks so slippery they had to dig footholds. Rocks, snags, and the ubiquitous prickly pears turned their feet into bleeding masses of flesh. Changing shoes from deerskin to buffalo hide did not help much, not even with double soles. It seemed prickly pears pierced anything except metal. One evening Clark picked seventeen thorns out of his feet.

There was more game now though. Lewis killed the largest elk he had ever seen—five feet three inches from hoof to shoulder. Pronghorns ran in large "gangues," followed by wolves and coyotes waiting to drag down an ailing or pregnant member of the herd. Lewis's dog Scammon killed a pronghorn swimming in the water. "The game is getting so plenty in this country," wrote one of the soldiers, "that some of the men has went up near enof to club them out of the way." Apparently there was a wolf that didn't even consider running away from the party. One of the men killed it with a halberd, an ancient weapon that looked like a combined axe and spear.

One morning, near the mouth of the Yellowstone River, Lewis walked to the top of a hill and saw spread out before him a timberless plain "exposing to the first glance of the spectator immense herds of buffalo, elk, deer, and antelopes feeding in one common and boundless pasture. We saw a number of beaver feeding on the bark of trees along the verge of the river, several of which we shot. Found them large and fat." The corps had seen beavers before, but after passing the mouth of the Little Missouri River a few miles back they had entered real beaver country.

To Indians the beaver was a prince among animals. Because of its industry and craft it was held up as a model for good natives to live by—"Con⸴ider the ways of the beaver and become wise." Indians lived on beaver meat and clothed themselves in its fur, but they took only what they needed and did not molest beaver colonies.

Some natives held the beaver in a sort of mystical awe, believing its life

and theirs somehow bound together. Others went farther, believing a Supreme Beaver had created the world and was in charge. This deity showed its displeasure with mortal men by thumping its great flat tail on heaven's floor causing thunder and earthquakes. Earthly beavers, in this theological scheme, were reincarnations of Indians sent back among the living to atone for their sins.

Presumably mortal beavers watched Lewis and Clark's expedition curiously as it passed, peeping out of the cylindrical holes they burrowed into the river bank. On the lower Missouri the men had caught a beaver and tamed it. The pet scampered around camp as if it belonged there. Another beaver severely wounded Scammon when its sharp teeth cut an artery in the dog's leg; it barely survived.

Beavers also provided the men with much food. They were especially fond of the animal's liver and tail. Beaver tail had long been a delicacy among Indians.

Buffalo now began appearing in larger and larger numbers. The corps had seen and killed them on the lower Missouri, but they thought five hundred was a large herd. The men were stunned to find the country black with them as far as the eye could see. A single herd might stretch for twenty-five miles—one could ride all day without seeing the end of it. Later frontiersmen declared they could tell when buffalo were over the horizon by the vapors arising from so many breaths.

Apparently it was mating season and the calls of the bulls led Lewis and

Clark to complain of the loud bellowing that disturbed their sleep. "The bulls keep up such a tremendious roaring," wrote Lewis, "we can hear them for many miles and there are such numbers of them there is a continual roar."

One night a wild buffalo careened into camp and created havoc. It had swum the river, climbed the bank, and clambered over one of the pirogues. It galloped past the sleeping men, its hooves only inches from the heads of some. Scammon averted a possible calamity. "My dog," wrote Lewis, "saved us by causing him to change his course a second time, which he did by turning a little to the right, and was quickly out of sight, leaving us, by this time, in an uproar, with our guns in our hands." An inspection showed the rampaging beast had broken York's rifle and damaged the rudder and a swivel gun on the pirogue. "I felt well content," continued Lewis, "happy indeed that we had sustained no further injury."

Attending the buffalo herds were the ever-present wolves, waiting for an opportunity to pick off a wounded cow or stray calf—buffalo cows showed little concern for their young. If a calf disappeared the mother took a cursory look around and then wedged herself back into the safety of the almighty herd. Once a calf attached itself to Lewis and followed him around until the captain returned to the river. Lewis decided it had been frightened by Scammon and was seizing on whatever comfort it could find.

In one spot on the Yellowstone the explorers found a large number of unusually fat wolves and a great stench that could only have come from rotting flesh. The reason for both was soon clear. Nearby was a high cliff with a large number of dead buffalo below it. Obviously Indians had stampeded the animals over the cliff's edge to their deaths, and left much of the prey for the wolves to glut themselves on. Lewis soon learned how this sort of carnage came about. A fleet-footed decoy, disguised in a buffalo skin, hid near "a precipice proper for the occasion." Other braves surrounded the herd and scared them in one direction. The decoy guided them to the precipice and then stepped quickly aside while the animals tumbled over the cliff like a great black waterfall.

There were two kinds of wolves. The larger ones did not differ much from those in the East. Lewis described them as "gray or blackish-brown and every intermediate shade from that to a cream-colored white." The wolves lived in the woodlands or plains, never burrowing into the ground like the smaller variety living only on the plains. The smaller ones, reddish-brown with eyes "of a deep sea-green color," had the erect ears and long pointed head of a fox and they weren't much bigger than that animal either. Wolves seemed unsure of themselves when alone and hunted in bands of ten or twelve. When pursued they hid in burrows and "made a note precisely like that of a dog."

Beyond the Yellowstone River the Missouri's banks were lined with bluffs and dwarf cedars. On one of these bluffs Clark spotted a bighorn sheep with one of its young. The party had seen bighorns from time to time, though the animals were always too high up on the terrain for hunters to get a good shot at them. Now Clark was to find out why the bighorn's agility was legendary. As his men approached "the noise we made alarmed them and they came down on the side of the bluff, which had but little slope, being nearly perpendicular. These animals ran and skipped about with great ease on this declivity and appeared to prefer it to the level bottom or plain." The men fired two shots and missed.

The party continued to see many bighorns, eyeing the men cautiously from their lofty perches, until they passed into the higher uplands of Montana.

The corps was now entering the grounds of the grizzly bear, a frightful beast they had been hearing more and more about. "The men, as well as ourselves, are anxious to meet with some of these bear," wrote Lewis. "The Indians give a very formidable account of the strength and ferocity of this animal." Indeed, natives never hunted the grizzly in parties of less than eight or ten, and even then were frequently defeated with the loss or one or more warriors: "When the Indians are about to go in quest of the white bear, previous to their departure they paint themselves and perform all those superstitious rites commonly observed when they are about to make war on a neighboring nation."

The Americans, knowing Indians had no weapons other than bows and

arrows and the "indifferent guns" the traders furnished them, had doubts about the ferocity of a grizzly. They felt the big beasts, formidable as they might be, were no match for their long rifles. They soon learned otherwise.

The party's first sign of a grizzly was a huge footprint—eleven by seven and a half inches—beside the carcasses of some dead buffalo. They saw other tracks almost daily and once in a while glimpsed a bear or two, but they never got close enough to shoot. It was astonishing how quickly these large creatures moved—as fast as a horse up to a hundred yards, it was said.

Lewis and one of his hunters were first to encounter a grizzly bear face to face and, for the captain, it was the first of two harrowing experiences with them. On this first occasion there were two bears. Unused to this sort of hunting—where they might become the hunted themselves—Lewis and his companion made the mistake of firing at the same time. Both shots struck home, but did not kill either bear. One of the animals fled, but the other charged Lewis and chased him some seventy-five yards. Fortunately the grizzly was so seriously wounded it couldn't pursue closely, giving Lewis time to reload his weapon and dispatch it. To his chagrin the bear turned out to be only an adolescent weighing a mere three-hundred pounds or so.

Lewis found this half-grown grizzly not much different from the average brown bear except that it had longer talons, tusks, legs, and hair. Its color was puzzling too. Grizzlies were said to be white or silvery gray, yet this one was yellowish brown. Later the party found out that most of them were this color—the men called them "yaller bears." In any case, Lewis admitted, the grizzly was "a much more furious and formidable animal" than he had thought.

Still the men remained confident of their ability to kill these animals, but after the next encounter some doubt seemed to creep into their minds. This incident concerned a single bear, and though it had five shots in its lungs and five more elsewhere, the grizzly had the strength to swim out to a sandbar in the river and remain alive for twenty minutes. It had made "the most tremendious roaring" from the first shot on. Clark thought it weighed about five-hundred pounds, but others believed it to be six hundred or seven hundred. It was eight feet seven and a half inches from nose to hind feet, almost six feet around the breast, and its talons were a little over four inches long.

By now the corps was well into Montana, a land swarming with yaller bears. A man stumbled into camp one day with a wild story about how he had shot a bear then it turned on him and chased him for half a mile. The captains sent some men after the animal and found it in a hole it had dug with its great talons; it was still alive. After the men shot it through the skull they found the soldier's slug had pierced the animal's lungs.

By this time Lewis had changed his mind about grizzlies: "This bear, being so hard to die, rather intimidates us all. I must confess I do not like the gentleman and had rather fight two Indians than one bear." He realized now that a quick bullet in the brain was the only way to "conquer the ferocity of these tremendious animals." This was no easy matter even for skilled marksmen—the brain was protected in front by thick bone, on the sides by large muscles.

The fury of a wounded grizzly knew no bounds, as six of the expedition's hunters found out when they accosted one on the Missouri's banks. Four men fired at once, the other two saving their fire in case the animal was not killed. (They had learned the fine points of grizzly hunting by this time.) When the wounded beast charged the hunters emptied their weapons at it, yet the bear kept coming; there was no time to reload. All six tore out for the river, the grizzly galloping after them on three legs. Two men got to their boat while the others hid in the bushes and reloaded. When their bullets hit their mark the bear merely turned and advanced on them. Two men threw down their weapons and jumped over a twenty-foot bank into the river, the bear right behind them. A sharpshooter on the bank fired just in time, putting a shot directly in the grizzly's brain.

Lewis's second close escape from a grizzly came when he was hunting alone. He had just shot a buffalo, forgetting to reload his rifle. Before he realized it a bear came up within twenty feet of him: "In the first moment I drew up my gun to shoot, but at the same instant recollected that she

An American having struck a Bear but not killed him, escapes into a Tree.

was not loaded and that he was too near for me to hope to perform this operation before he reached me, as he was then briskly advancing on me." The captain was in an open plain, not a single tree or even a bush within three hundred yards. The river bank sloped and the water was shallow; there was no place to hide. Lewis wrote:

> In this situation I thought of retreating in a brisk walk as fast as he was advancing until I could reach a tree about three hundred yards below me. But I had no sooner turned myself about but he pitched at me, open-mouthed and full speed. I then ran . . . hastily into the water about waist deep, and faced about and presented the point of my espontoon [halberd]. At this instance he arrived at the edge of the water within twenty feet of me. The moment I put myself in this attitude of defense he suddenly wheeled about, as if frightened, and declined the combat on such unequal grounds and retreated with quite as much precipitation as he had just before pursued me.

Returning to shore, Lewis quickly recharged his gun; but it was not necessary. The grizzly bear had hightailed it across the plain and disappeared into the woods, now and then glancing back as if afraid of pursuit. Lewis could not account for this singular behavior, but expressed himself "not a little gratified that he had declined combat."

Though grizzlies could be eaten, they were not as palatable as black or brown bears. They tasted like coarse pork, the men thought. Their oil was valuable in cooking—better than hog's lard—and a big grizzly "in good order" yielded up to thirty gallons of it.

Lewis remained puzzled by the bear's color until his men killed "a cream-colored white while the other in company with it was of the common bay or reddish brown, which seems to be the most usual color of them." The whitish one convinced Lewis these really were grizzly bears they were so often dealing with now, and that there were several shades of them.

On the way back to camp one day Lewis had an unnerving experience with another brownish-yellow creature, one that "crouched itself down like a cat, looking immediately at me as if it designed to spring on me." When he shot at it the creature disappeared into its burrow. From its tracks the captain was convinced it was an animal "of the tiger kind."

This was probably a cougar, or puma as it would often be called in the West. Another time some men wounded what they knew was a cougar—it had just killed a deer, eaten part of it, and was trying to hide the remains when it was seen.

Lewis and Clark were astonished by how much meat it took to feed their men. When game was abundant it took a buffalo a day, or four deer, or at least a deer and an elk. That figured out to eight or ten pounds of meat per day for each man, not always easy to come by. Always on the move, the expedition had no time to make use of all of an animal. Generally they took only the prime pieces—beaver tail or the hump and tongue of a buffalo—and left the rest for the wolves to fight over.

The Indian woman Sacagawea, of no use as a guide so far, helped supplement this flesh diet with vegetables of her acquaintance—prairie turnips and wild onions in particular. But the prairie turnips turned out not to be turnips at all. Often called white apples, they were legumes with a tuberous, turnip-shaped root. Lewis thought them a "tasteless, insipid food," but admitted epicures back home "would admire this root very much; it would serve them in their ragouts and gravies instead of truffles morella." Sacagawea taught them to look for these roots where the gophers stored them away. Wild onions, about the size of a bullet, were "very agreeable" when boiled.

Shrubs on the banks of the Missouri and its tributaries were covered with gooseberries, serviceberries, chokeberries, and red, yellow, and black currants. Lewis thought these small fruits very good, particularly the currants. Apparently he was cured of some feverish ailment by a concoction made from the chokeberry shrub. After boiling some of its leaves and twigs he drank two pints after supper and another pint in the morning. In no time he was "entirely relieved from pain and in fact every symptom of the disorder forsook me."

Lewis and Clark's expedition now came to a part of the Missouri that forked into two branches. One branch ran south, the other north. Which was the true Missouri? Lewis believed it was the northern branch, but Clark and most of the men disagreed. Lewis and a handful of men went up the northern stream far enough for him to realize he was wrong.

What Lewis saw from this vantage point was a rich and fertile land:

One of the most beautifully picturesque countries I have ever beheld, through the wide expanse of which innumerable herds of living animals are seen, its borders garnished with one continuous garden of roses, while its lofty and open forests are the habitations of myriads of the feathered tribes who salute the passing traveler with their wild and simple yet sweet and cheerful melody.

Somehow this panorama reminded Lewis of a cousin and so he named the stream Maria's River, a name it still bears today.

For the first time on their journey the expedition saw the Rocky Mountains rising magnificently into view, though only the snow-capped tops of the highest peaks were visible. "Whilst I viewed these mountains I felt a secret pleasure in finding myself so near the head of the—heretofore conceived—boundless Missouri," Clark confided to his journal. "But when I reflected on the difficulties which this snowy barrier would most probably throw in my way to the Pacific Ocean, and the sufferings and hardships of myself and party in them, it in some measure counterbalanced the joy I had felt in the first moments in which I gazed on them."

One day, when Lewis was out in front of the rest of the party, his ears "were saluted with the agreeable sound of a fall of water." Looking around he saw a great spray rising above the plain like a column of smoke. Hurrying forward he gazed on "a sublimely grand spectacle. . . . The grandest sight I ever beheld." It was the Great Falls of the Missouri, a prime landmark the expedition had looked forward to seeing for months.

Lewis climbed up to a high rock opposite the middle of the falls and gazed raptly as "the projecting rocks below receive the water in its passage down, and break it into perfect white foam which assumes a thousand forms in a moment, sometimes flying up in jets of sparkling foam to the height of fifteen or twenty feet, which are scarcely formed before large rolling bodies of the same beaten and foaming water are thrown over and conceal them."

The falls were about eighty feet high, the captain estimated. Below were several Indian lodges and "a handsome little bottom of about three acres which is diversified and agreeably shaded with some cottonwood trees." Down there lay the skeletons of several buffalo which Lewis assumed had been swept over by the strong current.

For supper that night the party had whitefish from the river and speckled trout from the falls. The trout's specks were "of a deep black instead of the red or gold color of those common to the U. States." As for describing his surroundings Lewis wished for the pen of a poet or the brush of an artist so he "might be enabled to give to the enlightened world some just idea of this truly magnificent and sublimely grand object which has, from the commencement of time, been concealed from the view of civilized man."

The next day, after hearing a great roaring, Lewis investigated and "was

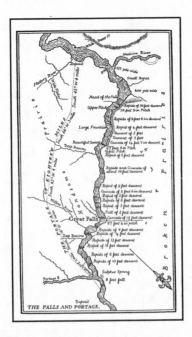

THE FALLS AND PORTAGE.

again presented by one of the most beautiful objects in nature, a cascade of about fifty feet perpendicular stretching at right angles across the river from side to side to the distance of at least a quarter of a mile." This new cascade, Rainbow Falls, came down in an even sheet, rose up from the rocky bottom in foaming billows of great height, and then glided away hissing, flashing, and sparkling. "If a skillful painter had been asked to make a beautiful cascade he would most likely have presented the precise image of this one," Lewis recorded.

Above Rainbow Falls was a huge spring that must have poured out several hundred thousand gallons of clear, bluish water a day. Today this pool, one of the largest natural springs in America, is part of a park in the city of Great Falls, Montana.

Around the falls were several smaller cascades and rapids, all forming the Great Falls of the Missouri. From a hill Lewis surveyed the country-side: "I overlooked a most beautiful and extensive plain, reaching from the river to the snow-clad mountains to the S. and S. West. I also observed the Missouri stretching its meandering course to the south through this plain to a great distance, filled to its even and grassy brim."

Though the waterfalls were "sublimely grand spectacles," they were also sublimely grand obstacles that had to be somehow gotten around. After reconnoitering Clark estimated that a portage would take sixteen days. The men then started to build two wagons to transport supplies and equipment. Cross sections of a large cottonwood tree made wheels and the mast of one boat became axles.

The portage turned out to be an ordeal. Pulling the two rickety wagons in harnesses of elk hide, the men grabbed onto whatever would give them leverage—grass, knobs, or stones. Prickly pears were a torment. They had to walk on ground that seemed frozen from the millions of buffalo hooves that had packed it. The axle trees kept breaking, making necessary long halts for repairs.

Lewis and Clark's men were working on one of the breakdowns, sweating in the summer sun, when they were visited by one of the prairie's sudden vicious hailstorms. Lumps of hail, some as large as seven inches in diameter and "driven with almost incredible violence," pelted them for twenty minutes. Though some were bruised and bleeding, the men saved themselves from more serious mishap by hiding under boats or covering their heads with baggage. Lewis took the occasion to make a bowl of punch with the largest hailstone he could find.

Two days later Clark, Sacagawea and her baby, and Charbonneau narrowly escaped death in another storm. They had sought cover in a ravine not realizing how quickly one of these plains tempests could overflow such a shelter. Suddenly water came rushing down the ravine "like a rolling torrent . . . driving rocks, mud, and everything before it." The inhabitants all scampered up the bank, Sacagawea cradling the baby in her arms, as the water rose in the ditch almost as fast as they could climb. Looking down they saw fifteen feet of water "with a current tremendious to behold."

A few days later the expedition was back on the Missouri again, the men working the boats harder than ever. They were tired most of the time and constantly annoyed by "our trio of pests": mosquitoes, eye gnats, prickly pears. They were "equal to any three curses that ever poor Egypt laboured under."

No one realized it, but this part of Montana was one of the richest lands in North America. Gold was found here later, but the men of Lewis and Clark were too concerned with their own problems to notice the occasional flecks of yellow in the river sands.

Soon the expedition passed through what Lewis named the Gates of the Mountain, "the most remarkable cliffs we have yet seen." Black granite rose straight up for what the captain guessed was twelve hundred feet: "Every object here wears a dark and gloomy aspect. The towering and projecting rocks in many places seem ready to tumble on us. The river appears to have forced its way through this immense body of solid rock for the distance of five and three-quarters miles, and where it makes its exit below had thrown on either side vast columns of rocks mountains high."

There was no place to land. The party had to travel some miles after dark to find a decent camping spot.

Beyond the Gates of the Mountains the Missouri River separated into three branches, the captains naming them Jefferson, Madison, and Gallatin. Here at Three Forks "the country opens suddenly to extensive and beautiful plains and meadows which appear to be surrounded in any direction with distant and lofty mountains."

The mountains were the Rockies, and the expedition desperately needed to get over these high ridges before winter snows clogged the passes. To do that the men would have to have pack horses, and they hoped to trade for those with the Shoshone Indians they knew could not be far away.

"If we do not find them," Lewis reported, "I fear the successful issue of our voyage will be very doubtful, or at all events much more difficult in its accomplishment. We are now several hundred miles within the bosom of this wild and mountainous country, where game may rationally be expected shortly to become scarce and subsistence precarious."

Sacagawea was expected to help now—she was a Shoshone and supposedly knew the country. But by no means did she guide Lewis and Clark across the continent, as the schoolbooks often imply. In fact she had been little help on the journey at all, yet she did remember Three Forks—it was where her tribe had camped when she was captured and carried off as a girl.

Lewis and Clark chose the "noblest" of the Three Forks' rivers—the Jefferson—to traverse and shortly Sacagawea noticed a familiar landmark, Beaver Head Rock. She told them they were not far from the summer retreat of her nation: "She assures us that we shall either find her people on this river, or on the river immediately west of its source, which, from its present size, cannot be far distant."

The Jefferson, growing shallower, soon forked into three branches. Lewis, out in front of the others, correctly picked the middle branch to follow. Soon he found himself astride a mere rivulet running down a hillside. At long last he had come to the humble origins of the Missouri, "in search of which we have spent so many toilsome days and restless nights."

Over the crest of the hill Lewis next found a "handsome bold running creek of clear cold water." It was running handsome and bold to the *west*—he had reached the Continental Divide. Taking a sip from the little stream Lewis exulted, "Here I first tasted the water of the great Columbia River,". only in a sense was this true. It was not the Columbia that Lewis found but the Lemhi River, a tributary of the Salmon River which was a tributary of the Snake River which was a tributary of the Columbia.

At Lemhi Pass—on what is today the Montana-Idaho boundary—Lewis and Clark found Sacagawea's people, the Shoshones. They were now in the Bitterroot Range of the Rockies where these peaceful Indians had been pushed back by their forceful enemies, the Blackfeet.

The Shoshones were inclined to be friendly, especially after the explorers gave presents to their leaders. Lewis wrote of their first meeting: "These men advanced and embraced me very affectionately in their way, which is by putting their left arm over your right shoulder, clasping your back while they apply their left cheek to yours. . . . We were all caressed and besmeared with their grease and paint until I was heartily tired of the native hug." Goodwill seemed certain when Chief Cameahwait, amazingly, turned out to be Sacagawea's brother.

Straddling the Rockies as they did, the Shoshones had to struggle to stay alive—there was not much game in the mountains at any time. In the spring the natives lived on the salmon that ran in the streams coming down the west side of the mountains and in the fall ventured to the western edge of the plains to hunt buffalo. For the rest of the year food was scarce and August—when the Corps of Discovery arrived—was a time of virtual starvation.

Despite the Americans' help—immediately they shot three deer—and the goodwill prevailing, the Shoshones proved difficult in the matter of horses. They knew how desperately the party wanted them, so the natives became stubborn. But Lewis and Clark played their ace in the hole—the partners told them about the black man with them. The Indians were eager to see such a marvel so York was duly trotted out and the Shoshones were as enchanted with this "black white man" as other Indians had been. After this trading for horses was no trouble.

After getting what they needed, Lewis and Clark's party was ready to move on. But how should they proceed from here? The Shoshones told the men that the Salmon River, into which the Lemhi flowed, was not navigable. After Clark verified this by a short excursion, the captains decided to go north and find a usable pass leading to a navigable river. They crossed the lower range of the Bitterroot Mountains where their Indian guide took them over a peak "nearly as steep as the roof of a house." Horses stumbled and fell and some men had to go ahead and clear a way through fallen timber and pine thickets. There was "much fatigue and hunger" every night.

A few Shoshones, including some women, went along as caretakers of the pack horses. Scarcely had the party started when it was reported to the captains that one of the squaws had dropped out back on the trail. Lewis wanted to know what was the matter with her. Nothing important, an Indian told him, she was just taking a few minutes out to have a baby. "In about half an hour," reported Lewis, "the woman arrived with her newborn babe and passed us on her way to camp, apparently as well as she ever was."

When the expedition emerged into the Bitterroot River valley they were greeted by a tribe of Flathead Indians. They were different from other natives they had seen, shorter and with a lighter complexion. The Flatheads' language was different, too, and they spoke with a sort of gurgling sound as if they had "an impediment in their speech or a brogue or burr on their tongue." These observations convinced some of the party that they had come upon the descendants of the Welsh prince Madoc, according to legend the founder of a colony in America in the twelfth century.

After bartering with the Flatheads for more horses, the expedition moved up the Bitterroot valley. When almost to present-day Missoula, Montana, they swerved west to face the northern range of the Bitterroot Mountains, including that terror known as Lolo Pass. They were in high, rugged country and the going was slow and treacherous, especially for the horses. The animals fell many times, one rolling a hundred yards down a hillside "nearly perpendicular and strewed with large irregular rocks." Amazingly the horse was scarcely injured.

Twice an Indian guide became disoriented and precious time slipped away. It was already late in the season and one September morning the men woke up to find the ground covered with several inches of snow. Out in front of the others, Clark spent much of his time searching for the trail while it continued to snow.

Spruce, fir, tamarack, and eight different kinds of pine trees filled the hollows. All the trees, Clark said, were "so covered with snow that in passing thro' them we are continually covered with snow. I have been as wet and cold as ever I was in my life. Indeed I was at one time fearful my feet would freeze in the thin mockirsons which I wore." Some men no longer had even "mockirsons" and, like the soldiers of Valley Forge, wrapped their feet in rags.

Game, scarce from the beginning, became almost nonexistent. The men were reduced to eating soup made with melted snow, parched corn, wolf meat, and an occasional crawfish caught in a brook, and finally three colts bought from the Flatheads. On one occasion there was nothing to eat except bear oil and twenty pounds of candles.

The Corps of Discovery descended to the western side of the Rockies almost dropping and famished. Besides empty stomachs, they suffered severely from boils and dysentery. Hurrying ahead with a small hunting party, Clark suddenly found spread out in front of him the lovely valley of the Kooskooske River, now the Clearwater. It was a swift, smooth stream lined with thick forests, plains, and majestic hills. Here the party met the Chopunnish Indians who gave them berries, salmon cakes, and roots. The men ate so much they made themselves sick.

The Chopunnish were better known by the name the French gave them: Nez Percé (Pierced Noses). Like other tribes of the Northwest, they were short and squat with broad faces.

Rest and an improved diet soon had the men of the expedition back on their feet and their surge toward the Pacific continued. They traded for canoes and dugouts and traveled down the Clearwater to the Snake River and finally to the Columbia River, pausing only long enough to buy fish and dogs from the natives. Dogs were becoming a large part of the men's diet and they were learning to appreciate them. In the Columbia, salmon were running in huge numbers, but the fish had laid their eggs and were dying. No one wanted to eat them.

The food situation was improving. Ducks, geese, and cranes were added to the menu. When the Indians saw a crane suddenly knocked from the

sky by a bullet they decided the Americans "came from the clouds
. . . and were not men."

The expedition moved forward quickly now. Everyone was eager because the long trail was nearing an end. New peaks appeared in the
distance: Mt. Adams, Mt. St. Helens, Mt. Hood.

It was also the beginning of a series of furious rapids. Below Celilo Falls
the entire Columbia, compressed and angry, poured through a channel of
rocks no wider than forty-five yards. The leaders paused to take stock of
the situation. It would take days to portage here and the captains didn't
think they could afford the time. Lewis, naming this the Short Narrows,
was determined "to pass through this place notwithstanding the horrid
appearance of this agitated gut, swelling, boiling, and whorling in every
direction."

Once the men were in this "agitated gut" it didn't seem as bad as it
looked. With a crowd of enthralled Indians watching with astonishment
from the cliffs above, the Americans negotiated the whole expanse without losing a man or a boat. Shortly they also passed through, with equal
success, what Lewis named the Long Narrows. This twelve-mile strip of
furious water was later named La Grande Dalle de la Columbia, or the
Dalles for short.

Quieter waters beyond the Dalles brought the expedition from the
Columbian Plain into the rain forests of the Northwest. Beyond the
shores lay green expanses of trees—Douglas firs, red cedars, spruce, and
hemlock—much bigger than the explorers had ever seen. Trees that had
been uprooted by immense swells and strong winds and tossed into the
river were a constant threat to navigation. According to Clark: "Every
exertion and the strictest attention by the party was scarcely sufficient to
defend our canoes from being crushed to pieces between those immensely
large trees."

The adventurers were not finished with the treachery of rapids. As the
Columbia surged along a deep gorge it again compressed its waters into
roiling cascades. Later these waters were known as the Upper and Lower
Cascades, though now they have disappeared into the reservoir of the
Bonneville Dam.

The men partly shot these waters, partly portaged them. When they
emerged they could for the first time feel the pull of Pacific tides. The
expedition was jubilant, not realizing the ocean was still more than a
hundred miles away. Soon they were plagued by fog and almost constant
rain. But on the morning of November 7, 1805, the fog lifted and to the
Americans' delighted eyes revealed what appeared to be an endless ex-

panse of water. "Ocian in view! O! the joy!" wrote Clark in his journal.

He was wrong. What he and the others saw was not the Pacific Ocean, but the wideness of Gray's Bay, named for Captain Robert Gray. The "ocian" was still twenty miles away.

For the next few days the Corps of Discovery fought wind and rain and giant breakers. For a period of eleven days and nights rain fell without ceasing, rotting clothing and moccasins, spoiling the party's little bit of food, and generally making life miserable. Yet the men were not totally downcast, for they knew their long-sought destination was not far away.

The expedition camped for a time at a site across the river from the present-day city of Astoria, Oregon. The local Indians, Chinooks, called on them hoping to sell some of their wares, especially otter skins. The natives wore conical hats of tightly woven twigs to keep off the rain.

The Chinooks were short and squat. Their legs were often lumpy and misshapen from so much sitting in dugout canoes, for these Indians were as dependent on boats as Plains Indians were on horses. The Chinook's dugouts, made of redwood and handsomely carved, were made in different sizes—some only big enough for one or two men, others holding twenty or more. The explorers marveled at how skillfully these Indians maneuvered them, even in open, choppy waters. "The best canoe navigators I ever saw," wrote Clark.

The women, though not unhandsome in the face, were in the same shape, that is, "low and badly made with large legs and thighs, which are generally swelled from a stoppage of circulation in the feet (which are small) by many strands of beads or curious strings which are drawn tight around the leg above the ankle." The legs or arms of some of the women were tattooed. On the arm of one was *J. Bowman*, proof enough that British or American sailors had visited this area. Further evidence that Europeans or Americans had already been here was the smattering of English words the Chinooks knew: musket, powder, shot, knife, damned rascal, son of a pitch [sic].

One day a handful of Clatsop Indians appeared and offered their own lands as a better campsite. They lived on the south side of the Columbia, on the coast. Lewis and Clark accepted, knowing that on the coast they could make salt for their usually tasteless food and watch for ships. The one drawback was that they would have to put up with dreadful weather.

And so the men built Fort Clatsop in a stand of lofty pine trees seven miles from the sea, on the Oregon side of the Columbia. Here they would remain until spring when they could begin the return trip to civilization. It was a miserable, rainsoaked winter.

The Clatsops lived in long lodges made of cedar and bark, some sunk deep into the ground. A dozen or so families might abide in the same lodge, sleeping on shelves or bunks built into the walls. Like many tribes, they had a sweat house. Their kind was made by damming up a creek, digging a hole in it about eight feet deep, and covering this with a conical roof of branches and mud. Bathers entered through a hole in the top, taking heated stones and a jug of water for creating steam. Afterward they took a cold dip in the creek. Steam bathing was essentially a social amusement and it was insulting to decline another's offer to bathe with him.

Like others of the Columbia River basin, these Indians were part of a salmon and root culture. When the salmon were running food was plentiful, but in the winter it was a different story. The Clatsops lived on whatever was available: pounded salmon, tainted elk or deer meat, roots of several sorts.

The staple roots of this tribe were tubers of the camass (a wild member of the Hyacinth family) plus wapatoo plants and the curiously sweet root of a thistle these natives called *shanataque*. Indian women prepared the bulbs by first steaming them in a hole lined with hot stones and covered with green leaves and dirt. The bulbs could then be eaten raw or pounded into flour for bread. The Americans' stomachs were not conditioned to eating camass and sometimes it threw them into purgative fits.

Wapatoo—Clark called it wap-to—was the Indian name for arrowhead, a plant with a tuberous root like a potato (early settlers called it swamp potato). It was found in ponds and marshes almost anywhere in North America, growing biggest in the Willamette River valley of Oregon. Wapatoo was never out of season. Indian women gathered it by

wading into shallow water and breaking off the roots with their toes. "They are nearly equal in flavour to the Irish potato and afford a very good substitute for bread," was Lewis's opinion.

Come Christmas Day, 1805, there was no feast for there was nothing to feast on. Lewis reported, "Our dinner consisted of pore elk, so much spoiled that we ate it through mere necessity, some spoiled pounded fish, and a few roots." The Clatsops ate tainted meat without complaint. In fact, they seemed to enjoy it.

Before winter was over Lewis discovered anchovies, the little smeltlike fish that became his favorite snack. "I find them best when cooked in Indian style, which is by roasting a number of them on a wooden spit without any previous preparation whatever. They are so fat that they require no additional sauce and I think them superior to any fish I ever tasted." They were so delicate, he found, that they spoiled quickly if not smoked or pickled.

When the captains heard a dead whale had washed up on the coast a few miles away, they were interested in getting some of its blubber, for eating and for boiling into oil. Clark and some men set out for the beach, taking Sacagawea who had begged to go and get a look at the big fish she had heard about. When the party arrived they found the whale "already pillaged of every valuable part by the Tillamook Indians in the vicinity, at whose villages it lay on the strand."

Clark soon found these Tillamooks boiling blubber by throwing it into long troughs filled with hot stones. The oil they extracted by this method they tied up in the whale's intestines. For eating the natives warmed blubber over a fire and then dipped it in oil or ate it with *shanataque* roots.

The captains managed to buy about three hundred pounds of blubber from the reluctant Tillamooks. After cooking some of it on a wooden spit in imitation of the Indians, most of the men found it "very palatable and

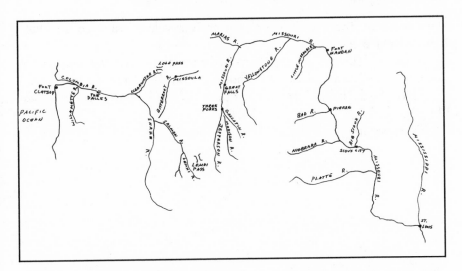

tender." It tasted something like pork fat, though spongier and a little coarse. Clark was glad for the blubber nonetheless and thanked God for being "much more kind to us than he was to Jonah, having sent this monster to be swallowed *by* us, instead of swallowing *of* us, as Jonah's did."

During those long, rainy winter months, dog was the main dish at the fort. The men devoured so many dogs they became fond of them; Lewis said the meat reminded him of beaver tail. "While we lived principally on the flesh of this animal," he wrote, "we were much more healthy, strong and fleshy than we had been since we left the buffalo country. For my own part I have become so perfectly reconciled to the dog that I think it is an agreeable food and would prefer it vastly to lean elk or venison."

When spring came the expedition began its return, though going off on some exploring tangents. They arrived safely back in St. Louis on September 23, 1806, having discovered, as Lewis wrote Jefferson, "the most practicable route which does exist across the continent by means of the navigable branches of the Missouri and Columbia Rivers."

Congress rewarded the men with 320 acres of land each and double pay for the time of their trip. To the two captains it also gave double pay and sixteen hundred acres of land apiece. Clark also became commanding general of the militia of the Louisiana Territory and Lewis was appointed governor.

Unfortunately Lewis was not temperamentally fit for such a job and was soon in trouble, most of it involving the financial affairs of the territory. While on a trip to Washington, D.C. to discuss these problems, at a lonely inn on the Natchez Trace near Nashville, Tennessee, he shot himself twice and died.

Clark and Jefferson were not surprised when they heard the news. Both were painfully aware of Lewis's tendency toward melancholia and hypochondria. Said Clark: "I fear 0! I fear the weight of his mind has overcome him."

So, apparently, it had.

EPILOGUE

With the return of Lewis and Clark the glory days of North American exploration ended. Except for a few mountain men later in the century, there would be no more bold spirits searching for the secrets of an exotic wilderness: no more Champlains, De Sotos, La Salles, Coronados, or Radissons. Yet the indomitable spirit of the explorers and *voyageurs* lived on in the hearts of the spunky American pioneers who "westered" during the later nineteenth century.

It was in the second half of the nineteenth century that a change came in the attitude of man toward the world he was so much a part of but had generally denied. Charles Darwin's *The Origin of Species* in 1859 encouraged him to look at his world not as a random collection of separate species, but as a web of life with one species dependent on another.

Three years later Darwin's *The Descent of Man* aroused feelings of another sort. Like plants, Darwin wrote, humans too developed from a lower form of life. He suggested the lower form was "a hairy animal of the great anthropoid group," a scientific man's way of saying an ape.

This was an imminently disturbing idea in the Victorian world. A bishop's wife in England probably summed up the general uneasiness when she said, "Let us hope it is not true, but if it is let us pray it does not become well known." It did become well known of course, and the theory of man's evolution caused some tottering in the religious and moral foundations of society.

Nevertheless Darwin's pair of books spawned an interest in natural science such as the stodgy old world had not seen since the days of Aristotle. Zoos, museums, and menageries by the hundreds opened. Schools began courses in nature study. Animal and bird books poured off the new steam-powered presses.

In America the groundwork for this change had been laid earlier by Ralph Waldo Emerson, Henry David Thoreau, and the painters John

James Audubon and George Catlin. *Walden*, published a generation earlier, now became standard reading for many. In it Thoreau wrote:

> We need the tonic of wildness—to wade sometimes in marshes where the bittern and the meadow-hen lurk, and hear the booming of the snipe, to smell the whispering sedge where only some wilder and more solitary fowl builds her nest, and the mink crawls with its belly close to the ground. At the same time that we are earnest to explore and learn things, we require that all things be mysterious and unexplorable, that land and sea be infinitely wild, unsurveyed, and unfathomed by us because unfathomable. We can never have enough of Nature.

Strangely, the dawning of an ecological consciousness in the second half of the nineteenth century coexisted with some of the most senseless devastation ever in the natural kingdom. The great forests that once stretched in grandeur from the East Coast to the plains were rapidly vanishing, chewed up by the insatiable maw of industrial civilization. Animals, birds, and reptiles disappeared in a holocaust of commercial exploitation fed by greed, the hunts often accompanied by savage violence.

Hunters—and sometimes sportsmen shooting from train windows—brought down buffalo until the plains were black with their carcasses. Unmercifully, bird hunters slaughtered their prey just for the feathers, an indispensable accessory to women's clothes in that age. Said the humor magazine *Puck*:

> We have the horseless carriage,
> The wireless and all that,
> Also the loveless marriage,
> But not the birdless hat.

By 1900 voices—faint at first but growing in volume—rose in protest. Societies were formed, wildlife reservations created, the National Park Service organized. Conservationists, first led by Theodore Roosevelt, bought land and tried to educate the public to the needs—and the rights—of wildlife.

These efforts have continued and have grown, especially since 1960. Yet the biggest problem remains, and will for a long time: how to reconcile man with his natural surroundings. It isn't that man should not use the environment for his own needs, but that he must strike a balance between his needs and the needs of nature.

BIBLIOGRAPHY

General Works:

Bakeless, John, *The Eyes of Discovery*, J.B. Lippincott, New York, 1950. This book was the inspiration for *Wilderness*, and its main source.

De Voto, Bernard, *The Course of Empire*, Houghton Mifflin, Boston, 1952. This classic is still good for explorations west of the Mississippi.

Eifert, Virginia, *Of Men and Rivers*, Dodd, Mead, New York, 1966.

Franklin, Wayne, *Discoverers, Explorers, Settlers: the Diligent Writers of Early America*, University of Chicago Press, Chicago, 1979.

Hooker, Richard J., *Food and Drink in American History*, Bobbs-Merrill, Indianapolis, 1981.

Nash, Gary B., *Red, White, and Black: The Peoples of Early America*, Prentice-Hall, Englewood Cliffs, New Jersey, 1974. (Second edition, 1982. Third edition, 1991).

Page, Evelyn, *American Genesis*, Gambit, Boston, 1973.

Platt, Rutherford, *Wilderness: the Discovery of a Continent of Wonder*, Dodd, Mead, 1961. Another main source. There are no explorers in this book, just wilderness and Indians.

Reid, Alan, *Discovery and Exploration: a Concise History*, Gentry Books, London, 1980.

Tindall, George Brown, *America: a Narrative History*, W. W. Norton, New York and London, 1984. Volume one is a good general history, though there are plenty of others.

General Works on Indians:

Adair, James, *History of the American Indians*, Promontory Press, New York, 1986. This book, originally published in London in 1775, is about Southeastern Indians only.

Catlin, George, *Letters and Notes on the Manners, Customs, and Conditions of the North American Indians*. Dover, New York, 1973. Originally published in London in 1844, this deals with Plains Indians of the mid-nineteenth century. This is beyond the time frame of *Wilderness*, but Indian customs and manners don't change much.

Hayes, Wilma P. and Vernon R., *Foods the Indians Gave Us*, Ives Washburn, New York, 1973.

Kroeber, A.L., *Handbook of the Indians of California*, Dover, New York, 1976. Originally published in 1925 by the United States Government Printing Office, Bureau of American Ethnology of the Smithsonian Institution.

Schoolcraft, Henry R., *History of the Indian Tribes of the United States*, J.B. Lippincott, Philadelphia, 1857.

Swanton, John R., *The Indians of the Southeastern United States*, United States Government Printing Office, 1946.

Turner, Geoffrey, *Indians of North America*, Blandford Press, Poole, England, 1979.

Waldman, Carl, *Atlas of the North American Indian*, Facts on File, New York, 1985. An invaluable reference guide.

Washburn, Wilcomb E., *The Indian in America*, Harper and Row, New York, 1975.

Wilbur, C. Keith, *The New England Indians*, Globe Pequot Press, Chester, Connecticut, 1978. Lots of good drawings.

General Works on Wildlife and Plants:

Coon, Nelson, *Using Wildlife and Wayside Plants*, Dover, New York, 1980.

Densmore, Frances, *How Indians Use Wild Plants for Food, Medicine and Crafts*, Dover, New York, 1974.

Eifert, Virginia, *River World: Wildlife of the Mississippi*, Dodd, Mead, New York, 1959.

Gibbons, Euell, *Stalking the Wild Asparagus*, David McKay, New York, 1962.

Griggs, Barbara, *Green Pharmacy: a History of Herbal Medicine*, Viking, New York, 1981.

Martin, Alexander C.; Zim, Herbert S.; and Nelson, Arnold L., *American Wildlife and Plants: a Guide to Wildlife Food Habits*, Dover, New York, 1961.

Matthiesson, Peter, *Wildlife in America*, Viking Penguin, New York, 1987 revised edition. A classic on American wildlife, originally published in 1959.

McClung, Robert, *Lost Wild America: the Story of Our Extinct and Vanishing Wildlife*, William Morrow, New York, 1969.

Medsger, Oliver Perry, *Edible Wild Plants*, Macmillan, New York, 1966. An indispensable reference, probably the best book of its kind dispite its age.

Verney, Peter, *Homo Tyrannicus: a History of Man's War Against Animals*, Mills and Boon, London, 1979.

Chapter 1:

Beazley, Raymond, *John and Sebastian Cabot: the Discovery of North America*, Burt Franklin Resource and Source Works Series, New York. First published in London, 1898. There is no publication date on this edition.

Costain, Thomas, *The White and the Gold*, Doubleday, New York, 1954. The making of Canada in an entertaining style.

Davies, Nigel, *Voyagers to the New World*, William Morrow, New York, 1979. A prehistory of the New World through the Norsemen.

Morison, Samuel Eliot, *The European Discovery of America: the Northern Voyages* (vol. 1), Oxford University Press, New York, 1971. The great historian covers all sea explorations on both coasts through the sixteenth century. No land explorers.

Mowat, Farley, *Sea of Slaughter*, Atlantic Monthly Press, Boston and New York, 1984. Early explorations of Newfoundland and the Gulf of St. Lawrence, with attention to the killing of wildlife.

Quinn, David B., *North America from Earliest Discovery to First Settlements*, Harper and Row, New York, 1977.
Russell, Franklin, *The Secret Islands*, W.W. Norton, New York, 1965. A word picture of Funk Island today, showing that it hasn't changed much.
Sauer, Carl Ortwin, *Sixteenth Century North America*, University of California, Berkeley, 1971.

Chapter 2:
Criukshank, Helen G. (ed.), *John and William Bartram's America*, Devin-Adair, Greenwich, Connecticut, 1957.
Johnson, James R., *The Southern Swamps of America*, David McKay, New York, 1970.
Lorant, Stefan (ed.) *The New World*, Duell, Sloan and Pearce, New York, 1946. The main source for Chapter 2, this book tells the story in the words of Florida's earliest explorers and settlers.
Ribault, Jean, *The Whole and True Discovery of Terra Florida*, University of Florida reprint, Gainsville, 1964.
Van Doren, Mark (ed.), *The Travels of William Bartram*, Dover, New York, 1955. First published in 1791.

Chapter 3:
Bourne, Edward Gaylord (ed.), *Narratives of the Career of Hernando de Soto in the Conquest of Florida, etc.*, A.S. Barnes, New York, 1904. Where all De Soto studies begin, this book includes the narratives of the four members of the expedition known to keep a record.
De La Vega, Garcilaso, *The Florida of the Inca*, University of Texas Press, Austin, 1951. This version of De Soto's travels comes from a part Peruvian, part Spaniard—the "Inca" of the title—which he drew from reports by certain survivors of the expedition. It was not published until 1605, in Lisbon, and not all of it can be accepted as accurate.
Quinn, *North America from Earliest Discovery, etc., op. cit.*
Sauer, *Sixteenth Century North America, op. cit.*

Chapter 4:
Bolton, Herbert E., *Coronado: Knight of Pueblos and Plains*, University of New Mexico Press, Albuquerque, 1949. Old as it is, Bolton's account has never been surpassed. It is the starting point for all studies of the Coronado expedition.
Horgan, Paul, *The Heroic Triad*, Holt, Rinehart and Winston, New York, 1954.
———, *Great River: the Rio Grande in North American History*, Rinehart and Co., New York, 1954.
Quinn, *North America from Earliest Discovery, etc., op. cit.*
Sauer, *Sixteenth Century North America, op. cit.*
Wellman, Paul I., *Glory, God, and Gold*, Doubleday, Garden City, New York, 1954.

Chapter 5:
Barbour, Philip L., *The Three Worlds of Captain John Smith*, Houghton Mifflin, Boston, 1964.

Beeching, Jack (ed.), *Voyages and Discoveries*, Viking Penguin, New York, 1972. Taken from Richard Hakluyt's *The Principall Navigations, Voyages, Traffiques and Discoveries of the English Nation*, London, 1589–1590.

Gerson, Noel, *The Glorious Scoundrel: a Biography of Captain John Smith*, Dodd, Mead, New York, 1978.

Ingram, David, *The Relation of David Ingram*, Readex Microprint (no place of publication), 1966. Originally published in 1589 as part of Hakluyt's *Principall Navigations*, etc.

Lorant, Stefan (ed.), *The New World, op. cit.* Reports and pictures of the Roanoke settlers.

Morison, Samuel Eliot, *The Northern Voyages, op. cit.* Detailed accounts of English voyagers in the far north of America.

Quinn, *North America from Earliest Discovery, etc., op. cit.*

Sauer, *Sixteenth Century North America, op. cit.*

Starkey, Marion L. *Land Where Our Fathers Died: the Settling of the Eastern Shores, 1607–1735*, Doubleday, New York, 1962.

Willison, George F., *Behold Virginia: the Fifth Crown*. Harcourt, Brace 1951.

Chapter 6:

Barbour, *The Three Worlds of Captain John Smith, op. cit.*

Bishop, Morris, *Champlain: the Life of Fortitude*, Macdonald and Co., London, 1949. Old but probably the best book available on Champlain.

Brereton, John, *Discoveries of the North Part of Virginia*, Readex Microprint (no place of publication), 1966. Originally published in London in 1602. "North part of Virginia" refers to New England.

Cronon, William, *Changes in the Land: Indians, Colonists, and the Ecology of New England*, Hill and Wang, New York, 1983.

Dillon, Francis, *The Pilgrims, Their Journeys and Their World*, Doubleday, Garden City, New York, 1975.

Fleming, Thomas, *One Small Candle: the Pilgrims First Year in America*, W.W. Norton, New York, 1963.

Sauer, Carl Ortwin, *Seventeenth Century North America*, Turtle Island Foundation, Berkeley, California, 1980.

Starkey, *Land Where Our Fathers Died, etc. op. cit.*

Willison, George F., *The Pilgrim Reader*, Doubleday, New York, 1953.

———, *Saints and Strangers*, Reynal and Hitchcock, New York, 1945. The classic account of the Pilgrims.

Chapter 7:

Englebert, Omer, *The Last of the Conquistadors: Junípero Serra*, Harcourt, Brace, New York, 1956.

Lavender, David, *Land of Giants: the Drive to the Pacific, 1750–1950*, Doubleday, Garden City, New York, 1958. Good material on Russian adventuring in Alaska.

Morison, *The Northern Voyages, op. cit.* For Sir Francis Drake only.

Quinn, *North America from Earliest Discovery, etc., op. cit.*

Sauer, *Sixteenth Century North America, op. cit.*

Chapter 8:

Adams, Arthur T., *The Explorations of Pierre Esprit Radisson,* Ross and Haines, Minneapolis, 1961. Radisson's travels in his own words.

Bishop, *Champlain, op. cit.*

Kenton, Edna (ed.), *The Jesuit Relations and Allied Documents: Travels and Explorations of the Jesuit Missionaries in North America (1610–1791),* Albert and Charles Boni, New York, 1925. An invaluable source for exploration of the Great Lakes and the Mississippi River.

Quinn, *North America from Earliest Discovery, etc. op. cit.*

Sauer, *Seventeenth Century North America, op. cit.*

Chapter 9:

Eckert, Allan, *The Silent Sky: the Incredible Extinction of the Passenger Pigeon,* Little, Brown, Boston, 1965.

Joutel, Henri, *A Journal of La Salle's Last Voyage,* Corinth Books, New York, 1962. Originally published in Paris in 1713 and then in London in 1714, this is the story of La Salle's tragic expedition to find the Mississippi River again as told by his chief lieutenant on the trip.

Kenton, *The Jesuit Relations, op. cit.*

Le Page Du Pratz, Antoine Simon, *The History of Louisiana, or of the Western Parts of Virginia and Carolina,* Pelican Press, New Orleans, 1949. "Louisiana" refers to the southern part of the Louisiana Territory. The book was originally published in 1758.

Monette, John W., *History of the Discovery and Settlement of the Valley of the Mississippi* (two volumes), Harper and Brothers, New York, 1846.

Parkman, Francis, *The Discovery of the Great West: La Salle,* Rinehart and Co., New York and Toronto, 1965. Originally published in 1869.

Sauer, *Seventeenth Century North America, op. cit.*

Severin, Timothy, *Explorers of the Mississippi,* Knopf, New York, 1968.

Chapter 10:

Bakeless, John (ed.), *The Journals of Lewis and Clark,* New American Library, New York, 1964.

———, *Lewis and Clark: Partners in Discovery,* William Morrow, New York, 1947.

Dillon, Richard, *Meriwether Lewis: A Biography,* Coward-McCann, New York, 1965.

Gilbert, E.W., *The Exploration of Western America, 1800–1850: an Historical Geography,* Cooper Square Publishers, New York, 1966.

Hawke, David Freeman, *Those Tremendous Mountains: the Story of the Lewis and Clark Expedition,* W.W. Norton, New York, 1980. An excellent short version of the expedition.

Lavender, David, *The Way to the Western Sea: Lewis and Clark Across the Continent,* Harper and Row, New York, 1988. A thorough examination by an eminent historian of the West. Fine maps.

INDEX

Bill Lawrence is a former history teacher. Trying to make his classes more interesting, he began the research that eventually led to the publication of *Wilderness*. His other books are *Then Some Other Stuff Happened*, a history of America compiled from answers on the test papers of his eighth grade students; *Fascinating Facts From American History*; and *A Social History of America*.

He lives in Pine Bluff, Arkansas, with his wife Joyce, a dog named Pooh-Baby, and too many cats.